CONTEMPORARY
FREUD

Turning Points & Critical Issues

CONTEMPORARY FREUD
Turning Points & Critical Issues

Series Founded by Robert Wallerstein

On Freud's "Analysis Terminable and Interminable"
Edited by Joseph Sandler

Freud's "On Narcissism: An Introduction"
Edited by Joseph Sandler, Ethel Spector Person, and Peter Fonagy

On Freud's "Observations on Transference-Love"
Edited by Ethel Spector Person, Aiban Hagelin, and Peter Fonagy

On Freud's "Creative Writers and Day-dreaming"
Edited by Ethel Spector Person, Peter Fonagy, and Sérvulo Augusto Figueira

ON FREUD'S

"A Child Is

Being Beaten"

Edited by Ethel Spector Person

for the International

Psychoanalytical Association

Yale University Press

New Haven and London

Grateful acknowledgment is made to Sigmund Freud Copyrights, Ltd.; the Institute of Psycho-Analysis, London; the Hogarth Press; and Basic Books for permission to reprint "A Child Is Being Beaten" as published in *The Standard Edition of the Complete Psychological Works of Sigmund Freud,* vol. 17, trans. and ed. James Strachey; and in *The Collected Papers of Sigmund Freud,* vol. 2, authorized translation under the supervision of Joan Riviere, published by Basic Books, Inc., by arrangement with the Hogarth Press, Ltd. and the Institute of Psycho-Analysis, London. Reprinted by permission of Basic Books, a division of HarperCollins Publishers, Inc.

Printed in the United States of America.

Library of Congress Cataloging-in-Publication Data

On Freud's "A child is being beaten" / edited by Ethel Spector Person
for the International Psychoanalytical Association.
p.   cm. — (Contemporary Freud turning points & critical issues,
Includes English translation of Ein Kind wird geschlagen.
Includes bibliographical references and index.
ISBN 0-300-07161-2 (cloth : alk. paper). — ISBN 0-300-07162-0 (pbk. : alk. paper)
1. Freud, Sigmund, 1856–1939. Kind wird geschlagen.   2. Sadomasochism.
I. Person, Ethel Spector.   II. Freud, Sigmund, 1856–1939. Kind wird geschlagen.
English.   III. International Psycho-Analytical Association.
IV. Series: Contemporary Freud.
RC560.S2305   1997
616.85'835—dc21   97–8960
CIP

A catalogue record for this book is available from the British Library.

The paper in this book meets the guidelines for permanence and durability of the Committee on Production Guidelines for Book Longevity of the Council on Library Resources.

10   9   8   7   6   5   4   3   2   1

Contents

Preface

The IPA monograph series "Contemporary Freud: Turning Points and Critical Issues" is designed to foster the exchange of psychoanalytic ideas among the several regions of the psychoanalytic world. Given the somewhat different emphases within regions and even within one region, the idea is to disseminate the regions' unique perspectives—and their congruences and divergences—through bringing together a number of distinguished psychoanalysts to discuss one of Freud's essays, Freud embodying our common heritage.

Each volume opens with one of Freud's classic papers, followed by contributions from a panel of leading analysts, analytic teachers, and theoreticians. Each of our contributors is asked to use Freud's observations and theories to link up with issues of current interest and concern to the reviewer. What is remarkable about this volume (and the preceding ones as well) is the wide array of variations played on Freud's original score and the superimposition of some rich new melodies.

The process for selecting the Freud paper that will serve as the springboard for the discussions has been amended for this volume. In previous years, the Advisory Board to the IPA Publications Committee, composed of scores of people from around the world, was called upon to supply suggestions for the subject of the monograph. For this monograph, however, because of time constraints, rather than solicit the Advisory Board for suggestions, we asked the Executive Committee of the IPA Council to make suggestions. Their list of three papers was then sent around to the members of the Advisory Board, who were asked to rank order their preferences. "A Child Is Being Beaten" was the paper most frequently endorsed. It seems particularly appropriate this year because it dovetails with the topic of sexuality, which is the major theme of the IPA Conference to be held in Barcelona in the summer of 1997.

I am doubly grateful for the suggestions of the Advisory Board members because, in addition to making the final selection of Freud's paper, they also recommended those psychoanalysts from around the world who they felt might best discuss "A Child Is Being Beaten" and address its relevance to contemporary psychoanalysis. The wisdom of their choices is, I think, self-evident in the pages that follow.

Each volume of the monograph series is first published in English and has been (or will be) translated into the other three official languages of the IPA: French, German, and Spanish. In addition, the series is published in Italy.

I have been fortunate to work for a number of years with Valerie Tufnell, administrative director of the IPA, and Janice Ahmed, IPA publications administrator. Only through their concerted efforts, dedication, skill, and patience is it possible to manage an international publishing venture such as this. Linda Dagnell, my administrative assistant on this volume as well as the previous one, has taken responsibility for transcribing the manuscripts, updating corrections, checking bibliographies, and keeping track of deadlines. This series would never have prospered without the unflagging commitment and dedication of Gladys Topkis, our editor at Yale University Press, who was involved from the very inception of our project. She is a great enthusiast, supporter, and friend of psychoanalysis and, in my opinion, one of the great psychoanalytic editors of this decade. She can spot (and often make more readable) what is the very best in our field. Thanks, too, to Janyce Beck, Gladys's administrative assistant, who has provided us with editorial input, care, and skill in bringing this volume to its conclusion; and to Jane Zanichkowsky for her thorough and tactful copyediting.

ETHEL SPECTOR PERSON

Introduction

ETHEL SPECTOR PERSON

Although our search for pleasure is self-evident, the quest for pleasure through suffering seems counterintuitive. The theoretical problem of how pleasure and suffering become linked is the question Freud struggles with in "A Child Is Being Beaten." Jack Novick and Kerry Kelly Novick observe that Freud's efforts to conceptualize sadomasochism prompted each of his major theoretical shifts, which suggests just how important sadomasochism phenomena are to psychoanalytic reasoning. In "A Child Is Being Beaten" Freud explores the childhood beating fantasy, its transformational stages, its changing cast of protagonists, and the differences between girls and boys in the sequences and meanings of the fantasy.

For Freud, the "child-is-being-beaten" fantasy appears in a three-stage sequence in girls: (1) the fantasizer sees her father beating another child, her rival; (2) she is beaten by her father; (3) a father substitute such as a teacher is beating children, usually boys, and the fantasizer is present, as in the first stage, in the role of a spectator rather than as a participant. Although the first and third stages of the fantasy are consciously remembered, the second stage is not. It is the third stage that generally accompanies sexual arousal. Ultimately, Freud suggests that the beating fantasy condenses a girl's debased

ix

genital love for her father with punishment for her incestuous wishes. In contrast, for the boy, Freud posits only two stages. Although the conscious fantasy is one of being beaten by the mother (or other women), the unconscious fantasy, like that of the girls, is "I am being beaten by my father." Thus, Freud believed the boy's beating fantasy, like the girl's, was stoked by sexual love for the father. No stage similar to the girl's first stage was described for the boy.

In more general terms, Freud uses the "child-is-being-beaten" fantasy to explore the genesis and structure of fantasy, its developmental sequencing, and the interplay between unconscious and conscious fantasy, and he extends his discussion to encompass masochism and perversion.

The contributors to this volume amply demonstrate that masochism and sadomasochism remain vital concerns from both the therapeutic and the theoretical perspectives. But the contributors differ as to whether beating fantasies themselves are as prevalent today as in Freud's day. Some observe the fantasy in their patients with some regularity. Others, who observe it in only a few patients, theorize that in Freud's patients an underlying masochistic fantasy took the conscious form of "a child is being beaten" as a result of children's witnessing the school floggings that were commonplace at that time. But not one of our authors questions the continuing prevalence of masochistic fantasies, sexual and otherwise, in diverse forms. The prevalence of masochistic fantasies may be gleaned by a glance at the *Diagnostical and Statistical Manual of Mental Disorders (DSM-III),* which suggests that "the diagnosis of sexual masochism is made only if the individual engages in masochistic sexual acts, not merely fantasies" (273–74). Yet this is not a requirement applicable to other paraphilias, including sadism. (This prerequisite is not maintained, however, in *DSM-IV.*) Masochistic fantasies are so widely dispersed that to diagnose a patient as perverse on the basis of fantasy alone would be to award the label to too many of us, suggesting, perhaps, that masochistic fantasies alone (as opposed to masochistic perversions) are not necessarily the result of contingent events in one's childhood but may be embedded in the human condition.

Freud's essay proves peculiarly relevant to a subject of intense current debate—namely, the etiologic importance of actual beatings or other forms of abuse in masochistic perversions and masochistic character pathology. Today's acknowledgment of the widespread prevalence of physical and sexual abuse of children and our greater knowledge about the impact of infantile experience and internalized object relations on emotional development have precipitated a divergence in theoretical viewpoints about pathogenesis. Some analysts have relinquished their reliance on unconscious conflict or biological predisposition as the major etiologic agents in masochism in favor of a new belief in acute or cumulative trauma as its major causative factor. Consequently, the etiological question of whether masochistic fantasy is primarily the product of an autonomously generated fantasy (or conflictual wish), as Freud suggested, or largely the derivative of a real event, often forgotten, and the technical question of how to distinguish between these possibilities are matters of current concern to therapists and theorists. Similarly, therapists now must assess whether an apparent memory of abuse is a memory of a real event, a derivative of fantasy, or an implanted memory. Remarkably, by 1919, Freud had already begun a sophisticated consideration of the relation of fantasy to memory and of how external triggers may determine the conscious forms of fantasy.

Not only is "A Child Is Being Beaten" relevant to current theoretical and technical questions, but I believe it provides a framework within which to try to conceptualize some contemporary cultural trends (a topic this volume can only touch on lightly). We live in a time when sadomasochistic fantasies (and perhaps enactments as well) are being increasingly mainstreamed. Although sadomasochistic fantasies and enactments may not be more common today, they are surely more frequently discussed, shared, or publicly enacted.

This cultural trend has been documented for heterosexuals, gays, and lesbians, but it first achieved prominence in the open establishment in the 1970s of gay leather and S&M bars. According to Frank Browning, by the 1970s, the South Market District in San Francisco "housed the world's largest collection of leather bars and S&M clubs" (1994, 82). As AIDS researchers began to explore the various expressions of homosexual desire, "they were stunned by matter-of-fact accounts of men whose nipples were attached to chains and stretched, whose testicles were twisted in leather thongs, whose mouths were gorged on the penis of one unknown man while another would plunge his fist and forearm so deeply into their bowels that he could feel on his fingers the contractions of the heart" (84). In essence, then, the AIDS epidemic opened the eyes of many straights to the escalating and publicly performed sadomasochistic practices of the gay world.

But sadomasochism is hardly the province of gays only. Browning describes how a CBS reporter interviewing the owner of an S&M shop in order to find out about gay sadomasochism discovered that 90 percent of its clientele was heterosexual. The differences between straights and gays may have more to do with how public the practices are than in how prevalent they are. Organized S&M groups of heteros and of lesbians have begun to surface over the past two decades. In the 1980s, the emergence of S&M lesbian groups led to an odd confrontation within feminism: S&M lesbian groups claiming that S&M sex was liberating came into open political conflict with the organized feminist position that S&M pornography was antiwoman (see Faderman, 1991).

Although it is well known that there are cultural swings in the degree to which sexual acts are suppressed or allowed expression, the cultural background for the escalation of sadomasochistic acts in the public realm has yet to be explored in any extensive way by cultural critics. But we do know something of the iconography involved and of its contagiousness. In her 1974 essay "Fascinating Fascism," Susan Sontag writes that "never before was the relation of masters and slaves so consciously aestheticized. Sade had to make up his theater of punishment and delight from scratch, improvising the decor and costumes and blasphemous rites. Now there is a master scenario available to everyone. The color is black, the material is leather, the seduction is beauty, the justification is honesty, the aim is ecstasy, the fantasy is death" (1980 [1974], 105). Sontag (1980) calls attention to the way in which the insignia of fascism—leather, nazi helmets, steel spike collars, caps, chains—were recruited to sadomasochistic sexuality, particularly among gays. But these props are not specific to S&M gays; they are also the regalia of choice of many bikers. Sadomasochistic iconography made its way into the general population via the incorporation into high fashion in the 1970s of the conventions of hardcore pornography, such as black leather, studs, and dominatrix spike-heeled shoes, as well as in fashion photographs suggesting sadomasochistic interactions.

Close relatives of the contemporary sadomasochistic strain in our culture are the practices that constitute the "body modification" movement, which includes not only the now-rampant tattooing and piercing crazes but also corsetry, branding, and scarring by knives (Leo, 1995). Body piercing first appeared in the gay community but then was picked up by punk rockers in big cities such as New York and San Francisco and was mainstreamed when it was adopted by major fashion models. In contrast, tattooing was originally associated with the biker crowd. Although some young practitioners may be merely conforming to a current fashion or trying to appear "bad," the symbolism of the various body modifications is not lost on some of them. For example, the imagery of body piercing symbolizes sexual slavery and sometimes affords a specifically masochistic pleasure. When one of my friends, a professor of psychology, asked a female graduate student why she wore a lip ring, she responded without hesitation, "For the pleasure."

Many works of popular culture now utilize sadomasochism as a leading theme rather than a subsidiary one. In 1967, when the film *Belle de Jour* was released, it was considered shocking (the connection it makes between childhood sexual abuse and masochism appeared before the connection was pointed out in the psychological literature). Although *Belle de Jour* still retains its filmic qualities, the shock is gone in the wake of the proliferation of films and novels now explicitly depicting sadomasochistic sex and relationships. In the English-speaking world, consider, for example, such recent movies as *Blue Velvet; Basic Instinct; The Cook, the Thief, His Wife, and Her Lover;* and the documentary *Crumb* or novels such as A. M. Homes's *The End of Alice* and Susanna Moore's *In the Final Cut*.

I would go so far as to say that the frequently encountered self-labeling as a "survivor," signaling triumph over victimhood of one or another sort, has emerged as one of the most important heroic scripts now culturally available to us. And yet, the survivor script (excluding, of course, the life stories of actual survivors of concentration camps and other disasters, from whom the term *survivor* has been borrowed) often conceals an underlying masochistic narrative, one of redemption through suffering.

Freud's depiction of the layering of fantasy shows how contemporary events and novels provide the content of conscious sadomasochistic fantasy, insofar as reality stimuli offer imagery for unconscious wishes and fantasies —hence today's permeation of S&M sex and motorcycle gang bravura with emblems of fascism and their leakage into the larger population. Freud's description of the third stage of the beating fantasy, in which arousal is achieved by witnessing two other people engaged in a sadomasochistic encounter, suggests how many of us not involved in sadomasochistic perversions may nonetheless be drawn to the S&M scene as voyeurs or, if you will, as fellow travelers. One of our contributors, Arnold Modell, analogizes the relation between the conscious beating fantasy and the unconscious masochistic fantasy to the relation between the manifest dream and the latent dream thought: in Freud's "specimen" fantasy (the beating fantasy), the day residue, as Freud suggests, was comprised of experiencing or witnessing a beating on the buttocks ("birchings") or of exposure to such literature as *Uncle Tom's Cabin*. Although today's "specimen" fantasy is different, the underlying fantasy may remain much the same.

As has been customary in previous volumes, our commentators place our theme paper, "A Child Is Being Beaten," in a dual historical perspective: personal and theoretical. During World War I (1914–18), Freud's personal life was filled with concern for his family, particularly his soldier sons, and fears about maintaining an adequate means of support. Professionally, he had reached a stumbling block in trying to understand the essence of masochism. But "A Child Is Being Beaten," unlike the essays addressed in previous volumes in our series, incorporates a unique drama. As Patrick Joseph Mahony observes, there were two well-known figures among the clinical sample of six described in this paper—not only the Wolf Man but also Freud's daughter Anna. Several of our essayists suggest that Anna's analysis hovers over Freud's text, pointing out specifically that the exploration of beating fantasies was central to her treatment. Several also note that Anna Freud's paper "Beating Fantasies and Daydreams" (presented to the Vienna Society in 1922 in order to qualify as a member) was, like her father's paper, almost certainly based on her own analysis, insofar as she had not seen any patients before she wrote it (Young-Bruehl, 1988). A few of our essayists explicitly propose that this famous father-daughter analysis and the different theoretical renditions of it by each of its principals may stand as evidence of a specific transference-countertransference and that perhaps the analysis itself constituted a sadomasochistic enactment.

When ten essayists are asked to review the same paper and to track Freud's ideas as they have evolved up to the present, there will inevitably be some overlap. But each of our essayists emphasizes different aspects of Freud's essay and the direction taken in his later formulations on masochism, and each focuses on the ways in which Freud's important themes find expression today in different theoretical frameworks.

Jack Novick and Kerry Kelly Novick, in the opening essay, suggest that the large number of ideas contained in "A Child Is Being Beaten" provides ample reason to revisit it in depth. These include Freud's assertion of the centrality of fantasy "as the organizer of internal and external experience"; the "transformations and the vicissitudes of fantasy"; and the "centrality of the Oedipus complex to the formation of neurosis." The Novicks point out how Freud emphasizes the importance of post-oedipal development and the incompatibility of ideas as a motive for repression.

They show how the 1919 paper better expresses some key insights—for example, the narcissistic component of sadomasochism—than his later paper on the subject (1924), insofar as he emphasizes object relations and the child's narcissistic trauma in being demoted vis-à-vis a younger sibling—"cast down from all the heavens of their imaginary omnipotence" (187). Thus, Freud suggests that competition and resentment fuel the first phase of the girl's beating fantasy; her pleasure is connected to her father's beating a rival child whom she hates. Freud also demonstrates how an unconscious beating fantasy implicates character, often resulting in authority problems in later life.

But Freud's basic ideas about the origins of sadomasochism changed over time. Later he came to propose erotic masochism as primary, not just sadism turned against the self; but he still invoked the sense of guilt and the need for punishment as its central mechanism. As the Novicks put it: "Freud finds his two solutions to the theoretical problems of sadomasochism by expanding both ends of the developmental sequence, extending back to the oral phase with primary masochism and forward through the end of the infantile period with the structural model formulation of the sadistic superego and masochistic ego."

Freud's 1919 essay presents "radical formulations about the operation of memory." The second phase of the girl's beating fantasy, "I am beaten by my father," is a transformation of its first phase, but this second phase is generally reconstructed rather than remembered. Thus, according to Freud, "in a certain sense . . . it has never had a real existence" (185). The Novicks note how "Freud's emphasis on the complexity, the malleability, and the tendentious nature of memory is central to the current controversy raging in psychology and psychiatry regarding the reliability of recovered memories."

The fantasy in its third phase often appears under the stimulus of reality factors, such as reading *Uncle Tom's Cabin* or witnessing beatings in school. In the fantasy, a teacher (or other father substitute) beats children while the fantasizer looks on; the fantasy is generally accompanied by sexual excitement. Here Freud utilizes the theory of *Nachträglichkeit,* or deferred action, to explain the transformation the fantasy has undergone. Thus Freud posits a developmental framework implicit in his transformational schema and "a complex transformation of both memory and fantasy in his description of the clinical phenomenology of the stages of the beating fantasy."

The Novicks confirm Freud's observations of some differences in males and females, which they observed in their own data. They identify a transitory beating fantasy that can be part of "normal post-oedipal development in girls." But a *fixed* beating fantasy "that becomes a permanent part of the child's psychosexual life" indicates some masochistic pathology in both sexes. (This distinction is perhaps analogous to the distinction sometimes made between a transient nonpathological stage of penis envy in girls and a fixed stage of penis envy, which is considered pathological.)

The Novicks also discuss the limitations of Freud's 1919 essay, an important omission being the role of the pre-oedipal mother in the genesis of masochism in both sexes. In error is Freud's equation of femininity, passivity, and masochism, a relation the Novicks were unable to demonstrate in their empirical studies. But the 1919 paper has the distinction of being the only one of Freud's papers to use the female rather than the male as the model for understanding development.

Patrick Joseph Mahony proposes that Freud's essay merits our attention because it contains Freud's fullest elaboration of the phasic transformations of an erotic fantasy; features Freud's most detailed explanation of the motives leading to repression; represents a watershed in Freud's recognition of different developmental lines for boys and girls; proposes an explanation of masochism as secondary, which is a way station to his later theory (Freud, 1924); and foreshadows the discovery of the superego (Freud, 1923).

Mahony notes that a "taxonomy" of unconscious phantasies and their derivatives has yet to be "drawn up." He suggests that sadomasochistic masturbation phantasies and beating phantasies are "subtypes" of the underlying masochistic fantasy. Mahony asks why beating fantasies, only peripheral issues for some patients, are of central importance in others, either continuing unconsciously and significantly influencing character in a sadomasochistic direction or continuing consciously (in which case they may be acted out). Mahony reviews the evidence in the literature on the influence—or lack of influence—that beatings and enemas may have on beating fantasies. He believes that in cases of overt physical masochism there is likely to be a childhood history of actual beatings or, alternatively, "pre-oedipal problems with the phallic mother."

Most particular to Mahony's approach is his textual analysis. He emphasizes the passivity conveyed by the title of the paper: "A Child Is Being Beaten." He is among those of our essayists who suggest that Freud's analysis of Anna constituted an enactment. As confirmatory evidence, he adduces Freud's very title: "The grammatically present progressive in the title suggests that in his iatrogenic seduction and abuse of his daughter, Freud was in the process of symbolically beating her and compounding her beating fantasies." He also notes many contradictions in Freud's text that may be related to his compromised position as Anna's analyst.

Also of note is Mahony's categorization of some "noteworthy throwaway assertions" in Freud's paper. Among these are "Freud's timely reminder—so often forgotten since—that a proof of congenital homosexuality cannot be based on memories of a sexual inclination that are limited by one's amnesia and do not go earlier than the sixth year of life." Freud also observes the narcissism involved in sadomasochism and links beating phantasies to paranoid phenomena. And Freud insists that guilt over masturbation in the neurotic is related to the childhood activity and not the adolescent one.

Arnold Modell, too, gives us an insightful reading of Freud's essay with his own special twist. In his practice, he says, he has rarely encountered a beating fantasy, but he has often observed a masturbation fantasy in women—sometimes obligatory—in which the fantasizer is being humiliated, controlled, and degraded. If a patient eroticizes a humiliation fantasy, Modell suggests, she is able to bring humiliation "within the sphere of the mastery of the self." What he regards as the core of perversion is the eroticization of painful affects. Moreover, to the degree that one keeps the obligatory sexual fantasies to oneself, the other is excluded. Thus, paradoxically, the wish to surrender is expressed in fantasy, but withholding the fantasy provides "a way of remaining alone in the presence of the other."

Modell questions whether the context of the guilt attached to masochistic fantasies is "as uniformly incestuous as Freud describes." He suggests another possibility: that the guilt may be the product of a "primitive or elemental" fantasy. "The elemental experience is as follows: when something 'good' is taken into the body/self, it is 'all gone' and not available to other members of the family. For some individuals, having something good—that is to say, something pleasurable—means that some other person has been deprived or depleted." Since Modell identifies that other as the child's damaged mother, he suggests that the child requires her permission to experience pleasure. If she is unable to communicate that permission, "then the specimen fantasy may be thought of as a symptom in which there is a compromise formation—the pursuit of sexual pleasure must be negated by the pain of humiliation." Consequently, for Modell, masochistic fantasies—including fantasies of humiliation—are more complex and enigmatic in their genesis and their variations much broader than Freud's essay suggests.

Modell raises the question of what it might mean that the second stage of the beating fantasy "is never remembered, . . . has never succeeded in becoming conscious" (185), asking if Freud is suggesting that the incestuous fantasy of being beaten by the father is a "primal fantasy." He notes that it is in this paper that Freud introduces the idea of guilt as the mechanism that transforms instinctual sadism into masochism. Modell, like several of our other contributors, wonders whether the publication of Freud's paper may represent "a collusive enactment between Freud and his daughter."

In his approach to "A Child Is Being Beaten," Leonard Shengold, well known for his contributions to our understanding of anal eroticism and soul murder, emphasizes the role of aggression in understanding sadomasochism. As he insists, the Oedipus complex involves not just sex but also murder. Shengold refers to the psychic realm "beyond the pleasure principle" as that metaphorical place "of illogical and self-destructive mystery [where] lie the murky paths to the understanding of human aggressive phenomena— murder and cannibalism, not only aimed at others (where they can some- times make defensive and adaptive sense) but also turned inward toward the self, in contradiction to our insistent assumptions of being motivated by instinctual self-preservation." He emphasizes, too, the pre-oedipal ante- cedents in sadomasochism.

Shengold notes that beating fantasies are to be observed in both those who have been beaten in childhood and those who have no such memories. Noting currently accepted ideas in neurology and psychology about the "shifting nature of memory," he concludes that the recovery of historical truth is "an impossible goal to aim for in our impossible profession."

Given Freud's primary focus on the beating fantasy in girls, it is of some importance that Shengold presents two cases and a biographical example of males that demonstrate some of the variations to be found in the genesis and functions of the beating fantasy. Among other factors, he highlights the role of separation and the rage it engenders as contributing factors in the genesis of the masochistic fantasy and the fantasy's function in trying to stabilize object relations. The vignette of his Patient C demonstrates how C's "pro- vocative masochism seems designed to hold onto parental objects whom he expected to lose—especially to preserve them from the destructive rage associated with such expectations." Patient D illustrates how sadomasochistic fantasies impinge upon the transference, especially how the regressive retreat from oedipal conflicts extends beyond the anal libidinal regression to the wish for oral merging, with the danger of loss of identity and loss of self. As Shen- gold puts it: "What is dangerous is also desired—the trap of narcissistic regressive defense."

Shengold presents some interesting material from the life of the poet Algernon Swinburne, who in his life and writing provides confirmation for

Freud's and Anna Freud's insight that "fits" of beating fantasies are regressive substitutes for incestuous longings. Swinburne, never married, developed a submissive relationship with his roommate, though probably not a sexual one. Shengold points to an "unconscious parent-child identification" in Swinburne's occasional tendency to write as though he were a schoolboy, "with frequent allusions to birchings." There is some suggestion that Swinburne frequented a brothel that specialized in flagellation delivered by women. Edmund Wilson writes that swimming in the ocean in dangerous waters also afforded Swinburne pleasure and that "he liked to be pounded and slapped about by the inexorable 'great sweet mother.'" Swinburne's pattern seems to confirm Freud's observations that masochistic men have fantasies of being beaten by women. Though Freud would have said that on an unconscious level the figure of the father lurked behind that of the mother, Shengold believes that there is a greater layering of meanings involving both parents. (There is, of course, ample clinical and cultural evidence that some men consciously desire to be beaten by women, some by men, and some by both sexes.) Shengold invokes Chasseguet-Smirgel's remark that "anal-sadomasochistic phenomena can aim at the denial of the differences between the sexes and the generations."

Like Shengold, Marcio de F. Giovannetti makes good use of Chasseguet-Smirgel's insights into perversion. Although he gives credence to the incestual core of perversion, he emphasizes the discovery of mortality (and the inability to come to terms with it) as closely linked to the genesis of perversion.

Giovannetti suggests that Freud's writings must be read in the context of the whole oeuvre because each paper is but "a mooring on the long voyage represented by the chain of associations of one of mankind's great thinkers." Giovannetti refers to Meltzer's observation that Freud had two major periods of genius, from 1899 to 1904 and from 1919 to 1922. For Giovannetti this shift does not stem primarily from Freud's move away from the topographic theory to the structural theory or from an emphasis on the sexual and ego instincts to an emphasis on the life and death instincts. Giovannetti contends, rather, that the second period of genius was ushered in by Freud's ability to overcome a resistance that had to do with his contemplation of the role of mortality. Consequently, he views "A Child Is Being Beaten" as "one of the most stimulating, disconcerting, and difficult works in the entire Freudian canon." Freud's new conceptual fantasy "is woven from the threads of infantile memories, infantile sexual theories, the primal scene, the

Oedipus complex, the castration complex, the phallus, and pleasure—with pleasure here showing its darkest face." By this Giovannetti means knowledge of the limits of the self through knowledge of one's beginning and one's end. He believes that the themes of curiosity, birth, oedipal rivalry, possessiveness, and jealousy become more prominent in Freud's work until, in 1919, he overcomes his resistance, whereupon the great works that stress the dark side of sexuality—namely, perversion and death—emerge. In "Beyond the Pleasure Principle," Freud acknowledges death, whereupon, Giovannetti believes, it takes center stage. Discovering the difference between the generations, the child confronts its own mortality. In Giovannetti's view, the child must accept the idea of waiting its turn to propagate, thus acknowledging its ultimate fate; alternately, the child constructs a perverse fantasy and a perverse world. The tense of the "child-is-being-beaten" fantasy Giovannetti refers to as the tense of the unconscious, which holds in it the denial of both past and future.

Thus, for Giovannetti, as for Chasseguet-Smirgel, the heart of perversion is denial of the difference between the sexes and between the generations. At the root of the perverse structure he sees "rejection of the knowledge as a result of which the human being discovers what constitutes both his greatness and his most drastic limitation—that is, the erogenous and mortal body."

Jean-Michel Quinodoz's "virtual" seminar provides an exemplary model of how one might conduct an actual teaching seminar. He begins by placing the paper in the context of Freud's "real" external world—the "dark" years of World War I but, more important, in the context of his analysis of his daughter Anna. Citing Pragier and Faure-Pragier, Quinodoz suggests that "in reintroducing the real, the anatomical, and making penis envy the major factor in women's libidinal development, Freud was defending himself against unresolved oedipal feelings toward his daughter during her two analyses and thereby denying his guilt as a father (and simultaneously introducing the concept of denial into his theory in his paper 'Negation' [1925])." Even so, Quinodoz argues, "A Child Is Being Beaten" is important for the way in which Freud begins to conceptualize masochism, the nature of perversion, and bisexuality. He also sees as a strength of the paper Freud's beginning approach to understanding the structure of fantasy.

Of particular interest are his discussions of four cases that he uses to update our ideas on masochism and perversion. More than our other contributors, Quinodoz brings important Kleinian perspectives to bear, especially in his emphasis on the major role of splitting in perversion. He notes how, in the Kleinian view, perversion is characterized by "the importance of psychic fragmentation resulting from multiple splitting, and . . . the role played by omnipotence in the intensity of projective identification." He quotes Hanna Segal to the effect that the factors "likely to reverse the course of pathological projective identification and thereby to facilitate the process of introjection and identification" include the patient's capacity to recognize that, "to some extent, . . . what he is projecting is separate and different from the object receiving and containing his projections." Perhaps one of Quinodoz's most significant contributions is to show through his case studies how the beating fantasies in Freud's paper, rather than being esoteric and timebound, sensitize us to unconscious masochistic fantasies in today's patients.

Thus far our contributors have ranged broadly, greatly expanding our understanding of the genesis of masochism and its impact on the masochist—not just in terms of sexual fantasies and practices but also in terms of character pathology and relationships. Although our next three contributors also deal insightfully with these issues, in addition they address how the beating fantasy and masochism in general affect some more general aspects of relationships and how they may interface with the larger social fabric. Isidoro Berenstein deals with the issue of the battered child, Rivka Eifermann with the way derivatives of the beating fantasy may be subtly enacted in psychoanalytic institutes during teaching and training, and Marcelo N. Viñar with the way in which sadomasochism may sometimes become part of the social field.

Berenstein presents an insightful commentary on Freud's personal circumstances and psychoanalytic conundrums at the time he wrote "A Child Is Being Beaten" and offers a very astute section-by-section commentary. What is unique to his paper, however, is its detailed presentation of a case in which the patient's "masochistic structure culminated in the apparent carelessness whereby he contracted HIV, eventually leading to his death after enormous suffering." This is a beautiful clinical example of the interplay between masochism and the circumstances of the patient's current and past life.

Berenstein also deals more fully than our other contributors with the possible intersection between the fantasy "A Child Is Being Beaten" and child beating. Going beyond the question as to whether beating fantasies depend on the experience of having been beaten or having witnessed beating, he describes the psychological situation when real battering occurs. Here he describes "a transgenerational model of identification" that may run though a family. Battering is encoded in such a way that the battered child often becomes a batterer. Berenstein notes that "the person inflicting the punishment does so out of an excess of excitation" and that the intensity of the event is something the child cannot conceptualize, "so that, rather than constituting the meaningful event, it often gives rise to a memory in the form of an act." Thus a chain of violence is constructed from generation to generation. But this is not the inevitable outcome of being beaten. Alternatively, being beaten may be "cathected secondarily as masochism, in which the wish is directed toward the father as the ultimate expression of survival."

Berenstein is particularly insightful in his discussion of the object relationship of the battering father: "The child is not accepted as other, and the father tries to transform him into an extension of an inner object relationship. If the child cries or does not behave as the father wishes, he hits him, with a view to silencing him and suppressing him as an intolerable stimulus, an intolerable other. That, however, is precisely the quality of what we call an object, so that we are once again in the world of fantasy and not of the link with the other." He extends the problem of the battered child to an exploration of sexual abuse. Whether or not Berenstein is correct in his assessment that fathers rather than mothers are by and large the batterers, he has brought an important area of research to our attention and related it to psychoanalytic thinking and theory.

Berenstein's paper reminded me of a woman I once treated who had "fits" of beating her male child—not her daughters—and remembered, in the course of discussing this completely ego-alien symptom (which was the proximate cause of her entering treatment), that as a child she had had a discrete, pleasurable (though not sexual) fantasy of beating a male infant. The origins of that fantasy are beyond my discussion here, but the question came up in treatment as to whether the fantasy itself (engendered in childhood, with no history of herself having been beaten) served as a stimulus to an enactment. Making a cause-and-effect correlation in a specific case is always problematic, though the patient herself experienced her fantasy and her beating "fits" as connected. This raises the possibility that beating a child, although sometimes the product of being beaten or of poor impulse control, may sometimes be the enactment of an autonomously engendered beating fantasy. In such a case, the beating fantasy is not recognizably incorporated into sexual behavior, but as a repeating fantasy is later enacted (Person, 1996).

Eifermann makes exceptionally clear and convincing her idea that sadomasochistic fantasies were enacted in the Freud-Freud analysis. Within the frame story of feeling herself under "considerable (and friendly) pressure" to produce a commentary on Freud's paper, she discusses how the Freud father-daughter analysis constituted an enactment, using as evidence a juxtaposition and detailed examination of Sigmund Freud's 1919 paper "A Child Is Being Beaten" and Anna Freud's 1922 paper "Beating Fantasies and Daydreams." She pinpoints distortions in S. Freud's paper that she argues are direct results of his countertransference. Part of that countertransference is manifest in his utilization of an "active" technique.

Eifermann uses her findings from this unique analysis to suggest that similar biases may exist in other analyses. Derivatives of the beating fantasy or other sadomasochistic fantasies may be enacted though covert force in analytic institutes today, not just in overactive analytic interventions but in methods of teaching. Eifermann sees the study of violations occurring early in the history of our field as useful for what they can tell us about the potential for contemporary transgressions, including "showing," "inducing," "seducing," and "beating out" in teaching. She uses her sense of being pressured to write her commentary—for this volume—to connect with important insights about teaching, supervising, and analyzing a candidate. In addition, she presents an interesting viewpoint about "didactic" training.

Although Viñar does not find the beating fantasy in his own practice in the form in which it appeared in Freud's patients, he insists that, even so, "Freud's concerns are . . . still valid, and . . . our present-day culture retains at its core the universal psychic experience of algolagnia—sexual excitation through pain—even if no longer in the form of beating fantasies." He goes on to focus on the structure of fantasy and in a real tour de force connects the third stage of the fantasy (in which the fantasizer is spectator) not just to individual psychology but to the whole social field.

But this is not his only major insight or even his primary focus. Viñar emphasizes the hierarchic architecture of fantasy in Freud's essay: "In the midst of the ostensible theme of perversion and masochism, I discovered a key of unparalleled clarity to the genesis and architecture of fantasy—that is, to the constitution of the subject—that emerges from the vicissitudes of the Freudian experience."

Viñar notes that the second phase of the beating fantasy, "I am being beaten by my father"—the phase Freud considers "the most important and momentous of all"—is nonetheless reported as "in a certain sense" never having had a "real existence." As Viñar points out, this "constitutes one of those clear instances in which Freud breaks with the naturalistic realism of clinical medicine." He argues that the second phase, "being unobservable, would have remained but an arbitrary, dilettantish, and capricious solipsism had Freud not imposed a necessary structure on it—not now from the point of view of clinical observation but in terms of his metapsychological hypothesis—and thereby achieved a unified understanding of the narrative." (Thus, for Viñar, psychoanalytic thinking must be distinguished from "pure" scientific thinking.) Viñar quotes Lacan to the effect that the sequence of phases Freud proposes is logical rather than genetic. He emphasizes that Freud's treatment and development of his theme have more to offer us than the correctness or incorrectness of his specific findings.

The third phase of the beating fantasy has particular relevance to the social field. For Lacan, as Viñar tells us, the salient feature of this phase is that the subject is "reduced to an eye, a mere unconcerned spectator, no longer a symbolic mediator between the punishing figure and the victim." This Lacan regards as the essence of the perverse structure. The oscillation of responsibility in the fantasy "between extraneous characters—anonymous characters or family members—and the fantasizer himself" is important to Viñar because of its link to a "universal human attitude toward intolerable violence." Here we have what I believe to be the strongest hint in the entire volume about the link between sexual sadomasochism and our interest in and tolerance of violence in the social field.

Despite the richness of the many insights presented in this volume, the ultimate mystery of sadomasochism lingers. Mahony offers comfort. He singles out as extremely important to all theory-making Freud's metatheoretical position that "all the signs on which we are accustomed to base our distinctions tend to lose their clarity as we come nearer to the source" (187). Mahony elaborates: "The closer we get to sources, the more our descriptive terms are a fabric of fiction, and what started out as speculation soon risks being hardened into definitive assertions." Insistence on knowing first causes sometimes entails a reductionism that obscures more than it reveals.

Just as many people read a novel for its plot and are not so well attuned to other aspects, so too is there the temptation to read a psychoanalytic paper in order to become acquainted with its ideas without rigorously evaluating them or placing them in some overall framework. In addition to the many topics addressed in this volume, several of the essays rigorously attend to how to systematically read a paper, with relevance not just to "A Child Is Being Beaten" but to the whole psychoanalytic corpus.

A note: in the fourth volume of this series—"On Freud's 'Creative Writers and Day-dreaming'"—I made the decision to leave the spelling of *fantasy* (with an *f*) or *phantasy* (with a *ph*) as each author used it rather than standardize the spelling, since the meanings are specific to the tradition in which the author was trained and the theoretical position from which he or she speaks. This policy has been extended to the current volume, in which one of the central foci is on fantasy and phantasy.

REFERENCES

Browning, F. 1994. *The culture of desire: Paradox and perversity in gay lives today.* New York: Vintage.

Diagnostical and statistical manual of mental disorders (DSM-III). 1980. Washington, D.C.: American Psychiatric Association.

Faderman, L. 1991. *Odd girls and twilight lovers: A history of lesbian life in twentieth-century America.* New York: Columbia University Press.

Freud, S. 1917. Mourning and melancholia. *S.E.* 14:237–56.

———. 1919. A child is being beaten. *S.E.* 17:175–204.

———. 1924. The economic problem of masochism. *S.E.* 19:157–70.

Leo, J. 1995. The modern primitives. *U.S. News and World Report* V.119 (July 31).

Person, E. 1996. *By force of fantasy: How we make our lives.* New York: Basic Books.

Sontag, S. 1980. *Fascinating fascism,* reprinted in *Under the sign of Saturn.* New York: Anchor Books/Doubleday.

Young-Bruehl, E. 1988. *Anna Freud: A biography.* New York: Summit.

PART ONE

A Child Is Being Beaten (1919)

SIGMUND FREUD

events exhibited clearly marked individual traits of obsessional neurosis. The fourth case, it must be admitted, was one of straightforward hysteria, with pains and inhibitions; and the fifth patient, who had come to be analysed merely on account of indecisiveness in life, would not have been classified at all by coarse clinical diagnosis, or would have been dismissed as 'psychasthenic'.[1] There is no need for feeling disappointed over these statistics. In the first place, we know that not every disposition is necessarily developed into a disorder; in the second place, we ought to be content to explain the facts before us, and ought as a rule to avoid the additional task of making it clear why something has *not* taken place.

The present state of our knowledge would allow us to make our way so far and no further towards the comprehension of beating-phantasies. In the mind of the analytic physician, it is true, there remains an uneasy suspicion that this is not a final solution of the problem. He is obliged to admit to himself that to a great extent these phantasies subsist apart from the rest of the content of a neurosis, and find no proper place in its structure. But impressions of this kind, as I know from my own experience, are only too willingly put on one side.

III

Strictly considered—and why should this question not be considered with all possible strictness?—analytic work deserves to be recognized as genuine psycho-analysis only when it has succeeded in removing the amnesia which conceals from the adult his knowledge of his childhood from its beginning (that is, from about the second to the fifth year). This cannot be said among analysts too emphatically or repeated too often. The motives for disregarding this reminder are, indeed, intelligible. It would be desirable to obtain practical results in a shorter period and with less trouble. But at the present time theoretical knowledge is still far more important to all of us than therapeutic success, and anyone who neglects childhood analysis is bound to fall into the most disastrous errors. The emphasis which is laid here upon the importance of the earliest experiences does not imply any underestimation of the influence of later ones. But the later impressions of life speak loudly enough through

[1] [Nothing is said here of the sixth case.]

the mouth of the patient, while it is the physician who has to raise his voice on behalf of the claims of childhood.

It is in the years of childhood between the ages of two and four or five that the congenital libidinal factors are first awakened by actual experiences and become attached to certain complexes. The beating-phantasies which are now under discussion show themselves only towards the end of this period or after its termination. So it may quite well be that they have an earlier history, that they go through a process of development, that they represent an end-product and not an initial manifestation.

This suspicion is confirmed by analysis. A systematic application of it shows that beating-phantasies have a historical development which is by no means simple, and in the course of which they are changed in most respects more than once— as regards their relation to the author of the phantasy, and as regards their object, their content and their significance.

In order to make it easier to follow these transformations in beating-phantasies I shall now venture to confine my descriptions to the female cases, which, since they are four as against two, in any case constitute the greater part of my material. Moreover, beating-phantasies in men are connected with another subject, which I shall leave on one side in this paper.[1] In my description I shall be careful to avoid being more schematic than is inevitable for the presentation of an average case. If then on further observation a greater complexity of circumstances should come to light, I shall nevertheless be sure of having before us a typical occurrence, and one, moreover, that is not of an uncommon kind.

The first phase of beating-phantasies among girls, then, must belong to a very early period of childhood. Some features remain curiously indefinite, as though they were a matter of indifference. The scanty information given by the patients in their first statement, 'a child is being beaten', seems to be justified in respect to this phase. But another of their features can be established with certainty, and to the same effect in every case. The child being beaten is never the one producing the phantasy, but is invariably another child, most often a brother or a sister

---

[1] [Freud does in fact discuss beating-phantasies in men below (p. 196 ff.). Their specifically feminine basis is what he probably has in mind in speaking of 'another subject'.]

if there is any. Since this other child may be a boy or a girl, there is no constant relation between the sex of the child producing the phantasy and that of the child being beaten. The phantasy, then, is certainly not masochistic. It would be tempting to call it sadistic, but one cannot neglect the fact that the child producing the phantasy is never doing the beating herself. The actual identity of the person who does the beating remains obscure at first. Only this much can be established: it is not a child but an adult. Later on this indeterminate grown-up person becomes recognizable clearly and unambiguously as the (girl's) *father*.

This first phase of the beating-phantasy is therefore completely represented by the phrase: '*My father is beating the child.*' I am betraying a great deal of what is to be brought forward later when instead of this I say: 'My father is beating the child *whom I hate.*' Moreover, one may hesitate to say whether the characteristics of a 'phantasy' can yet be ascribed to this first step towards the later beating-phantasy. It is perhaps rather a question of recollections of events which have been witnessed, or of desires which have arisen on various occasions. But these doubts are of no importance.

Profound transformations have taken place between this first phase and the next. It is true that the person beating remains the same (that is, the father); but the child who is beaten has been changed into another one and is now invariably the child producing the phantasy. The phantasy is accompanied by a high degree of pleasure, and has now acquired a significant content, with the origin of which we shall be concerned later. Now, therefore, the wording runs: '*I am being beaten by my father.*' It is of an unmistakably masochistic character.

This second phase is the most important and the most momentous of all. But we may say of it in a certain sense that it has never had a real existence. It is never remembered, it has never succeeded in becoming conscious. It is a construction of analysis, but it is no less a necessity on that account.

The third phase once more resembles the first. It has the wording which is familiar to us from the patient's statement. The person beating is never the father, but is either left undetermined just as in the first phase, or turns in a characteristic way into a representative of the father, such as a teacher. The figure of the child who is producing the beating-phantasy no longer itself appears in it. In reply to pressing enquiries the patients only declare: 'I am probably looking on.' Instead of the one child that is being beaten, there are now a number of children present as a rule. Most frequently it is boys who are being beaten (in girls' phantasies), but none of them is personally known to the subject. The situation of being beaten, which was originally simple and monotonous, may go through the most complicated alterations and elaborations; and punishments and humiliations of another kind may be substituted for the beating itself. But the essential characteristic which distinguishes even the simplest phantasies of this phase from those of the first, and which establishes the connection with the intermediate phase, is this: the phantasy now has strong and unambiguous sexual excitement attached to it, and so provides a means for masturbatory satisfaction. But this is precisely what is puzzling. By what path has the phantasy of strange and unknown boys being beaten (a phantasy which has by this time become sadistic) found its way into the permanent possession of the little girl's libidinal trends?

Nor can we conceal from ourselves that the interrelations and sequence of the three phases of the beating-phantasy, as well as all its other peculiarities, have so far remained quite unintelligible.

IV

If the analysis is carried through the early period to which the beating-phantasies are referred and from which they are recollected, it shows us the child involved in the agitations of its parental complex.

The affections of the little girl are fixed on her father, who has probably done all he could to win her love, and in this way has sown the seeds of an attitude of hatred and rivalry towards her mother. This attitude exists side by side with a current of affectionate dependence on her, and as years go on it may be destined to come into consciousness more and more clearly and forcibly, or else to give an impetus to an excessive reaction of devotion to her. But it is not with the girl's relation to her mother that the beating-phantasy is connected. There are other children in the nursery, only a few years older or younger, who are disliked on all sorts of other grounds, but chiefly because the parents' love has to be shared with them, and for this reason they are repelled with all the wild energy characteristic of the emotional life of those years. If the child in question is a younger brother or sister (as in three of my four cases) it is despised as well as hated; yet it attracts to itself the share of affection which the blinded parents are always ready to give the youngest child, and this is a spectacle the sight of which cannot be avoided. One soon learns that being beaten, even if it does not hurt very much, signifies a deprivation of love and a humiliation. And many children who believed themselves securely enthroned in the unshakable affection of their parents have by a single blow been cast down from all the heavens of their imaginary omnipotence. The idea of the father beating this hateful child is therefore an agreeable one, quite apart from whether he has actually been seen doing so. It means: 'My father does not love this other child, *he loves only me*.'

This then is the content and meaning of the beating-phantasy in its first phase. The phantasy obviously gratifies the child's jealousy and is dependent upon the erotic side of its life, but is also powerfully reinforced by the child's egoistic interests. Doubt remains, therefore, whether the phantasy ought to be described as purely 'sexual', nor can one venture to call it 'sadistic'.

As is well known, all the signs on which we are accustomed to base our distinctions tend to lose their clarity as we come nearer to the source. So perhaps we may say in terms recalling the prophecy made by the Three Witches to Banquo: 'Not clearly sexual, not in itself sadistic, but yet the stuff from which both will later come.' In any case, however, there is no ground for suspecting that in this first phase the phantasy is already at the service of an excitation which involves the genitals and finds its outlet in a masturbatory act.

It is clear that the child's sexual life has reached the stage of genital organization, now that its incestuous love has achieved this premature choice of an object. This can be demonstrated more easily in the case of boys, but is also indisputable in the case of girls. Something like a premonition of what are later to be the final and normal sexual aims governs the child's libidinal trends. We may justly wonder why this should be so, but we may regard it as a proof of the fact that the genitals

s.f. xvii—n

have already begun playing their part in the process of excitation. With boys the wish to beget a child from their mother is never absent, with girls the wish to have a child by their father is equally constant; and this in spite of their being completely incapable of forming any clear idea of the means for fulfilling these wishes. The child seems to be convinced that the genitals have something to do with the matter, even though in its constant brooding it may look for the essence of the presumed intimacy between its parents in relations of another sort, such as in their sleeping together, micturating in each other's presence, etc.; and material of the latter kind can be more easily apprehended in verbal images than the mystery that is connected with the genitals.

But the time comes when this early blossoming is nipped by the frost. None of these incestuous loves can avoid the fate of repression. They may succumb to it on the occasion of some discoverable external event which leads to disillusionment—such as unexpected slights, the unwelcome birth of a new brother or sister (which is felt as faithlessness), etc.; or the same thing may happen owing to internal conditions apart from any such events, perhaps simply because their yearning remains unsatisfied too long. It is unquestionably true that such events are not the *effective* causes, but that these love-affairs are bound to come to grief sooner or later, though we cannot say on what particular stumbling block. Most probably they pass away because their time is over, because the children have entered upon a new phase of development in which they are compelled to recapitulate from the history of mankind the repression of an incestuous object-choice, just as at an earlier stage they were obliged to effect an object-choice of that very sort.[1] In the new phase no mental product of the incestuous love-impulses that is present unconsciously is taken over by consciousness; and anything that has already come into consciousness is expelled from it. At the same time as this process of repression takes place, a sense of guilt appears. This is also of unknown origin, but there is no doubt whatever that it is connected with the incestuous wishes, and that it is justified by the persistence of those wishes in the unconscious.[2]

[1] Compare the part played by Fate in the myth of Oedipus.
[2] [*Footnote added* 1924:] See the continuation of this line of thought in 'The Dissolution of the Oedipus Complex' (1924*d*).

The phantasy of the period of incestuous love had said: 'He (my father) loves only me, and not the other child, for he is beating it.' The sense of guilt can discover no punishment more severe than the reversal of this triumph: 'No, he does not love you, for he is beating you.' In this way the phantasy of the second phase, that of being beaten by her father, is a direct expression of the girl's sense of guilt, to which her love for her father has now succumbed. The phantasy, therefore, has become masochistic. So far as I know, this is always so; a sense of guilt is invariably the factor that transforms sadism into masochism. But this is certainly not the whole content of masochism. The sense of guilt cannot have won the field alone; a share must also fall to the love-impulse. We must remember that we are dealing with children in whom the sadistic component was able for constitutional reasons to develop prematurely and in isolation. We need not abandon this point of view. It is precisely such children who find it particularly easy to hark back to the pregenital, sadistic-anal organization of their sexual life. If the genital organization, when it has scarcely been effected, is met by repression, the result is not only that every psychical representation of the incestuous love becomes unconscious, or remains so, but there is another result as well: a regressive debasement of the genital organization itself to a lower level. 'My father loves me' was meant in a genital sense; owing to the regression it is turned into 'My father is beating me (I am being beaten by my father)'. This being beaten is now a convergence of the sense of guilt and sexual love. *It is not only the punishment for the forbidden genital relation, but also the regressive substitute for that relation,* and from this latter source it derives the libidinal excitation which is from this time forward attached to it, and which finds its outlet in masturbatory acts. Here for the first time we have the essence of masochism.

This second phase—the child's phantasy of being itself beaten by its father—remains unconscious as a rule, probably in consequence of the intensity of the repression. I cannot explain why nevertheless in one of my six cases, that of a male, it was consciously remembered. This man, now grown up, had preserved the fact clearly in his memory that he used to employ the idea of being beaten by his mother for the purpose of masturbation, though to be sure he soon substituted for his own mother the mothers of his school-fellows or other women who in some way resembled her. It must not be forgotten that when a boy's incestuous phantasy is transformed into the corresponding masochistic one, one more reversal has to take place than in the case of a girl, namely the substitution of passivity for activity; and this additional degree of distortion may save the phantasy from having to remain unconscious as a result of repression. In this way the sense of guilt would be satisfied by regression instead of by repression. In the female cases the sense of guilt, in itself perhaps more exacting, could be appeased only by a combination of the two.

In two of my four female cases an elaborate superstructure of day-dreams, which was of great significance for the life of the person concerned, had grown up over the masochistic beating-phantasy. The function of this superstructure was to make possible a feeling of satisfied excitation, even though the masturbatory act was abstained from. In one of these cases the content—being beaten by the father—was allowed to venture again into consciousness, so long as the subject's own ego was made unrecognizable by a thin disguise. The hero of these stories was invariably beaten (or later only punished, humiliated, etc.) by his father.

I repeat, however, that as a rule the phantasy remains unconscious, and can only be reconstructed in the course of the analysis. This fact perhaps vindicates patients who say they remember that with them masturbation made its appearance before the third phase of the beating-phantasy (shortly to be discussed), and that this phase was only a later addition, made perhaps under the impression of scenes at school. Every time I have given credit to these statements I have felt inclined to assume that the masturbation was at first under the dominance of unconscious phantasies and that conscious ones were substituted for them later.

I look upon the beating-phantasy in its familiar third phase, which is its final form, as a substitute of this sort. Here the child who produces the phantasy appears almost as a spectator, while the father persists in the shape of a teacher or some other person in authority. The phantasy, which now resembles that of the first phase, seems to have become sadistic once more. It appears as though in the phrase, 'My father is beating the child, he loves only me', the stress has been shifted back on to the first part after the second part has undergone repression.

But only the *form* of this phantasy is sadistic; the satisfaction which is derived from it is masochistic. Its significance lies in the fact that it has taken over the libidinal cathexis of the repressed portion and at the same time the sense of guilt which is attached to the content of that portion. All of the many unspecified children who are being beaten by the teacher are, after all, nothing more than substitutes for the child itself.

We find here for the first time, too, something like a constancy of sex in the persons who play a part in the phantasy. The children who are being beaten are almost invariably boys, in the phantasies of boys just as much as in those of girls. This characteristic is naturally not to be explained by any rivalry between the sexes, as otherwise of course in the phantasies of boys it would be girls who would be being beaten; and it has nothing to do with the sex of the child who was hated in the first phase. But it points to a complication in the case of girls. When they turn away from their incestuous love for their father, with its genital significance, they easily abandon their feminine role. They spur their 'masculinity complex' (Van Ophuijsen, 1917) into activity, and from that time forward only want to be boys. For that reason the whipping-boys who represent them are boys too. In both the cases of day-dreaming —one of which almost rose to the level of a work of art—the heroes were always young men; indeed women used not to come into these creations at all, and only made their first appearance after many years, and then in minor parts.

V

I hope I have brought forward my analytic observations in sufficient detail, and I should only like to add that the six cases I have mentioned so often do not exhaust my material. Like other analysts, I have at my disposal a far larger number of cases which have been investigated less thoroughly. These observations can be made use of along various lines: for elucidating the genesis of the perversions in general and of masochism in particular, and for estimating the part played by difference of sex in the dynamics of neurosis.

The most obvious result of such a discussion is its application to the origin of the perversions. The view which brought into the foreground in this connection the constitutional reinforcement or premature growth of a single sexual component is not shaken, indeed; but it is seen not to comprise the whole truth. The perversion is no longer an isolated fact in the child's sexual life, but falls into its place among the typical, not to say normal, processes of development which are familiar to us. It is brought into relation with the child's incestuous love-object, with its Oedipus complex. It first comes into prominence in the sphere of this complex, and after the complex has broken down it remains over, often quite by itself, the inheritor of the charge of libido from that complex and weighed down by the sense of guilt that was attached to it. The abnormal sexual constitution, finally, has shown its strength by forcing the Oedipus complex into a particular direction, and by compelling it to leave an unusual residue behind.

A perversion in childhood, as is well known, may become the basis for the construction of a perversion having a similar sense and persisting throughout life, one which consumes the subject's whole sexual life. On the other hand the perversion may be broken off and remain in the background of a normal sexual development, from which, however, it continues to withdraw a certain amount of energy. The first of these alternatives was already known before the days of analysis. Analytic investigation, however, of such fully-developed cases almost bridges the gulf between the two. For we find often enough with these perverts that they too made an attempt at developing normal sexual activity, usually at the age of puberty; but their attempt had not enough force in it and was abandoned in the face of the first obstacles which inevitably arise, whereupon they fell back upon their infantile fixation once and for all.

It would naturally be important to know whether the origin of infantile perversions from the Oedipus complex can be asserted as a general principle. While this cannot be decided without further investigation, it does not seem impossible. When we recall the anamneses which have been obtained in adult cases of perversion we cannot fail to notice that the decisive impression, the 'first experience', of all these perverts, fetishists, etc., is scarcely ever referred back to a time earlier than the sixth year. At this time, however, the dominance of the Oedipus complex is already over; the experience which is recalled, and which has been effective in such a puzzling way, may very well have represented the legacy of that complex. The connections between the experience and the complex which is by this time repressed are bound to remain obscure so long as analysis has not thrown any light on the time before the first 'pathogenic' impression. So it may be imagined how little value is to be attached, for instance, to an assertion that a case of homosexuality is congenital, when the ground given for this belief is that ever since his eighth or sixth year the person in question has felt inclinations only towards his own sex.

If, however, the derivation of perversions from the Oedipus complex can be generally established, our estimate of its importance will have gained added strength. For in our opinion the Oedipus complex is the actual nucleus of neuroses, and the infantile sexuality which culminates in this complex is the true determinant of neuroses. What remains of the complex in the unconscious represents the disposition to the later development of neuroses in the adult. In this way the beating-phantasy and other analogous perverse fixations would also only be precipitates of the Oedipus complex, scars, so to say, left behind after the process has ended, just as the notorious 'sense of inferiority' corresponds to a narcissistic scar of the same sort. In taking this view of the matter I must express my unreserved agreement with Marcinowski (1918), who has recently put it forward most happily. As is well known, this neurotic delusion of inferiority is only a partial one, and is completely compatible with the existence of a self-overvaluation derived from other sources. The origin of the Oedipus complex itself, and the destiny which compels man, probably alone among all animals, to begin his sexual life twice over, first like all other creatures in his early childhood, and then after a long interruption once more at the age of puberty—all the problems that are connected with man's 'archaic heritage'—have been discussed by me elsewhere, and I have no intention of going into them in this place.[1]

Little light is thrown upon the genesis of masochism by our discussion of the beating-phantasy. To begin with, there seems to be a confirmation of the view that masochism is not the

[1] [Freud had discussed these questions at length, not long before, in his *Introductory Lectures* (1916–17), especially in Lectures XXI and XXIII. Cf. also below, pp. 261–2.]

manifestation of a primary instinct, but originates from sadism which has been turned round upon the self—that is to say, by means of regression from an object to the ego.[1] Instincts with a passive aim must be taken for granted as existing, especially among women. But passivity is not the whole of masochism. The characteristic of unpleasure belongs to it as well,—a bewildering accompaniment to the satisfaction of an instinct. The transformation of sadism into masochism appears to be due to the influence of the sense of guilt which takes part in the act of repression. Thus repression is operative here in three ways: it renders the consequences of the genital organization unconscious, it compels that organization itself to regress to the earlier sadistic-anal stage, and it transforms the sadism of this stage into masochism, which is passive and again in a certain sense narcissistic. The second of these three effects is made possible by the weakness of the genital organization, which must be presupposed in these cases. The third becomes necessary because the sense of guilt takes as much objection to sadism as to incestuous object-choice genitally conceived. Again, the analyses do not tell us the origin of the sense of guilt itself. It seems to be brought along by the new phase upon which the child is entering, and, if it afterwards persists, it seems to correspond to a scar-like formation which is similar to the sense of inferiority. According to our present orientation in the structure of the ego, which is as yet uncertain, we should assign it to the agency in the mind which sets itself up as a critical conscience over against the rest of the ego, which produces Silberer's functional phenomenon in dreams, and which cuts itself loose from the ego in delusions of being watched.[2]

We may note too in passing that the analysis of the infantile perversion dealt with here is also of help in solving an old riddle—one which, it is true, has always troubled those who have not accepted psycho-analysis more than analysts themselves. Yet quite recently even Bleuler regarded it as a remarkable and inexplicable fact that neurotics make masturba-

---

[1] Cf. 'Instincts and their Vicissitudes' (1915c).—[In *Beyond the Pleasure Principle* (1920g), *Standard Ed.*, 18, 54–5, Freud suggested that there might after all be a primary masochism.]

[2] [See Part III of Freud's paper on narcissism (1914c). This agency was, of course, later described as the 'super-ego'. Cf. Chapter III of *The Ego and the Id* (1923b).]

tion the central point of their sense of guilt. We have long assumed that this sense of guilt relates to the masturbation of early childhood and not to that of puberty, and that in the main it is to be connected not with the act of masturbation but with the phantasy which, although unconscious, lies at its root—that is to say, with the Oedipus complex.[1]

As regards the third and apparently sadistic phase of the beating-phantasy, I have already [pp. 190–1] discussed the significance that it gains as the vehicle of the excitation impelling towards masturbation; and I have shown how it arouses activities of the imagination which on the one hand continue the phantasy along the same line, and on the other hand neutralize it through compensation. Nevertheless the second phase, the unconscious and masochistic one, in which the child itself is being beaten by its father, is incomparably the more important. This is not only because it continues to operate through the agency of the phase that takes its place; we can also detect effects upon the character, which are directly derived from its unconscious form. People who harbour phantasies of this kind develop a special sensitiveness and irritability towards anyone whom they can include in the class of fathers. They are easily offended by a person of this kind, and in that way (to their own sorrow and cost) bring about the realization of the imagined situation of being beaten by their father. I should not be surprised if it were one day possible to prove that the same phantasy is the basis of the delusional litigiousness of paranoia.

VI

It would have been quite impossible to give a clear survey of infantile beating-phantasies if I had not limited it, except in one or two connections, to the state of things in females. I will briefly recapitulate my conclusions. The little girl's beating-phantasy passes through three phases, of which the first and third are consciously remembered, the middle one remaining unconscious. The two conscious phases appear to be sadistic, whereas the middle and unconscious one is undoubtedly of a masochistic nature; its content consists in the child's being beaten by her father, and it carries with it the libidinal charge

[1] [See for example a discussion in the 'Rat Man' case history (1909*d*), *Standard Ed.*, **10**, 202 ff.]

and the sense of guilt. In the first and third phantasies the child who is being beaten is always someone other than the subject; in the middle phase it is always the child herself; in the third phase it is almost invariably only boys who are being beaten. The person who does the beating is from the first her father, replaced later on by a substitute taken from the class of fathers. The unconscious phantasy of the middle phase had primarily a genital significance and developed by means of repression and regression out of an incestuous wish to be loved by the father. Another fact, though its connection with the rest does not appear to be close, is that between the second and third phases the girls change their sex, for in the phantasies of the latter phase they turn into boys.

I have not been able to get so far in my knowledge of beating-phantasies in boys, perhaps because my material was unfavourable. I naturally expected to find a complete analogy between the state of things in the case of boys and in that of girls, the mother taking the father's place in the phantasy. This expectation seemed to be fulfilled; for the content of the boy's phantasy which was taken to be the corresponding one was actually his being beaten by his mother (or later on by a substitute for her). But this phantasy, in which the boy's own self was retained as the person who was being beaten, differed from the second phase in girls in that it was able to become conscious. If on this account, however, we attempt to draw a parallel between it and the *third* phase of the girl's phantasy, a new difference is found, for the figure of the boy himself is not replaced by a number of unknown, and unspecified children, least of all by a number of girls. Therefore the expectation of there being a complete parallel was mistaken.

My male cases with an infantile beating-phantasy comprised only a few who did not exhibit some other gross injury to their sexual activities; again they included a fairly large number of persons who would have to be described as true masochists in the sense of being sexual perverts. They were either people who obtained their sexual satisfaction exclusively from masturbation accompanied by masochistic phantasies; or they were people who had succeeded in combining masochism with their genital activity in such a way that, along with masochistic performances and under similar conditions, they were able to bring about erection and emission or to carry out normal intercourse.

In addition to this there was the rarer case in which a masochist is interfered with in his perverse activities by the appearance of obsessional ideas of unbearable intensity. Now perverts who can obtain satisfaction do not often have occasion to come for analysis. But as regards the three classes of masochists that have been mentioned there may be strong motives to induce them to go to an analyst. The masochist masturbator finds that he is absolutely impotent if after all he does attempt intercourse with a woman; and the man who has hitherto effected intercourse with the help of a masochistic idea or performance may suddenly make the discovery that the alliance which was so convenient for him has broken down, his genital organs no longer reacting to the masochistic stimulus. We are accustomed confidently to promise recovery to psychically impotent patients who come to us for treatment; but we ought to be more guarded in making this prognosis so long as the dynamics of the disturbance are unknown to us. It comes as a disagreeable surprise if the analysis reveals the cause of the 'merely psychical' impotence to be a typically masochistic attitude, perhaps deeply embedded since infancy.

As regards these masochistic men, however, a discovery is made at this point which warns us not to pursue the analogy between their case and that of women any further at present, but to judge each independently. For the fact emerges that in their masochistic phantasies, as well as in the performances they go through for their realization, they invariably transfer themselves into the part of a woman; that is to say, their masochistic attitude coincides with a *feminine* one. This can easily be demonstrated from details of the phantasies; but many patients are even aware of it themselves, and give expression to it as a subjective conviction. It makes no difference if in a fanciful embellishment of the masochistic scene they keep up the fiction that a mischievous boy, or page, or apprentice is going to be punished. On the other hand the persons who administer chastisement are always women, both in the phantasies and the performances. This is confusing enough; and the further question must be asked whether this feminine attitude already forms the basis of the masochistic element in the *infantile* beating-phantasy.[1]

[1] [*Footnote added* 1924:] Further remarks on this subject will be found in 'The Economic Problem of Masochism' (1924c).

Let us therefore leave aside consideration of the state of things in cases of adult masochism, which it is so hard to clear up, and turn to the infantile beating-phantasy in the male sex. Analysis of the earliest years of childhood once more allows us to make a surprising discovery in this field. The phantasy which has as its content being beaten by the mother, and which is conscious or can become so, is not a primary one. It possesses a preceding stage which is invariably unconscious and has as its content: '*I am being beaten by my father.*' This preliminary stage, then, really corresponds to the second phase of the phantasy in the girl. The familiar and conscious phantasy: 'I am being beaten by my mother', takes the place of the third phase in the girl, in which, as has been mentioned already, unknown boys are the objects that are being beaten. I have not been able to demonstrate among boys a preliminary stage of a sadistic nature that could be set beside the first phase of the phantasy in girls, but I will not now express any final disbelief in its existence, for I can readily see the possibility of meeting with more complicated types.

In the male phantasy—as I shall call it briefly, and, I hope, without any risk of being misunderstood—the being beaten also stands for being loved (in a genital sense), though this has been debased to a lower level owing to regression. So the original form of the unconscious male phantasy was not the provisional one that we have hitherto given: 'I am being beaten by my father', but rather: '*I am loved by my father*'. The phantasy has been transformed by the processes with which we are familiar into the conscious phantasy: '*I am being beaten by my mother*'. The boy's beating-phantasy is therefore passive from the very beginning, and is derived from a feminine attitude towards his father. It corresponds with the Oedipus complex just as the female one (that of the girl) does; only the parallel relation which we expected to find between the two must be given up in favour of a common character of another kind. *In both cases the beating-phantasy has its origin in an incestuous attachment to the father.*[1]

It will help to make matters clearer if at this point I enumerate the other similarities and differences between beating-phantasies in the two sexes. In the case of the girl the un-

[1] [A beating-phantasy plays some little part in the analysis of the 'Wolf Man' (1918*b*). See above, pp. 26 and 47.]

conscious masochistic phantasy starts from the normal Oedipus attitude; in that of the boy it starts from the inverted attitude, in which the father is taken as the object of love. In the case of the girl the phantasy has a preliminary stage (the first phase), in which the beating bears no special significance and is performed upon a person who is viewed with jealous hatred. Both of these features are absent in the case of the boy, but this particular difference is one which might be removed by more fortunate observation. In her transition to the conscious phantasy [the third phase] which takes the place of the unconscious one, the girl retains the figure of her father, and in that way keeps unchanged the sex of the person beating; but she changes the figure and sex of the person being beaten, so that eventually a man is beating male children. The boy, on the contrary, changes the figure and sex of the person beating, by putting his mother in the place of his father; but he retains his own figure, with the result that the person beating and the person being beaten are of opposite sexes. In the case of the girl what was originally a masochistic (passive) situation is transformed into a sadistic one by means of repression, and its sexual quality is almost effaced. In the case of the boy the situation remains masochistic, and shows a greater resemblance to the original phantasy with its genital significance, since there is a difference of sex between the person beating and the person being beaten. The boy evades his homosexuality by repressing and remodelling his unconscious phantasy: and the remarkable thing about his later conscious phantasy is that it has for its content a feminine attitude without a homosexual object-choice. By the same process, on the other hand, the girl escapes from the demands of the erotic side of her life altogether. She turns herself in phantasy into a man, without herself becoming active in a masculine way, and is no longer anything but a spectator of the event which takes the place of a sexual act.

We are justified in assuming that no great change is effected by the *repression* of the original unconscious phantasy. Whatever is repressed from consciousness or replaced in it by something else remains intact and potentially operative in the unconscious. The effect of *regression* to an earlier stage of the sexual organization is quite another matter. As regards this we are led to believe that the state of things changes in the unconscious as well. Thus in both sexes the masochistic phantasy of being

23

beaten by the father, though not the passive phantasy of being loved by him, lives on in the unconscious after repression has taken place. There are, besides, plenty of indications that the repression has only very incompletely attained its object. The boy, who has tried to escape from a homosexual object-choice, and who has not changed his sex, nevertheless feels like a woman in his conscious phantasies, and endows the women who are beating him with masculine attributes and characteristics. The girl, who has even renounced her sex, and who has on the whole accomplished a more thoroughgoing work of repression, nevertheless does not become freed from her father; she does not venture to do the beating herself; and since she has herself become a boy, it is principally boys whom she causes to be beaten.

I am aware that the differences that I have here described between the two sexes in regard to the nature of the beating-phantasy have not been cleared up sufficiently. But I shall not attempt to unravel these complications by tracing out their dependence on other factors, as I do not consider that the material for observation is exhaustive. So far as it goes, however, I should like to make use of it as a test for two theories. These theories stand in opposition to each other, though both of them deal with the relation between repression and sexual character, and each, according to its own view, represents the relation as a very intimate one. I may say at once that I have always regarded both theories as incorrect and misleading.

The first of these theories is anonymous. It was brought to my notice many years ago by a colleague with whom I was at that time on friendly terms.[1] The theory is so attractive on account of its bold simplicity that the only wonder is that it should not have found its way into the literature of the subject except in a few scattered allusions. It is based on the fact of the bisexual constitution of human beings, and asserts that the motive force of repression in each individual is a struggle between the two sexual characters. The dominant sex of the person, that which is the more strongly developed, has repressed the mental representation of the subordinated sex into the

[1] [Near the end of Freud's 'Analysis Terminable and Interminable (1937c), where he refers back to the present passage, he attributes this theory to Wilhelm Fliess.]

unconscious. Therefore the nucleus of the unconscious (that is to say, the repressed) is in each human being that side of him which belongs to the opposite sex. Such a theory as this can only have an intelligible meaning if we assume that a person's sex is to be determined by the formation of his genitals; for otherwise it would not be certain which is a person's stronger sex and we should run the risk of reaching from the results of our enquiry the very fact which has to serve as its point of departure. To put the theory briefly: with men, what is unconscious and repressed can be brought down to feminine instinctual impulses; and conversely with women.

The second theory is of more recent origin.[1] It is in agreement with the first one in so far as it too represents the struggle between the two sexes as being the decisive cause of repression. In other respects it comes into conflict with the former theory; moreover, it looks for support to sociological rather than biological sources. According to this theory of the 'masculine protest', formulated by Alfred Adler, every individual makes efforts not to remain on the inferior 'feminine line [of development]' and struggles towards the 'masculine line', from which satisfaction can alone be derived. Adler makes the masculine protest responsible for the whole formation both of character and of neuroses. Unfortunately he makes so little distinction between the two processes, which certainly have to be kept separate, and sets altogether so little store in general by the fact of repression, that to attempt to apply the doctrine of the masculine protest to repression brings with it the risk of misunderstanding. In my opinion such an attempt could only lead us to infer that the masculine protest, the desire to break away from the feminine line, was in every case the motive force of repression. The repressing agency, therefore, would always be a masculine instinctual impulse, and the repressed would be a feminine one. But symptoms would also be the result of a feminine impulse, for we cannot discard the characteristic feature of symptoms—that they are substitutes for the repressed, substitutes that have made their way out in spite of repression.

Now let us take these two theories, which may be said to have in common a sexualization of the process of repression,

[1] [Adler's theory of repression was discussed briefly in the case history of the 'Wolf Man' (1918*b*), p. 110 f. above.]

and test them by applying them to the example of the beating-phantasies which we have been studying. The original phantasy, 'I am being beaten by my father', corresponds, in the case of the boy, to a feminine attitude, and is therefore an expression of that part of his disposition which belongs to the opposite sex. If this part of him undergoes repression, the first theory seems shown to be correct; for this theory set it up as a rule that what belongs to the opposite sex is identical with the repressed. It scarcely answers to our expectations, it is true, when we find that the conscious phantasy, which arises after repression has been accomplished, nevertheless exhibits the feminine attitude once more, though this time directed towards the mother. But we will not go into such doubtful points, when the whole question can be so quickly decided. There can be no doubt that the original phantasy in the case of the girl, 'I am being beaten (i.e. I am loved) by my father', represents a feminine attitude, and corresponds to her dominant and manifest sex; according to the theory, therefore, it ought to escape repression, and there would be no need for its becoming unconscious. But as a matter of fact it does become unconscious, and is replaced by a conscious phantasy which disavows the girl's manifest sexual character. The theory is therefore useless as an explanation of beating-phantasies, and is contradicted by the facts. It might be objected that it is precisely in unmanly boys and unwomanly girls that these beating-phantasies appeared and went through these vicissitudes; or that it was a trait of femininity in the boy and of masculinity in the girl which must be made responsible for the production of a passive phantasy in the boy, and its repression in the girl. We should be inclined to agree with this view, but it would not be any the less impossible to defend the supposed relation between manifest sexual character and the choice of what is destined for repression. In the last resort we can only see that both in male and female individuals masculine as well as feminine instinctual impulses are found, and that each can equally well undergo repression and so become unconscious.

The theory of the masculine protest seems to maintain its ground very much better on being tested in regard to the beating-phantasies. In the case of both boys and girls the beating-phantasy corresponds with a feminine attitude—one, that is, in which the individual is lingering on the 'feminine line'—and both sexes hasten to get free from this attitude by repressing the phantasy. Nevertheless, it seems to be only with the girl that the masculine protest is attended with complete success, and in that instance, indeed, an ideal example is to be found of the operation of the masculine protest. With the boy the result is not entirely satisfactory; the feminine line is not given up, and the boy is certainly not 'on top' in his conscious masochistic phantasy. It would therefore agree with the expectations derived from the theory if we were to recognize that this phantasy was a symptom which had come into existence through the failure of the masculine protest. It is a disturbing fact, to be sure, that the girl's phantasy, which owes its origin to the forces of repression, also has the value and meaning of a symptom. In this instance, where the masculine protest has completely achieved its object, surely the determining condition for the formation of a symptom must be absent.

Before we are led by this difficulty to a suspicion that the whole conception of the masculine protest is inadequate to meet the problem of neuroses and perversions, and that its application to them is unfruitful, we will for a moment leave the passive beating-phantasies and turn our attention to other instinctual manifestations of infantile sexual life—manifestations which have equally undergone repression. No one can doubt that there are also wishes and phantasies which keep to the masculine line from their very nature, and which are the expression of masculine instinctual impulses—sadistic tendencies, for instance, or a boy's lustful feelings towards his mother arising out of the normal Oedipus complex. It is no less certain that these impulses, too, are overtaken by repression. If the masculine protest is to be taken as having satisfactorily explained the repression of passive phantasies (which later become masochistic), then it becomes for that very reason totally inapplicable to the opposite case of active phantasies. That is to say, the doctrine of the masculine protest is altogether incompatible with the fact of repression. Unless we are prepared to throw away all that has been acquired in psychology since Breuer's first cathartic treatment and through its agency, we cannot expect that the principle of the masculine protest will acquire any significance in the elucidation of the neuroses and perversions.

The theory of psycho-analysis (a theory based on observation) holds firmly to the view that the motive forces of repression must not be sexualized. Man's archaic heritage forms the

s.f. xvii—o

nucleus of the unconscious mind; and whatever part of that heritage has to be left behind in the advance to later phases of development, because it is unserviceable or incompatible with what is new and harmful to it, falls a victim to the process of repression. This selection is made more successfully with one group of instincts than with the other. In virtue of special circumstances which have often been pointed out already,[1] the latter group, that of the sexual instincts, are able to defeat the intentions of repression, and to enforce their representation by substitutive formations of a disturbing kind. For this reason infantile sexuality, which is held under repression, acts as the chief motive force in the formation of symptoms; and the essential part of its content, the Oedipus complex, is the nuclear complex of neuroses. I hope that in this paper I have raised an expectation that the sexual aberrations of childhood, as well as those of mature life, are ramifications of the same complex.

[1] [See for instance Freud's paper 'Formulations on the Two Principles of Mental Functioning' (1911*b*).]

PART TWO

Discussion of "A Child Is Being Beaten"

Not for Barbarians

An Appreciation of Freud's "A Child Is Being Beaten"

JACK NOVICK AND

KERRY KELLY NOVICK

Psychoanalysis is unlike other scientific disciplines. In physics or astronomy, for instance, the work of earlier years is often at best a curiosity, but history is central to psychoanalysis, in relation to both the individual and the field. Psychoanalysts assume that we all carry our pasts into the present and constantly revise the past in the light of subsequent experience. Thus we pass on to the future both the strengths and the weaknesses of our adaptations, accommodations, and conflict resolutions. In individual analyses or in the study of our theories analysts try to see what we can learn from the past and to correct errors so that they are not perpetuated. It is in this spirit that we feel it important to continue to study historical psychoanalytic papers, particularly those that are as central to the development of psychoanalytic thinking as "A Child Is Being Beaten."

Not everyone finds this paper important. Peter Gay (1988), the most recent Freud biographer, does not even mention it. Even though Jones described the paper as a "masterly analytic study" (1955, 308), it seems to us that he dismisses the importance of the work by saying, "In 1919, at a time when he was more engrossed with theory, Freud turned aside to publish a purely clinical study that reminds one of his earlier days" (308). Jones's comment appears in the context of his description of Freud's burst of theoretical creativity culminating in the development of libido theory. Jones seems to have felt that "A Child Is Being Beaten" added nothing to Freud's evolving theoretical formulations. We find, however, that a major strength of this paper is the very number of ideas contained in it. Freud describes the empirical base for his formulations—a series of six cases—and uses this relatively short, clinically descriptive piece to state, restate, or amplify major clinical and theoretical concepts: (1) the centrality of fantasy as the organizer of internal and external experience and as a product of synthesis; (2) the link between fantasy and gratification of masturbatory impulses; (3) the transformations and the vicissitudes of fantasy—repression and regression; (4) the centrality of the Oedipus complex to the formation of neurosis and in the sexualization of the beating fantasy; (5) the vicissitudes of memory, its complexity, and the reorganization of memory (*Nachträglichkeit*); (6) the importance of post-oedipal development and the crucial role of guilt and shame in the dynamics of sadomasochism, with the experience of humiliation linked to the motive power of "incompatible ideas"; (7) the incompatibility of ideas as a motive for repression; (8) the importance of the role of the father in the Oedipus complex; and (9) the unconscious effect of fantasy on character and pathology, including severe pathology, such as paranoia, and the concept of sublimation are also elaborated. Moreover, this is Freud's only paper in which the female is the model for understanding and development.

The choice of emphasis for this essay is difficult, for each of these points warrants separate discussion. But many of them are interrelated and can be included as we address the ongoing clinical and theoretical problems of sadomasochism. We can read a psychoanalytic paper in much the same way that we listen to patients: mindful of its strengths and capacities, of the conflicts that emerge, of the formal characteristics of the material, and of the present and past contexts. As we discuss Freud's paper, we will touch on each of these four dimensions to examine the continuing relevance of this paper for our current understanding of sadomasochism in its manifold manifestations.

In examining a historical paper we have a benefit analogous to the reflection available in the clinical setting: errors, like conflicts, will be repeated unless they are noticed, remembered, and tested against current reality. Insights gained can sometimes be forgotten and have to be rediscovered. Just as self-analysis is repeatedly necessary, so we reread old papers to find lost points, to notice what went unacknowledged at the time of writing, and to highlight what Freud either did not develop or did not realize was the starting point of a further theoretical development.

Empathy is another clinical skill of the consulting room that may usefully be brought to the reading of a paper. Empathy has come to be enshrined in various theories but was discussed very early and extensively by Freud (1912, 1913) and Ferenczi, both separately and with each other (Ferenczi, 1955 [1928]; Grubrich-Simitis, 1986). Part of what Freud called *Einfühlung* involves the active apprehension of the context, past and current, of the patient's productions. So we might ask where Freud was in his theory-building when writing this paper.

By 1919, Freud was at a point of some frustration in his theorizing. The topographical theory was proving inadequate to explain sadomasochistic phenomena and functioning. He was faced in his clinical work and in the events of the world with things that went beyond the explanatory power of the pleasure principle. He was in a creative crisis—his planned book on metapsychology was not yet written, and seven of the twelve metapsychological papers had disappeared or had been destroyed. We may infer that he felt escalating tension over the limitations of prestructural theory. Freud wrestled with the problems of sadomasochism throughout his career; indeed, each major shift in theory derived from continuing struggle to understand and address this pathology.

His personal life too provides important understanding of the context of this work. Freud's three sons, his sons-in-law, and his nephew all served in the army during World War I. His letters show his constant concern for their safety. Toward the end of the war, Freud's son Martin was imprisoned by the Italians, and the family had no word of his whereabouts for months. By 1915 most of Freud's younger colleagues were in the army, and he complained to Lou Andreas-Salomé that he was once again alone. He had no patients and from 1916 until two years after the end of the war often had difficulty buying food for his family. His wife contracted influenza and pneumonia after the war, and her state of malnutrition made her recovery slow. As late as 1920, Freud's work was affected by a shortage of paper.

So, in the face of theoretical frustration and personal privation, suffering, and anxiety, Freud turned to an empirical study of what he called the "essence of masochism" (1919, 189). He described the beating fantasy as representing both debased genital love for the father and punishment for incestuous wishes. For ease of study and comparison of Freud's ideas with later developments, we will use here the summary of Freud's ideas from our 1970 study of beating fantasies in children (Novick and Novick, 1996 [1972]).

From adult analytic material Freud reconstructed the sequential vicissitudes of the beating fantasy in boys and girls. He suggested that the fantasy first appears in the preschool years and no later than five or six years of age. It has three phases in girls:

1. "My father is beating the child whom I hate." Freud questions whether this can be called a fantasy and notes that it may represent rather a recollection of "desires which have arisen" (p. 185). The motive for this first phase is the child's jealousy of and rivalry with a sibling. Freud doubts that this first phase can be described as sexual and gives its full meaning as "My father does not love this other child, he loves only me."

2. "I am being beaten by my father." According to Freud this second phase is the result of a profound transformation of the first phase. Although the beater remains the father, the one being beaten is invariably the child producing the fantasy. This fantasy is of an "unmistakably masochistic character" and represents both debased genital love for the father and punishment for incestuous wishes. This phase of the fantasy is never remembered and, Freud adds, "in a certain sense . . . has never had a real existence" (p. 185).

3. "A [father substitute] teacher beats children" (usually boys). This phase, like the first, is consciously remembered. Unlike the first phase, but like the second and thus linked with it, is the strong and unambiguous sexual excitement attached to it.

Freud expected but did not find a parallel sequence in the beating fantasies of boys. He described the third (conscious) phase of the fantasy in males as "I am being beaten by my mother (or other woman)." This is preceded by the unconscious fantasy: "I am being beaten by my father." This corresponds with the second phase in girls; thus the beating fantasy in both sexes has its origin in oedipal attachment to the father. Freud did not find evidence of a first phase in boys in which the beating bears no sexual significance but is motivated by jealousy. However, he felt that further observation might reveal that boys too have such a first phase. (3–4)

It is interesting to note, in the light of current feminist critiques of Freud, that in this paper he clearly distinguishes between the psychologies of his female and his male patients. He uses the female fantasy as the model but cautions against drawing too close a parallel between the two sexes, a distinction often elided by other writers on the beating fantasy.

The evolution of the beating fantasy as Freud describes it includes radical formulations about the operation of memory. Freud notes that analysis of the conscious fantasy (the manifest content) led to the recollection of events that were witnessed or desires that had arisen involving a father beating his child (the latent content). This describes physical abuse, but did it really happen? Freud is underscoring the complex interaction of memory and desire: desire not only can determine what is perceived and recalled but can also constitute the memory itself and be confused with reality. The intensely pleasurable thought of the second phase may represent a memory of sexual abuse or a "recovered memory" that garners publicity or is used in a lawsuit against parents. Freud makes it clear that this second phase is never remembered, is a construct of the analysis, something arrived at together by patient and therapist; "in a certain sense," as Freud states, "it has never had a real existence" (1919, 185). Freud's emphasis on the complexity, the malleability, and the tendentious nature of memory is central to the current controversy raging in psychology and psychiatry regarding the reliability of recovered memories. Recent research by Loftus (1993, 1994) on the implanting of false memories; Ganaway's (1989) work on the association of multiple personality disorder, suggestibility, hypnotizability, and the reporting of abuse; and Yapko's (1994) demonstration of the naiveté and ignorance of therapists who use hypnosis, drugs, and suggestion to recover memories—all substantiate Freud's basic theory of memory. At the end of his paper on screen memories, Freud states, "It may indeed be questioned whether we have any memories at all from our childhood. Memories relating to our childhood may be all that we possess" (1899, 322).

Current emphasis on technique and the interaction in the treatment relationship, at the expense of a focus on psychic mechanisms, seems to have led to a decline of interest in memory. In this paper Freud confronts us with the complexity of memory and its centrality to both theory and technique. In addition, he uses the theory of *Nachträglichkeit,* or deferred action, to account for the appearance, intensification, and modification of the beating fantasy in its third phase. He points out that the conscious fantasy of a teacher beating boys appears under the impetus of external experiences, such as witnessing beatings in school or reading books such as *Uncle Tom's Cabin,* memories of which appeared consistently in his patients' clinical material. The modern equivalent might be exposure to violent interactions on television at a time when the child is in a new phase of development, one that influences the memories and fantasies of earlier phases. Thus we see Freud positing a complex transformation of both memory and fantasy in his description of the clinical phenomenology of the stages of the beating fantasy. Freud's theory of deferred action may usefully be applied to transformations of memory, fantasy, and meaning throughout development, with changes in function reflecting changes in internal and external realities (Novick and Novick, 1994).

Freud wrote in 1913, "From the very first psychoanalysis was directed towards tracing a developmental process" (183). "A Child Is Being Beaten" illustrates his reliance on thinking within a developmental framework for generating both theory and clinical understanding. The impact of the developmental phase on how internal and external events are experienced has been noted above in the context of transformations. Note also Freud's empathy with the child's experience, his sense of what is felt and understood early in development, which comes through clearly in his description of the child's reaction to a younger sibling who has attracted the love of the parents: "Many children who believed themselves securely enthroned in the unshakable affection of their parents have by a single blow been cast down from all the heavens of their imaginary omnipotence" (1919, 187).

Later in the paper Freud makes the disclaimer that "little light is thrown upon the genesis of masochism by our discussion of the beating-phantasy" (193). Earlier, however, when describing the reconstructed fantasy of being beaten by the father as "a convergence of the sense of guilt and sexual love," Freud says, "Here for the first time we have the essence of masochism" (189). This apparent contradiction reflects a continuing difficulty in conceptualizing the origin of masochism, the genesis of phenomena that reside "beyond the pleasure principle." This puzzle leads in the paper on beating fantasies to a focus on the sense of guilt and an "agency in the mind which sets itself up as a critical conscience over against the rest of the ego" (194). Later Freud would describe this as the superego (1923, ch. 3). The "riddle of masochism," in Wurmser's (1993) apt phrase, led Freud to posit in 1924 another possible solution—the idea of a primary masochism in which pleasure in pain, or erotogenic masochism, is governed by the nirvana or constancy principle rather than by the pleasure principle.

One reason for the relative obscurity of the beating fantasy paper is that it was contradicted and in some ways superseded by Freud's 1924 paper "The Economic Problem of Masochism." In that paper he expands on the meanings of the beating fantasy. Again using a developmental framework, he notes the oral-phase fear of being eaten, the wish to be beaten by the father as an anal-sadistic impulse, castration as the masochistic content of the fantasies of the phallic stage, and the wish to copulate and to give birth as the transformation of primary masochism that appears in the final genital organization. In the 1924 paper he uses the concepts of fusion, defusion, superego, and moral masochism to address questions raised or avoided in the 1919 paper. It is still crucial, however, to look at the beating fantasy paper to see what was omitted or deemphasized in 1924 and so lost to later generations of psychoanalysts.

Earlier we listed some of the many important ideas contained in Freud's "A Child Is Being Beaten." Here we will focus on those ideas about sadomasochism that seem still relevant.

The narcissistic component of sadomasochism. After 1924, explanatory emphasis centered on the drive components of sadomasochism, but in the 1919 paper Freud highlights the role of shame, humiliation, and guilt. He describes the resistance of his patients to acknowledging and articulating the conscious fantasy of a child being beaten, and he relates this to feelings of shame over the umistakably sexual excitement produced by the fantasies. The first form of the fantasy ("My father is beating the child I hate") is seen as motivated both by humiliation at having to give up the position of sole recipient of parental love and by the wish to humiliate the hated rival. Recently, psychoanalysts have again turned their attention to the narcissistic components of masochistic phenomena (see Novick and Novick, 1996a, ch. 3 for a review).

Sadomasochism and object relations. Freud's 1924 concept of primary erotogenic masochism highlights the drive component of sadomasochism and has allowed many to forget that drives are manifest only in the context of an object relationship. In "A Child Is Being Beaten" Freud describes the shifts in the fantasy in terms of inner and outer determinants of the changing relation to parents. The beating fantasy implies a particular type of relationship—one of power and submission. Freud delineates how it emerges out of the child's rage and humiliation at being dethroned from the position of sole recipient of parental love: from internal feelings of help-lessness, hurt, and rage the child constructs the wish that the father should beat and so humiliate the despised rival. The transformation of the "sadistic" wish to the "masochistic" wish to be beaten by the father is spurred by the internal changes of the oedipal phase, which lead the child into the wish to be the recipient of the father's love and to have his baby. Thus the 1919 paper contains a clear model for the object-relational component of sadomasochism.

The character effects of the beating fantasy. Freud points out that the second, unconscious, phase of the fantasy, in which the child is being beaten by the father, has "effects upon the character" (195). He notes that people who harbor unconscious beating fantasies develop a special sensitivity and irritability toward father figures. They are easily offended by people in authority and so bring about the situation of being beaten by their father. He also suggests that the beating fantasy may be the basis of the "delusional litigiousness of paranoia" (195). This relation between sadomasochism and character is a good example of an idea that warrants further exploration. Along these lines, Blum (1980) described a dynamic connection between paranoia and the beating fantasy.

The sexualization of the beating fantasy. Freud repeatedly emphasizes the role of the Oedipus complex in his presentation of the developmental sequence of the fantasy. In the first phase the aim is not primarily sexual but aggressive toward the sibling. In the second phase, oedipal incestuous love for the father is repressed, and the fantasy of being beaten represents "not only the punishment for the forbidden genital relation, but also the regressive substitute for that relation, and from this latter source it derives the libidinal excitation which is from this time forward attached to it, and which finds its outlet in masturbatory acts" (189). This distinction between a presexual and a sexualized phase of the beating fantasy was confirmed in our 1970 study. Material from children observed in nursery school and children treated in analysis demonstrated a distinct sequence of beating wishes. There is a time in which almost all children form their concepts of relationships in terms of power and control. Active discharge of aggressive impulses to beat, hit, or overpower is linked with the anal phase. This stage in the development of the beating wish is similar to the first phase of the beating fantasy as Freud describes it: the important characteristics are that it is aggressive, not sexual, is discharged in action, is appropriate to the anal phase, and occurs in both sexes. The sadistic intercourse theory (Freud, 1908) is a persistence and generalization of anal-phase concepts of relationships to the impulses of the phallic phase. It is via the sadistic theory of intercourse that the beating wish becomes sexualized. At the phallic stage both boys and girls were seen playing hitting games or chasing and catching games, all accompanied by intense sexual excitement. In these games, the children alternated between playing attacker and victim. Diffuse sexual excitement and masturbation usually accompanied or followed the games. With the awareness of the difference between the sexes, being beaten acquires a further meaning. From the anal phase it carries the meaning of punishment and loss of love; from the early phallic phase it comes to represent parental intercourse, and, at this point, with differentiation between the sexes, it represents castration and the feminine position in intercourse. Here we regularly found a divergence between boys and girls. Such phenomena have recently been explored by Galenson (1988) and by Glenn (1984), with technical and theoretical insights into the complexity and richness of the layering of development. Freud continues the description of the transformations of the beating fantasy into post-oedipal phases, through the early and later school years. He then notes the overcoming or consolidation of sadomasochism at adolescence. This too is a fruitful area for further exploration that has implications for the technical importance of including work on patients' adolescent experience (Novick and Novick, 1994, 1996b).

Sadomasochism as a dynamic or nosological entity. There is a current debate (Panel, 1991) over this matter. Freud takes both sides in this paper but provides evidence that the beating fantasy, and hence sadomasochism, can be found in many diagnostic categories and arises out of a constellation of developmental and dynamic forces.

The beating fantasy is the essence of masochism. Freud's later writings on sadomasochism, although they add crucial dimensions, seem to lose this critical insight into the organizing role of the fantasy and how study of its history, vicissitudes, determinants, and functions can open the door to further understanding of sadomasochism.

We have sketched above some of the strengths of Freud's paper in relation to the theory of sadomasochism. But what of its deficiencies? Freud himself acknowledged that this study does not throw light on the *origins* of sadomasochism. In the effort to pursue that understanding he found one solution in revising drive theory, positing the role of primary erotogenic masochism (1924). Another solution is contained in the idea of the sense of guilt and the need for punishment, which Freud developed into the superego concept and the structural theory. Both of these evolutions have already been briefly discussed.

A glaring omission from "A Child Is Being Beaten" is the role of the pre-oedipal mother in the origins of sadomasochism and the beating fantasy. Freud does not mention the mother at all in relation to his female patients and refers to the oedipal mother only with the males. Freud finds his two solutions to the theoretical problems of sadomasochism by expanding both ends of the developmental sequence, extending back to the oral phase with primary masochism and forward through the end of the infantile period with the structural model formulation of the sadistic superego and masochistic ego. So for Freud the components of sadomasochism encompass the whole developmental span, a notion lost in later controversies over whether determinants of sadomasochism are oedipal or pre-oedipal (Novick and Novick, 1987). This makes the omission of the mother even more striking, as, for instance, even during the oral phase, Freud writes of the masochistic fear of being eaten by the father. Through subsequent developmental phases the primary object in sadomasochistic fantasies, as Freud describes them, is the father, who beats at the anal-sadistic level, castrates at the phallic, creates the baby at the oedipal, and is internalized as a sadistic prohibitor in the superego.

Along with Freud's omission of the mother is the assumption in the 1919 paper of the equation of femininity, passivity, and the masochistic position. This assumption, which leads to the concept of "normal" feminine masochism, continues to receive widespread cultural and psychoanalytic dissemination, despite bitter criticism from many quarters. We have been unable to substantiate this equation in any of our studies. We do not agree that the choice of an experience or activity that may include pain, such as childbirth or self-sacrifice, is necessarily masochistic. Thus we do not find any relation among feminine functions, passivity, and masochism. Freud and later analysts have used the term *passive* in many different ways, as described by Davis (1993). Freud's early and most consistent use of *passive* was in relation to the direction of drive impulses. The "passive" wish to be done to, beaten, and penetrated was linked to masochism (Freud, 1905) and equated with the feminine position in intercourse. These usages parallel grammatical distinctions between active and passive voice. However, *passive* is also used by Freud and others to refer to a quality of the ego, the opposite of purposeful, goal-directed, focused behavior. In our work we have found it helpful to distinguish between passive and receptive (Novick and Novick, 1996a [1987]). We see passivity as an ego quality linked in its pathological extreme manifestations to the experience of parental inability to sustain attention. On the other hand, "masochists are highly receptive and are ready to take in any stimuli from the outside world. . . . . Masochists are very active in their pursuit of pain and failure, in part to maintain the receptive relationship with an intrusive object" (31).

The finding of Freud's that we can confirm from our research is his description of differences in the beating fantasies of men and women and his clinical sense of a significant difference in degrees of pathology. Our studies demonstrated that a *transitory* beating fantasy can be part of normal post-oedipal development in girls (Novick and Novick, 1996a [1972]). A *fixed* beating fantasy, on the other hand, one that becomes a permanent part of the child's psychosexual life and serves multiple psychological functions after consolidation at puberty, is indicative of severe underlying sadomasochistic pathology in both men and women.

Another curious omission by Freud is reference to his own work of the same period; he does not link the beating fantasy with his description of the sexual theories of children, especially the sadistic theory of intercourse (Freud, 1908). In our own work on beating fantasies in children (Novick and Novick, 1972) and sadomasochism (Novick and Novick, 1987) we found that the sadistic theory of intercourse was universal and played a central role in the sexualization of the beating wish. We also found that children who constructed beating fantasies made stories that went beyond being beaten. Further analytic work revealed that the beating was always followed by parents' or parent substitutes' treating the child as a very special person, entitled to unusual and special treatment. "One child fantasied that the beating would be followed by both parents apologizing and the mother putting soothing lotion on his bottom" (Novick and Novick, 1996a [1972], 12). Nor does Freud refer in 1919 to his paper on character types, particularly his description of the "exception," the victim of fate who feels himself thereby entitled to be an exception to normal rules (Freud, 1916). Our data from child, adolescent, and adult analyses extends the concept of sadomasochism past its equation with adult sexual perversion alone to the experience of the self as a victim of others' injustice, a state of affairs that can then be used for narcissistic justification and entitlement. Thus Freud's suggestion of character ramifications of the presence of a beating fantasy is borne out by further work.

Freud made the point in 1919 that the beating fantasy is the essence of masochism, but he never pursued the idea further. Our application of his idea reveals the sadomasochism in the character type of the "exception." This holds true of the other two character types described by Freud in his 1916 paper, where an underlying beating fantasy can be discerned as the structure of the sadomasochistic character disturbance. "Criminals from a sense of guilt" have a sadistic superego attacking a masochistic ego and thus may fit easily into the extension we propose of Freud's ideas. "Characters wrecked by success" were eventually explained by Freud in terms of a negative therapeutic reaction, which he characterized as the clinical manifestation of a need for punishment derived from moral masochism (Freud, 1923, 1924). What emerges in those wrecked by success, unable to tolerate pleasure or achievement, is a history of a sadomasochistic relationship with the mother designed to protect an image of mother and child as omnipotently essential to each other. The operation of a negative therapeutic motivation in treatment (Novick, 1980), with the goal of wrecking the analysis, serves to protect the sadomasochistic character organization. But why does a patient work so hard to preserve this pathology? This in turn raises the question of the functions served by sadomasochism in the operation of the personality.

The multiple functions served by a sadomasochistic organization reflect its multilevel origins. In our view, each phase of development contributes to the clinical manifestations of sadomasochism. Painful experiences in infancy are transformed into a mode of attachment, then into an embraced marker of specialness and unlimited destructive power, then into a conviction of equality with the oedipal parents, and, finally, into an omnipotent fantasy of gratifying infantile wishes through the coercion of others. By school age, children who have found these solutions to the conflicts of earlier phases have established a magic omnipotent system of thought that undermines alternate means of competent interactions with reality. In adolescence and adulthood it becomes increasingly hard for them to deny, avoid, or distort reality without resorting to escalating self-destructive behaviors. All the elements of these formulations may be found in Freud's 1919 study, including reference to the influence of culture and to externalization as a crucial mechanism in sadomasochistic pathology, although many aspects of the views presented in this paper were later submerged or never followed up. We continue to find this paper a fruitful source of clinical and theoretical insights and suggestions, but it has taken much further elaboration to arrive at some ideas about the difficulties of working with patients who manifest sadomasochistic functioning.

The multiple functions served by a sadomasochistic organization lead to manifold and often seemingly intractable technical difficulties in treatment. To the end of his life, despite the many revisions of theory prompted by sadomasochistic phenomena, Freud was troubled by the problems of addressing sadomasochism. In 1940, he wrote that we are still "specially inadequate" in dealing with masochistic patients (180). Analysts ever since have experienced the same discouragement (see, for example, Meyers, 1988). The therapeutic impasses we often face with sadomasochistic patients make us feel stymied and helpless.

We noted earlier that it can be illuminating to read a psychoanalytic paper in ways analogous to the listening we do with patients: our knowledge of the context surrounding the material at hand is built up over time and includes the patient's past and present, the transferences and countertransferences of both people. If we look at the totality of Freud's life while he was working on "A Child Is Being Beaten" we can see what Annie Reich (1960) described as normal and pathological forms of self-esteem regulation. In the paper Freud describes a closed, sadomasochistic system. But his life exemplifies the operation of open, creative, resourceful solutions to serious problems. Faced with privation and isolation, helpless to protect and provide for his loved ones, Freud did not seek a solution in a sadomasochistic psychical formation. Rather, he made an active, competent response, finding ways to earn either money or payment in kind—potatoes in one instance! He worked to keep his anxieties conscious, actively analyzing his dreams in his effort to master his anxiety about his missing son, Martin.

In studying the sadomasochistic solution to conflict in child, adolescent, and adult patients we have concluded that sadomasochism is not a specific or separate diagnostic category but an integral part of all pathology. Our formulation assumes a developmental path in which "healthy" or "adaptive" solutions to conflict may be achieved throughout life, in an open, competent system of self-regulation based on mutually respectful, pleasurable, and growth-promoting relationships formed through realistic perceptions of separate, autonomous individuals. On the other hand, there is a closed, omnipotent sadomasochistic system based on the active search for pain with the change throughout development of the experience of helplessness into a hostile, omnipotent defense.

When we describe two systems, the competent one open to inner and outer realities, the omnipotent one closed within a self-perpetuating, sadomasochistic fantasy that follows the structure of the beating fantasy described by Freud in 1919, we are not referring to distinct psychic structures (such as id, ego, superego), to different developmental stages, or to distinct topographic dimensions of the conscious and unconscious regions of the mind, each with a different type of thought organization. Rather, we are referring to two modes of conflict resolution and self-esteem regulation, each of which is a possible response to conflict at any point in development.

"As we have stated elsewhere, one of the aims of treatment is to help the patient become aware of the system he is using, to face the way in which the omnipotent system destroys the reality of his capacities and achievements, and ultimately to realize that relinquishing the omnipotent source of self-esteem will not leave him with nothing. As the patient laboriously gets in touch with the alternative sources of self-esteem available through competent, empathic, and loving interactions with others, a conflict arises between the two systems" (Novick and Novick, 1996a, 68). Where there is conflict within the individual we have techniques for allying with the patient's ego to address the sources of the difficulty.

If we read Freud's 1919 paper from an analytic stance, the work becomes more than a historical curiosity. We see that there is much that has been ignored or lost in later theories; many of these lost ideas are relevant to a modern psychoanalytic theory of sadomasochism. Our analytic ear also notes omissions and distortions, and we work toward integration rather than repetition. In listening to a patient's material, we absorb the present, link it with the past, and extend it to the future. So with this paper we include earlier concepts and note the transformations of the 1919 ideas as they evolve in later formulations. Finally, our analytic listening to this paper includes the larger context of Freud the man, which directs us toward further expansion of theory and technique as we address the continuing riddle of sadomasochism.

To be a psychoanalyst is to be immersed in history—the history of the session, the analysis, the life of the individual and his family, one's own history, and the history of psychoanalytic thought. But we know only too well that history can be rewritten to suit the needs of the moment. We see this in our patients, and we spend our days combatting the tendentious rewriting of personal history. In a recent collection of essays, Isaiah Berlin (1991) noted, "Only barbarians are not curious about where they come from, how they came to be where they are, where they appear to be going, whether they wish to go there, and if so, why, and if not, why not" (2).

REFERENCES

Berlin, I. 1991. *The crooked timber of humanity: Chapters in the history of ideas.* New York: Knopf.

Blum, H. P. 1980. Paranoia and beating fantasy: An inquiry into the psychoanalytic theory of paranoia. *J. Amer. Psychoan.* 28: 331–62.

Davis, R. H. 1993. *Freud's concept of passivity.* Madison, Conn.: International Universities Press.

Ferenczi, S. 1955 [1928]. The elasticity of psycho-analytic technique. In *Final contributions to the problems and methods of psycho-analysis,* ed. M. Balint, trans. E. Mosbacher et al. New York: Basic.

Freud, S. 1899. Screen memories. *S.E.* 3:303–22.

——. 1905. Three essays on the theory of sexuality. *S.E.* 7: 125–243.

——. 1908. On the sexual theories of children. *S.E.* 9:207–26.

——. 1912. Recommendations to physicians practising psycho-analysis. *S.E.* 12:109–20.

——. 1913. The claims of psycho-analysis to scientific interest. *S.E.* 13:163–90.

——. 1916. Some character-types met with in psychoanalytic work. *S.E.* 14:311–36.

——. 1919. A child is being beaten. *S.E.* 17:175–204.

——. 1923. The ego and the id. *S.E.* 19:12–59.

——. 1924. The economic problem of masochism. *S.E.* 19:157–70.

——. 1940 [1938]. An outline of psychoanalysis. *S.E.* 23: 141–207.

Galenson, E. 1988. The precursors of masochism: Protomasochism. In *Masochism: Current psychoanalytic perspectives,* ed. R. A. Glick and D. I. Meyers, 189–204. Hillsdale, N.J.: Analytic.

Ganaway, G. K. 1989. Historical versus narrative truth: Clarifying the role of exogenous trauma in the etiology of MPD and its variants. *Dissociation* 2:205–20.

Gay, P. 1988. *Freud: A life for our time.* New York: Norton.

Glenn, J. 1984. A note on loss, pain and masochism in children. *J. Amer. Psychoan.* 32:63–73.

Grubrich-Simitis, I. 1986. Six letters of Sigmund Freud and Sandor Ferenczi on the interrelationship of psychoanalytic theory and technique. *Int. Rev. Psychoanal.* 13:259–77.

Jones, E. 1955. *The life and work of Sigmund Freud: Years of maturity.* Vol. 2. New York: Basic.

Loftus, E. F. 1993. The reality of repressed memories. *Amer. Psychol.* 48:518–37.

——. 1994. The repressed memory controversy. *Amer. Psychol.* 49:443–45.

Meyers, H. 1988. A consideration of treatment techniques in relation to the functions of masochism. In *Masochism: Current psychoanalytic perspectives,* ed. R. A. Glick and D. I. Meyers, 175–89. Hillsdale, N.J.: Analytic.

Novick, J. 1980. Negative therapeutic motivation and negative therapeutic alliance. *Psychoanal. Study Child* 35:299–320. New Haven: Yale University Press.

Novick, J., and Novick, K. K. 1972. Beating fantasies in children. *Int. J. Psycho-Anal.* 53:237–42.

———. 1996a. *Fearful symmetry: The development and treatment of sadomasochism.* Northvale, N.J.: Jason Aronson.

———. 1996b. A developmental perspective on omnipotence. *J. Clinical Psychoanal.* 5:129–74.

Novick, K. K., and Novick, J. 1987. The essence of masochism. *Psychoanal. Study Child* 42:353–84. New Haven: Yale University Press.

———. 1994. Postoedipal transformations: Latency, adolescence, and pathogenesis. *J. Amer. Psychoan.* 42:143–70.

Panel 1991. Sadism and masochism in character disorder and resistance. M. H. Sacks, reporter. *J. Amer. Psychoan.* 39:215–26.

Reich, A. 1960. Pathologic forms of self esteem regulation. *Psychoanal. Study Child* 15:215–32. New Haven: Yale University Press.

Wurmser, L. 1993. *Das Ratsel des Masochismus [The riddle of masochism].* Heidelberg: Springer Verlag.

Yapko, M. D. 1994. *Suggestions of abuse: True and false memories of childhood sexual trauma.* New York: Simon and Schuster.

"A Child Is Being Beaten"

A Clinical, Historical, and Textual Study

PATRICK JOSEPH MAHONY

Freud's essay "A Child Is Being Beaten" has elicited different critical reactions. In Jones's opinion, it is "a masterly analytic study of his experience" (1955, 308). For Bonaparte, "Freud has set more problems than he solves" (1953, 83). For Asch, Freud's essay "is one of his more speculative discourses, generalized from too few cases" (1980, 653). Whatever the evaluation, "A Child Is Being Beaten" merits our attention if for no other reason than that it contains Freud's fullest elaboration of the phasic transformations of a neurotic phantasy, features his most detailed explanation of the motives leading to repression, represents a watershed in his recognition of different developmental lines for boys and girls, proposes an explanation of masochism as secondary that is a way station to his later theory (Freud, 1924), and foreshadows the discovery of the superego (Freud, 1923).

Thus, "A Child Is Being Beaten," one of Freud's more complex essays, has much to offer us. I shall explore it in terms of its setting, its major and secondary content, its form, and its position in the context of subsequent psychoanalytic contributions.

THE SETTING AND IMMEDIATE
ENDING OF FREUD'S ESSAY

Although the general examination of beating phantasies occupies the major portion of Freud's essay, he particularly values his insights into the genesis of masochism. His correspondence clearly expresses this estimate and corrects Strachey's affirmation that the essay was finished and given its title by the middle of March 1919 (Strachey note, 1918, *S.E.* 17:177). Thus, on January 1, 1919, Freud wrote to Ferenczi: "I am still fully taken up. Soon I shall have brought out in fair copy some reliable novelties on the genesis of masochism." Less than two months later, he told Kata Levy, his patient and intimate acquaintance: "I am, moreover, in a creative mood and still hope to finish a little essay tonight" (unpublished letter of March 3, 1919). This hope was not realized, for Freud wrote again to Ferenczi two weeks later: "I have completed some twenty-six pages of a bold work on the genesis of masochism, which bears the title 'A Child Is Being Beaten.'"[1] The piece was published in the summer of 1919, but that was far, far from the end of the matter.

Another story was not long in the making. In the summer of 1920 Jones wrote a letter to Freud introducing Strachey as a patient and a potential translator in these reserved terms, which would be monumentally disproved by subsequent history: "I hope he may assist with translation of your works. I think [him] a good fellow but weak and perhaps lacking in tenacity." That fall Freud took both James and Alix Strachey into analysis; shortly after the treatments were under way, Freud shared Jones's letter with James Strachey (!) and then, only a few weeks later, instructed him and his wife to translate "A Child Is Being Beaten" (Jones, 1955, 410; Clark, 1980, 427–28; Strachey, *S.E.* 1:xxi). Extant letters from the period also show that, much as he did with Joan Riviere, Freud discussed the translation of his writings with James and Alix Strachey in their analyses (Steiner, 1995, 749). To be sure, discussion of the translation also occurred outside of analytic sessions; we find Freud reporting on February 7, 1921, that he would be consulted by Strachey the next day about some points in the translation he had just finished (Freud, 1993, 409). The discussion must have caused Freud to make

1. I am grateful to Ernst Falzeder for supplying me with the citations from the letters to Ferenczi and Kata Levy.

further revisions, for in a letter to Jones on February 23, he expressed the hope that he would finish the essay before Easter (414). Also on February 23, Jones sent Freud a criticism of Strachey's translation for both its English and its rendering of German; let it be said, however, that in Jones's sole attribution of error (207/187–88), Freud backed up Strachey's position (Freud, 1993, 412–13, 416). Not long thereafter, Strachey's translation was honored by its appearance in the inaugural issue of the *International Journal of Psycho-Analysis* (1921).

We discover a hidden punitive aspect of Freud's composition when we realize that it was written under bodily pain caused by a "bad pen" (letter to Jones of April 18, 1919; Freud, 1993, 341). Another hidden punitive aspect has a longer and more intriguing history and relates to external events that attended the conception and writing of "A Child Is Being Beaten." Without doubt, Freud was stimulated to explore beating phantasies because they were central in the dynamics of his daughter, whom he began analyzing in October 1918. (He finished her first analysis in the spring of 1922.) Thus, only when the analysis was fully under way did Freud set about composing "A Child Is Being Beaten." Anna was one of the six cases dealt with in her father's essay (Blass, 1993; compare Young-Bruehl, 1988). The grammatically present progressive in the title suggests that in his iatrogenic seduction and abuse of his daughter, Freud was in the process of symbolically beating her and compounding her beating fantasies (Mahony, 1992). I have also noticed that in "A Child Is Being Beaten" Freud did not use the term *identification,* a lexical absence and possible defensive trace of the dyad's strong mutual identification. Had Freud focused on identification, I muse, he might have expedited his groping discovery of the superego. A derivative of both the parental analysis and Freud's essay was Anna's disguised, autobiographical "Beating Fantasies and Daydreams" (1923). Oedipally engendered, that paper served also as her "write" of passage—it was a membership paper delivered to the Vienna Psychoanalytic Society, which was presided over by none other than her own father and analyst. Anna described how her oedipally incestuous phantasies regressed to the anal stage and then appeared as beating phantasies accompanied by masturbation; eventually those phantasies changed into punitive "nice stories," with sexual excitation as a possibility. (For some differences between Anna's and her father's understanding of beating phantasies, see Blass, 1993.)

FREUD'S ESSAY: WHAT IS BEING
SAID ABOUT THE PRINCIPAL MATTER

Freud's essay consists of six sections. The first four examine a subtopic of sadomasochism—namely, the evolution, form, and significance of beating phantasies, which can bear the contradictory meanings of feeling unloved and feeling loved in a genital sense.

Two great psychoanalytic personages figure among Freud's clinical sample: his daughter, as we know, and the Wolf Man, who, as a child, had numerous phantasies of himself and others being beaten on the penis (Freud, 1918, 26, 46–47, 63–64). The four female patients, Freud told Bonaparte, were all virgins (see Bonaparte, 1953); the male patients referred to either specifically or generally were largely what he classified as true perverts. Because of expository difficulties, however, Freud focused for the most part on female patients. As he confessed, "It would been quite impossible to give a clear survey of infantile beating-phantasies if I had not limited it, except in one or two connections, to the state of things in females" (1919, 195). Although he confines his descriptions to the female cases, for broader conclusions about perversion he also relies on a "fairly larger number" of less fully investigated cases (182, 184, 191).

In his orienting formulations Freud describes two crucial phases in the development of the parental complex (186–88; see also Freud, 1924, 173). In the first, children enjoy "the heavens of their imaginary omnipotence" and "love-affairs" with the parent of the opposite sex. That incestuous idyllic state comes to grief because of internal, phylogenetic or ontogenetic conditions or because of an external event such as the birth of a sibling.

Freud finds that the girl's beating phantasies, pivoting around oedipal conflicts and sibling rivalry, occur in three phases: first, the father beats a child, a sibling if one exists; then he beats the author of the phantasy; and finally, she observes a group of boys receiving the punishment. According to Freud's detailed understanding of the first phase, "A child is being beaten" is its "phantasy-representation."[2] Although Freud starts out by identifying "A child is being beaten" as the conscious phantasy representation of the first phase, he later states that it may be rather a desire or a recollection of actual

2. Whenever I use two sets of numbers separated by a slash, the first set refers to pages in the *Gesammelte Werke* and the second to pages in the *Standard Edition*.

events (204/185). Then he proceeds to render the latent verbal representation of the phantasy in a double proposition: "My father does not love this other child, *he loves only me.*"

We should also note that whereas Freud asserts that the first phase is not directly sexual, he hedges as to whether it is sadistic: "It would be tempting to call it sadistic, but one cannot neglect the fact that the child producing the phantasy is never doing the beating herself" (185). Two pages later Freud returns to the first phase and bluntly advances that no one can "venture to call it 'sadistic.'" But then, approximating his first formulation, he concludes that the first phase does "appear to be sadistic" (195).

The second phase of the phantasy is a reconstruction in which its author, identifying with a debased rival, is now "regularly" (*regelmässig,* 204/185; compare the mistranslation in *S.E.* 17: "invariably") beaten by her father. If egoistic interests reinforce the sexuality of the first-phase phantasy, the second phase reverses that narcissistic triumph into: "No, he does not love you, for he is beating you." The underlying message, however, is that being beaten is equated with intercourse with father. The first-phase phantasy, Freud insists, has "no special significance," but the second phase is the "most important and the most momentous of all," influencing later character pathology and causing girls to be antagonistic to anyone like their fathers (195).

The disparately described psychodynamic factors that are involved with the emergence of the second-phase phantasy may be synthesized as follows (181–82, 189, 191–94):

(1) The sadistic component of the sexual function has grown "prematurely independent" and, without apparent evidence of trauma, undergoes fixation.

(2) Once it is "no longer" independent, the sadism affects the incestuous oedipal wish to be loved by the father.

(3) A guilt-induced repression renders sequelae of the genital organization unconscious and changes the sadism into masochism.

(4) In that guilt-induced transformation, a primary sadism is turned against the self, thus constituting the passive nature of masochism.

(5) Together with the sense of guilt, the precocious sadistic component effects a regression to the anal-sadistic stage. The essence of masochism lies in the libidinal excitation over the regressive punishment for the forbidden genital relation.

Freud lapses into disorganization and even self-contradiction when he describes the psychodynamic features of the second phase. In an unsteady generalization, he starts out with a definite statement, which he then—in a rare gesture for him—forcefully repeats in two paraphrases: the phantasy "is never remembered, it has never succeeded in becoming conscious. It is a construction of analysis, but it is no less a necessity on that account" (185). Later, he is again forceful, but this time he twice modifies his generalization about the phantasy: it "remains unconscious as a rule. . . . I repeat, however, that as a rule the phantasy remains unconscious, and can only be reconstructed in the course of the analysis" (189–90). He later returns to his unqualified generalization that the second phase is "unconscious" (195). Freud's oscillation between "never" and "as a rule" is quite unsettling. This juggling with observational fact suggests how much, at the moment of writing, Freud's volatile affect could influence his memory and undercut the accuracy of his clinical reporting.

In the conscious phantasy of the third phase, the girl's father (most often) or a surrogate is beating a number of unknown boys. This phantasy bears the libidinal charge and sense of guilt attached to the repressed second portion of the first-phase phantasy, that is, "My father is beating the child, *he loves only me.*" Unconsciously, however, the girl in her penis envy identifies with the victim and enjoys a masochistic, disguised incestuous pleasure. The phantasy, Freud asserts, marks the girl's leaving her oedipal love for her father and her entrance into a masculine complex whereby she wants only to be a boy. In this transition, the superego replaces the father and child as original subjects with vague ones (authoritarian agents and male children).

According to Freud, the author of the phantasy report in all likelihood was in fact a spectator of the scene—she "probably" looked on (186). Freud then claims that she appears a spectator "at the most" (*höchstens;* compare the erroneous "almost" in *S.E.* 210/190). Finally Freud asserts the girl's spectatorship without qualification: the girl "is no longer anything but a spectator" (199). The issue of masturbation is also evidence of the partial inaccuracy of Freud's clinical description (a countertransferential disturbance of Anna's ongoing analysis?). At the climax of the imagined situation, we are told, beating phantasies are carried out "almost invariably" with masturbation (179; compare Freud's qualifier "regularly," *regelmässig,* on page 180, which is mistranslated as "invariably" in the *S.E.,* thus making Freud contradict himself). But Freud reverses himself when he later (190) states that two of his four female cases abstained from masturbation. (In 1925, let us note,

Freud stressed that beating fantasies are confessions of masturbation.) Freud is also erratic about the sadomasochism of the third phase: the phantasy is "sadistic" (186); only its form is sadistic, its satisfaction is masochistic (191); the phantasy is "apparently sadistic" (195); it does "appear to be sadistic" (195).

So far I have examined Freud's theses and some of their problematic presentation. Because this creates puzzlement, I have drawn up as a pedagogical guide a table that, for convenience, flattens out contradictory statements and depicts three intricate phases of girls' beating phantasies (see table 2.1).[3]

No table is necessary to clarify boys' beating phantasies because Freud's account of them is simpler and more concentrated (see 187–91, 196–200, 203). In the first phase, a boy's unconscious phantasy reads: "I am loved by my father." Here and in the two succeeding phases the boy evinces an inverted oedipal complex and adopts a passive, feminine attitude toward his father. Underscoring that the first phase of the boy's beating phantasy is not sadistic, as the girl's is, Freud wonders whether that fact will be modified by further research (198). In the light of Freud's imbalanced comparative understanding of beating phantasies, I conclude that the sexual life of boys (rather than that of girls) can be the darker continent!

The second phase of boys' beating phantasies has the wording "I am being beaten by my father." The masochistic, regressive phantasy of this phase is "regularly" unconscious (Strachey's mistranslation of *regelmässig* by "invariably," [219/198], makes Freud contradict a statement made nine pages earlier). The boy represses his homosexual love of his father in his otherwise conscious third-phase phantasy. Hence, it is worded "I am being beaten by my mother"; she, like the later maternal substitutes in the phantasy, has masculine attributes.

3. To complete my outline, I include a paginated guide to the core of Freud's essay. For convenience, I have the followed the notational policy of the English *Concordance to the Psychological Works of Sigmund Freud*. Hence, I have divided each page of Freud's essay into four parts (a, b, c, d) so that, for example, "186b" refers to matter appearing in the second quarter of page 186. After studying Freud's whole essay according to its own expository order, one might reread it according to the sequence of this selective plan: (A) the heavenly oedipal period prior to the girl's beating phantasies: 186d, 187b, 187d–88c; (B) heaven's next best—the purgatorial period of beating phantasies—(1) first phase: 184d–85b, 186b, 186d–87b, 188d–89a, 195d–96a, 199a; (2) second phase: 181c–82d, 185b, c, 186b, 189a–90c, 194a–c, 195b–96a; (3) third phase: 185d–86b, 190d–91c, 195b, 195d–96a, 199b–200a.

Table 2.1 Three intricate phases of girls' phantasies.

	Phase 1	Phase 2	Phase 3
The initial presentation of the phantasy	"A child is being beaten"		Strange boys are being beaten by an indeterminate person or a surrogate of the father
Latent verbal representation of the phantasy	"My father does not love this other child, *he loves only me*"	"No, he does not love you, for he is beating you"	
Author of phantasy	Author differs from victim, who is most often a sibling if one exists	Author is victim	Probably a spectator of the beating (the beaten children are surrogates for the author of the phantasy)
Aggressor in the phantasy	Father	Father	Father or his surrogate, such as a teacher
The aggressive act	Beating	Beating	The beating may be replaced by punishments or humiliations of other kinds; in the sophisticated phantasy of later years, the punished child is not seriously injured
Psychic status of the phantasy	Either a conscious phantasy, wish, or recollection of witnessed events rather than a reconstruction	Remains unconscious; can only be reconstructed	Conscious phantasy; the beater as father, however, is a reconstruction
General significance of the phantasy	The beating has "no special significance"	This phase of the phantasy, "the most important and the most momentous of all," influences the character of girls to be hostile to anyone like their fathers	

Table 2.1 (*continued*)

	Phase 1	Phase 2	Phase 3
Developmental matrix of the phantasy	An effect of the oedipal child's premature choice of an object	The masochistic phantasy gives much pleasure; may be attended by masturbation	The phantasy, sadistic only in form, is accompanied by strong sexual excitement and at its climax is "almost invariably" attended by masturbation
Libidinal import of the phantasy	The phantasy arises from the normal Oedipus complex, gratifies the child's jealousy and is reinforced by her egoistic interests	The phantasy marks the essence of masochism; sexual excitement is strong and unambiguous	Turning away from incestuous love of their fathers, girls see their own masculine complex spurred into activity and from that time on want only to be boys
Transformational dynamics	Emergence of guilt; repression of incestuous love-impulses	Repression transforms repression sadism into masochism; guilt and the sadistic component effect a regression to the anal-sadistic stage	Repression of the phantasy of being loved by father, allowing masochistic gratification

FREUD'S ESSAY: WHAT IS BEING SAID ABOUT OTHER MATTERS

At the outset of section 5, alluding to his clinical base of six main cases along with a considerable number of less thoroughly examined cases, Freud points to three general matters that remain to be considered: the origin of perversion (the subtitle of his essay), the origin of perverse masochism in particular (the original title of his essay), and the role of sexual difference in the dynamics of neurosis. Freud sets about modifying his previous notion that a sadistic component of the sexual function, if precociously developed, undergoes fixation and is then withdrawn from later development (181, 189); he now says that the sadistic component plays an integral role in oedipal development and then inherits oedipal libidinal charge and guilt (191–92). Freud goes on to posit, in a somewhat rambling way, that perversions derive from the Oedipus complex and that beating phantasies and similarly perverse fixations are its scars (193).

Freud admits that he can say little about the second issue—the origin of masochism. We read that this perversion results from guilt, which has caused sadism to turn upon the self; we also read that its essence lies in sexual pleasure derived from suffering. Yet we are still five years away from Freud's clarification of the three kinds of masochism.

In the final section of his essay, Freud proceeds to use Fliess and Adler as his own whipping boys since they distortedly sexualized the theory of repression (ironically, Freud himself perceived as masculine both libidinal and sadistic strivings—that is, the targets of repression). Freud alleges that he "always" rejected the respective biological and sociological theories of Fliess and Adler concerning the link between repression and sexual character. That is not quite correct. In the letter to Fliess of October 27, 1897, after quoting Hamlet's reflection that every man deserves a whipping(!), Freud expresses his indecision regarding Fliess's theory of repression (Freud, 1985, 273). Also, in Draft M, sent to Fliess on May 23, 1897, Freud endorses a position on the sexualization of repression similar to Adler's, only to abandon it by November 14 of the same year (Freud, 1985, 246, 281); he publicly criticized it in 1914 and 1918 (Freud, 1914, 54; 1918, 110–11). At any rate, Freud's later critical position was as follows: Fliess's theory that every person strictly represses the tendencies belonging to the opposite sex reductionistically equates one's sexual identification with the form of one's genitals. Adler's theory that masculine protest occurs in all persons, serving as a motive for the repression of everything intrapsychically feminine, explains neither the repression of "masculine" sadistic impulses nor boys' masochistic attitudes in their beating phantasies.

In every one of Freud's writings, there are a number of noteworthy throwaway assertions, and it is fitting to mention a few pertinent ones here. For one thing, we come across Freud's timely reminder—so often forgotten since— that a proof of congenital homosexuality cannot be based on memories of a sexual inclination that are limited by one's amnesia and do not go earlier than the sixth year of life (193). We also can appreciate Freud's evergrowing awareness of narcissism in his labeling the masochistic stage narcissistic and calling the effects of the superego a narcissistic scar (193–94). On another score, just before the profound insight that beating phantasies constitute the basis of paranoid phenomena (195), Freud insisted that the neurotic's guilt over masturbation relates not to guilt in puberty but rather to guilt in childhood and the unconscious oedipal phantasies accompanying masturbation. Freud's clinical technique concerning early pathology was such, let us remark, that he not only repeatedly stressed the decisive impact of childhood masturbation (as we see in the case histories—Freud, 1905, 56–57, 75–82; 1909a, 24; 1918, 24–26) but he also was given to its reconstruction even within the first two weeks of treatment (Freud, 1909b, 263).

Freud also made a crucial assertion about the possible existence of *wish* without phantasy that is, surprisingly, not cited in the Freud-Klein controversies (King and Steiner, 1991) or in the mass of critical literature on phantasy. Thus, in investigating the first phase of the beating phantasy, Freud downplayed the importance of whether it was a question of desire or memory: "One may hesitate to say whether the characteristics of a 'phantasy' can yet be ascribed to this first step towards the later beating-phantasy. It is perhaps *rather* a question of recollections of events which have been witnessed, *or* of desires which have arisen on various occasions. But these doubts are of *no importance"* (185, italics mine).

Finally, Freud formulated a theoretical and metatheoretical position that merits recitation: "All the signs on which we are accustomed to base our distinctions tend to lose their clarity as we come nearer to the source" (187). Said otherwise, the closer we get to sources, the more our descriptive terms are a fabric of fiction, and what started out as speculation soon risks being hardened into definitive assertions. All too often, when dealing with genetic issues, analysts have ignored the implication of Freud's wisdom to the effect that our very descriptive language is challenged. As if by the tender judgment of poetic justice, the most elaborate application of Freud's generalization is found years later in his daughter's reflection on defense mechanisms: "If you look at them microscopically they all merge into one another. . . . The point is that one should not look at them microscopically, but macroscopically, as big and separate mechanisms, structures, events, whatever you want to call them. They will stand out from each other, and the problems of separating them theoretically become negligible. *You have to take off your glasses to look at them, not put them on"* (A. Freud, in J. Sandler and A. Freud, 1983, 90, italics mine).

STYLE: FREUD'S ESSAY IS BEING FORMED

As I have often said, the expository manner that Freud typically adopted in writing generated and facilitated the associative and critical processes, his own in the act of writing and ours in the act of reading him. While tracking Freud's complex thought, we follow its linear progression with ease, but tracking his primary process—the eye of the storm—is another matter, with its cyclonic movement, its unpredictably rapid swerves that change between swirling outward and inward and spiraling upward and downward. To appreciate the crucial implications of Freud's expository tactics, we could not do better than to cite Shakespeare, who, bearing in mind his father's profession as a glover, wrote these immortal words about the peril in his own life as creator:

> My nature is subdued
> To what it works in, like the dyer's hand. (Sonnet 111)

In his expository method Freud took the risk of being either inventively brilliant or being confused and even handled by his own instrument. We turn first to the latter outcome.

In trying to describe how the child with beating phantasies is "entangled" (*vertrickt,* compare "involved in" *S.E.* 205/186) with them, Freud can become confused in his own exposition, as when he vacillates about the sadistic or masochistic quality of the beating phantasy. He sometimes continues his reconstruction with the reader, which can be quite appealing; at other times, as we have noted, he changes the clinical facts, which unsettles and baffles the careful reader. For instance, Freud's oscillation about the patient's spectatorship indicates that this element of the third phase is also, despite Freud's overt claim, a reconstruction.

Freud continues his somewhat disorganized description of psychodynamic features in section 6, some paragraphs of which require rereading in order to be understood. He even misidentifies "I am being beaten by my father" as the boy's original phantasy instead of the one in the second phase (202). Bonaparte (1953, 94) was confused enough in her reading of Freud to think that he saw two phases in boys' phantasies, whereas in fact he offered a triple progression, which can be set out this way: "I am loved by my father . . . I am being beaten by my father. . . I am being beaten by my mother" (198). Similarly, when Freud takes up the girl's original phantasy, he misidentifies it as "I am being beaten (i.e., I am loved) by my father"; that erroneous reformulation actually combines the latent meanings of the girl's beating fantasies in the first and second phases.

But we also can find a Freud in masterful control of his expressivity. In this essay as in other clinical material (Mahony, 1986, 1989, 1995, 1996) references to literature are constant in Freud's mind, which shuttles back and forth between saying that life is like literature and that literature is like life. For example, we read that in producing elaborate phantasies children compete with writers of fiction (180) and that beating phantasies had an artistic (*kunstvoller*, 210/190) superstructure in two cases. One of them, ranking almost as a work of art, moves Freud to write poetically about the subject: "The later impressions of life speak loudly enough through the mouth of the patient, while it is the physician who has to raise his voice on behalf of the claims of childhood" (183–84). We also hear Freud quoting *Macbeth* or giving echoes of his favorite poem, Milton's *Paradise Lost,* in which the devils, shorn of their majestic status, are cast down from heaven: "Children who believed themselves securely enthroned in the unshakable affection of their parents have by a single blow been cast down from all the heavens of their imaginary omnipotence" (187). Freud also poetically exclaims that for the child completely in love "the time comes when this early blossoming is nipped [*geschädigt,* "damaged"] by the frost" (207/188).

There is a noticeable amount of tentativeness crafted in Freud's essay that has been eliminated in the English translation (Ornston, 1982). Sometimes Strachey unnecessarily intensifies it, as when he renders *Regung* (stirring) by "excitement" or "impulse" (197 f./179 f.; 201/182; 208 f./188 f.; 216/195; 223/201; Ornston, 1982, 413–14). If one chooses to reject the delicate aspects of Freud's discourse as belletristic nuance, one will miss its psychodynamic dimension. In the first two paragraphs of Freud's essay, for instance, there are three clauses in which the passive voice was changed by Strachey into the active voice, thus erasing the introductory effect of passivity, in which the passive phantasy "a child is being beaten" is enveloped. Shortly afterwards, Freud insightfully describes phantasy as if it were a two-way mirror: not only does it draw on a child's observation, but it is also an internal witness (*Zeugnis,* 200/181) to the child's peculiar or abnormal constitution. And again, Freud refers to an event acting like "a single blow" (*einen einzigen Schlag,* my italics, 206/187) that can cause the child to have beating phantasies. The German text allows us to notice Freud's verbal genius in describing a *Schlag* (event) that resembles its very sequel, beating phantasies (*Schlagphantasien*).

In an even more extraordinary passage Freud artfully describes the intricacy of the girl's phantasy:

Das Mädchen entläuft dem Anspruch des Liebeslebens überhaupt, phantasiert sich zum Manne, ohne selbt männlich aktiv zu werden, und wohnt dem Akt, welcher einen sexuellen ersetzt, nur mehr als Zuschauer bei. (220–221/199)

Ornston (1982, 418) translates the text this way:

The little girl escapes the claim of love life as such: without becoming active in a masculine way she fantasies herself to be a man and lives within this act, which replaces a sexual one, only now as an observer.

According to Ornston's astute analysis, "Sie phantasiert sich zum Manne" signifies not only that the girl phantasies herself as a man but also that she gives herself to him sexually. And "sie wohnt dem Act bei" signifies not only that the girl lives within the act but also that she is copulating. Thus in Freud's fluid exposition, which subtly renders the primary-process-marked phantasies in which fluctuating roles can interchange as well as combine, the girl simultaneously observes and participates in an act of beating, which itself substitutes for sexuality and yet is plainly sexual.

Freud's sensitivity to time is another distinctive trait of clinical and textual genius. In the essay at hand, there are three interwoven narrative strands: the three-phase evolution of the beating phantasy, the affective and ideational nature of its gradual uncovering in analysis, and the pace of Freud's expository revelations. These individually intricate strands, reinforced by the temporal implications of Freud's numerous affect-laden references to surprise, wonder, expectation, hesitation, and suspicion, manifest a complex responsiveness I have found in no other analytic writing.

Worthy in its own right though less intricate, a minor narrative plot depicts Freud's progressive efforts to understand what he named the superego four years later. In describing the first phase of the beating phantasy, Freud merely says that repression occurs at the same time a sense of guilt emerges (188). In the second phase, however, guilt becomes a causative dynamic factor: it transforms sadism into masochism and takes part in the act of repression (189, 194). Arriving at this point in his exposition, Freud then tentatively invokes an agency that sets itself up in the ego as a critical conscience. On a somewhat different order, the alert reader may observe instances in which Freud, showing his nonobsessional attachment to the exact wording of beating phantasies, yet respecting the overall cast of their manifest and latent meanings, does not hesitate to offer slight, associative variants of them.

LATER ESSAYING: BEYOND "A CHILD IS BEING BEATEN"

Like so much else in psychoanalysis, phantasy, the main focus of clinical interest, still eludes our full comprehension. Indeed, a satisfactory taxonomy of unconscious phantasies and their derivatives has yet to be drawn up (Moore and Fine, 1990, 75). Closer to the subject at hand, we may still ask, What is the basic masochistic phantasy of which sadomasochistic masturbation phantasies and beating phantasies are, respectively, subtypes and sub-subtypes? Also, how widespread are undisguised beating phantasies or their derivatives, such as the dramatization of humiliation alluded to by Freud? Pertinently, our language abounds in the use of *beat* and such synonyms as *crush, vanquish,* and *rout* to mean "defeat" or "subdue" in many areas of life, ranging from politics, warfare, and sports to professional competition; we refer often to tongue lashing and to narcissistic blows. If I may go back to Freud's citation of Shakespeare, is not the punitive superego a symbolic whipping? Finally, who can overlook the contribution of guilt to the idiomatic expressions used by young male adolescents to describe masturbation such as "beating off" or "beating the meat"?

Seconded by many analysts, Freud (179) expressed surprise about the ubiquity of beating phantasies. A greater claim for their universality or nigh universality is found, inter alia, in the classic paper of the Kris Study Group (Joseph, 1965; see also Bonaparte, 1953, and Galenson, 1980), published almost midway between Freud's essay and our own reflections.[4] Kris himself suggested that in the light of the "almost ubiquitous" sado-masochistic fantasy of the primal scene whereby the father beats the mother, a child's beating fantasy expresses the desire to be loved sexually by the father and is "almost universal." It stands to reason—or better yet, to phantasy—that Kris's position is right and is borne out over time if one remains clinically alert to the changing emergence of beating phantasies and

---

4. For an account of the flagellation literature rampant in Victorian England, see the sixth chapter, entitled "A Child Is Being Beaten," in Marcus (1974).

their manifold derivatives, including those of humiliation and other narcissistic insults.

Much more than Freud ever conceived, the conscious or unconscious state of beating phantasies as well as their manifest and latent forms (both of which can be visual) may vary greatly according to the particular patient. In their fine clinical paper, Broden and Myers (1981) used data to show the dynamic connection between persistent hypochondriacal complaints that mollify superego demands and underlying unconscious beating phantasies that were activated by guilt. On another score, one of my adult patients, still terrified by memories of his uncontrollable father's beatings, tries to fend off surges of "nameless" guilt by overdetermined, highly controlled onanism, which he calls the "soft spank."

Although beating phantasies are usually sequestered from the rest of the clinical picture and are uncovered as peripheral issues during the analysis, the question remains as to why they retain considerable importance in some patients. Beating phantasies can continue unconsciously and influence character structure in a sadomasochistic way, or they may continue in a conscious state and even be acted out. Reviewing his material, Freud (1919, 180) could not establish any link between actual domestic beating and the phantasies. Asch (1980), contra Myers (1980), alleged that the influence of actual beatings and enemas on beating phantasies has not been clinically substantiated. More certainty exists, however, in the cases of overt physical masochism in adult life, where there is likely to be a childhood history of actual beatings (Hunt, 1973) or of pre-oedipal problems with the phallic mother. Then again, pathogenic indications of repetitively fixed beating phantasies have greater pathogenic indications than do benignly adaptive transitory ones (Novick and Novick, 1987).

It is fascinating to see Freud so often on the edge of a deeper insight but unable to proceed further, a circumstance determined in great part by the limitations of his self-analysis. In spite of his insistent belief in polymorphous infantile sexuality and his surmise that beating phantasies were an end product of previous development (184), he could not go beyond the father's oedipal role to the pre-oedipal mother's impact on beating phantasies. He could not reach beneath his own bedrock, which, appositely enough, he designated by the term *gewachsener Fels* instead of by the synonym *Muttergestein,* literally "mother-rock" (see Mahony, 1989). From early on, analysts, in correcting Freud's bias, have reported the actual or interpreted presence of the pre-oedipal mother in beating phantasies (Bergler, 1938,

1948). And the notions of Freud and Bonaparte (1953, 87) about a normal feminine masochism are more and more recognized for their historical datedness; feminine masochism is not a normal innate or developmental character trait but rather represents an unconscious phantasy distortive of woman's body and her ego ideal. One of the many questions that await further research, however, is why women with persistent beating phantasies tend to be less profoundly disturbed than their male counterparts (Novick and Novick, 1972; Ferber, 1975).

As could be expected, investigators have gone far beyond Freud's etiological factors of a precocious sadistic component, guilt, narcissistic injury, and penis envy disguised as sibling rivalry (Freud, 1924, 254). We have understood more about environmental pressures and stimulation (primal scene exposure, deficient parenting, disenabling separation-individuation, and so on) and intrapsychic development (faulty genital schematization, pathological superego formation, and so on) as determinants of beating phantasies. In addition, the functions of beating phantasies as complex compromise formations have been enlarged to include a range of strivings, from maintaining body boundaries or a symbiotic tie to forming psychic structures, atoning in advance for masturbatory pleasures (Lax, 1992), warding off more intense destructive wishes toward an ambivalently loved mother, and effecting an adaptational reparation.

In closing, a pair of brief technical considerations may be in order. Freud and a number of the early German-speaking analysts were given to formulating the patient's phantasy as part of an internal monologue in the first person. Formulating the experience–near interpretation in that way facilitates internalizability and is evidence of optimal clinical closeness (the synonymous epithet "optimal clinical distance," in my opinion, aims at a pseudo-scientific objectivity and can betoken an unempathic relation). The comparatively less internalizable interpretations reported nowadays tend to be removed from internal monologue, to be set in the second person, and to show more secondary process characteristics—for example, "It seems that because you hate your brother, you imagine that your father is beating him, a punishment that then leads you to infer that you are the only child loved by your father."

Just as an analysis of the facade of a phobia sheds light on its overdetermination, so particular attention to the manifest content of a beating phantasy uncovers its latent meanings and functions (compare Lewin, 1952; Ferber, 1975). We cannot attend too closely to the diversity of sensory modalities and other variables that abound in clinical material: memories of being forced into immobilization during the beating or of feeling numbness at the end; the substitution of the buttocks for the breasts of the frustrating pre-oedipal mother (Bergler, 1938, 1948); the symbolization of hand or beating instrument; the excitement of watching others being spanked or defeated; humiliation in daydreams. I think of a patient with long-standing bouts of depressive, physical paralysis that relate directly to his being held immobile during childhood spankings. On occasions when other patients were working through memories of the mother's warning of an anticipated beating by the father ("Wait until he comes home!"), I have also observed the emergence of new intracessional fears about subjection to the analytic setting or process, such as feeling compelled to lie on the couch or to free-associate; at other times the feelings of subjection were tied in with the unconscious wish to provoke a beating from the analyst.

In concluding, I should like to cite what Nietzsche wrote both in the first part of *Thus Spake Zarathustra* and in the preface to *Ecce Homo:* "One requiteth a teacher badly if one remains a mere student." Those who have mastered and integrated the clinical gains of the past must advance toward the future. Beaten are those who choose to stay on the path that is beaten.

REFERENCES

Asch, S. 1980. Beating fantasy: Symbiosis and child battering. *Int. J. Psychoanal. Psychother.* 8:653–58.
Bergler, E. 1938. Preliminary phases of the masculine beating fantasy. *Psychoanal. Quart.* 22:514–636.
———. 1948. Further studies on beating fantasies. *Psychiat. Quart.* 7:480–86.
Blass, R. 1993. Insights into the struggle of creativity: A rereading of Anna Freud's "Beating fantasies and daydreams." *Psychoanal. Study Child* 48:67–98.
Bonaparte, M. 1953. *Female sexuality.* New York: International Universities Press.
Broden, A., and Myers, W. 1981. Hypochondriacal symptoms; unconscious beating fantasies. *J. Amer. Psychoanal. Assn.* 29:535–57.
Clark, R. 1980. *Freud: The man and the cause.* New York: Random House.
Ferber, L. 1975. Beating fantasies. In *Masturbation, from infancy to senescence,* ed. I. Marcus and J. Francis, 205–22. New York: International Universities Press.
Freud, A. 1923. The relation of beating fantasies to a daydream. *Int. J. Psychoanal.* 4:89–102.
Freud, S. 1905. Fragment of an analysis of a case of hysteria. *S.E.* 7.

————. 1909a. Analysis of a phobia of a five-year-old boy. *S.E.* 10.

————. 1909b. Notes upon a case of obsessional neurosis. *S.E.* 10.

————. 1914. On the history of the psychoanalytic movement. *S.E.* 14.

————. 1918. From the history of an infantile neurosis. *S.E.* 17.

————. 1919. A child is being beaten. *S.E.* 17.

————. 1923. The ego and the id. 24. *S.E.* 19.

————. 1924. The economic principle of masochism. *S.E.* 19.

————. 1925. Some psychical consequences of the anatomical distinction between the sexes. *S.E.* 19.

————. 1937. Analysis terminable and interminable. *S.E.* 23.

————. 1985. *The complete letters of Sigmund Freud to Wilhelm Fliess: 1887–1904.* Cambridge, Mass.: Harvard University Press.

————. 1993. *The complete correspondence of Sigmund Freud and Ernest Jones 1908–1939.* Cambridge, Mass.: Harvard University Press.

Galenson, E. 1980. Preoedipal determinants of a beating fantasy. *Int. J. Psychoanal. Psychother.* 8:649–52.

Hunt, W. 1973. Beating fantasies and daydreams revisited: Presentation of a case. *J. Amer. Psychoanal. Assn.* 21:817–33.

Jones, E. 1955. *The life and work of Sigmund Freud.* Vol. 2. New York: Basic Books.

Joseph, E., reporter. 1965. Beating fantasies. In *Monograph Series of Kris Study Group.* 1965. Monograph I, 30–67. New York: International Universities Press.

King, P., and Steiner, R., eds. 1991. *The Freud-Klein controversies: 1941–45.* London: Tavistock.

Lax, R. 1992. A variation of Freud's theme in "A child is being beaten": Mother's role—some implications for superego development. *J. Amer. Psychoanal. Assn.* 40: 455–73.

Lewin, B. 1952. Phobic symptoms and dream interpretation. *Psychoanal. Quart.* 31:295–322.

Mahony, P. 1986. *Freud and the Rat Man.* New Haven, Conn.: Yale University Press.

————. 1989. *On defining Freud's discourse.* New Haven, Conn.: Yale University Press.

————. 1992. Freud as family therapist: Reflections. In *Freud and the history of psychoanalysis,* ed. T. Gelfand and J. Kerr. Hillsdale, N.J.: Analytic.

————. 1995. *Les hurlements de l'homme aux loups.* 2d. ed. Paris: Presses Universitaires de France.

————. 1996. *Freud's Dora: A psychoanalytic, historical and textual study.* New Haven, Conn.: Yale University Press.

Marcus, S. 1974. *The other Victorians.* New York: Norton.

Moore, B., and Fine, B., eds. 1990. *Psychoanalytic terms and concepts.* New Haven, Conn.: Yale University Press.

Myers, W. 1980. The psychodynamics of a beating fantasy. *Int. J. Psychoanal. Psychother.* 8:623–38.

Novick, K., and Novick, J. 1972. Beating fantasies in children. *Int. J. Psychoanal.* 53:237–42.

———. 1987. The essence of masochism. *Psychoanal. Study Child,* 42:353–84.

Ornston, D. 1982. Strachey's influence: A preliminary report. *Int. J. Psychoanal.* 63: 409–26.

Sandler, J., and Freud, A. 1983. Discussions in the Hampstead index of *The ego and the mechanisms of defence. J. Amer. Psychoanal. Assn.* 31 (Supplement): 19–146.

Steiner, R. 1995. "Et in Arcadia ego . . . ?" Some notes on methodological issues in the use of psychoanalytic documents and archives. *Int. J. Psychoanal.* 76:739–58.

Strachey, J. 1955. Editor's note to "A child is being beaten." S.E. 17:177–78.

———. 1966. General preface to the *Standard Edition. S.E.* 1:xiii–xxvi.

Young-Bruehl, E. 1988. *Anna Freud: A biography.* New York: Summit.

Humiliating Fantasies
and the Pursuit
of Unpleasure

ARNOLD H. MODELL

"A Child Is Being Beaten" can be read as an elaboration of Freud's discussion of perversion in *Three Essays on the Theory of Sexuality* (1905). In that book, Freud defined perversion as an exclusive fixation on an immature sexual aim, but he also indicated that we are all perverse as children. Children are "normally" polymorphous perverse in that they consciously derive sexual pleasure from the erotogenic zones of the mouth, the anus, and the genitals. It is only at puberty that one achieves sexual maturity through the organizing effect of genital primacy. Perversion is therefore defined as an immature sexual aim, a deviation from the norm of genital union.

In *Three Essays,* Freud expresses the view that it is not until puberty that sharp distinctions can be made between men and women. It is here that Freud outlines the mistaken views of female sexual physiology that have so enraged feminist authors and have been used as a justification for discrediting Freud as well as psychoanalysis. Freud believed that girls at puberty have the difficult task of transferring the zone of sexual arousal from the clitoris—an analogue of the penis—to the vagina. At puberty girls must give up the active masculine mode in order to become passive and feminine. Consequently, vaginal orgasm is the hallmark of mature femininity, whereas clitoral orgasm is an immature vestige of masculinity. Freud stated, "A man retains his leading zone unchanged since childhood . . . whereas women change their leading erotogenic zone, which as it were *puts aside their childish masculinity*" (Freud, 1905, 21; italics mine).

In 1910, five years after the publication of *Three Essays,* Freud was quoted in the minutes of the Vienna Psychoanalytic Society regarding a discussion of the "harmfulness of masturbation": "An additional factor appears in women, in whom sexual conflict arises in connection with the practice of masturbation. Whereas man's resistance is mainly of a social nature, in the woman it is a straight sexual conflict. Woman's [clitoral] masturbation, while being an infantile activity, has in addition a masculine character" (Nunberg and Federn, 1967, 562). Freud here implies that masturbation in women generates a conflict regarding their sexual identity. This theme reappears in "A Child Is Being Beaten," in which Freud explains that when girls fantasize that a boy is being beaten, this represents a masculine identification that is a consequence of clitoral masturbation (191). This explains Freud's otherwise puzzling statement that "between the second and third phases [of the beating fantasy] the girls change their sex, for in the phantasies of the latter phase they turn into boys" (196).

Freud's definition of perversion is complicated by his belief that neurotic symptoms are an expression of perverse—that is to say, immature—sexual aims. The difference between neurosis and perversion is then defined by the state of consciousness: in the pervert the immature sexual aim is conscious, whereas in the neurotic it is unconscious. This is expressed in the well-known formula that neuroses are the negative forms of perversions. Freud stated that behind the neurotic symptom lay unconscious infantile sexual aims, which would be described as *perverse* in the widest sense of the word if they could be "expressed directly in fantasy and action without being diverted from consciousness" (165). Given this definition of perversion, a fantasy can be labeled perverse if it is conscious. Freud stated that a beating fantasy retained for purposes of masturbation can "only be regarded as a primary trait of perversion" (181).

Freud's observations in "A Child Is Being Beaten" were based on six cases, four females and two males. The fifth patient, we are told, came to analysis because of indecisiveness in life and "would not have been classified at all by coarse clinical diagnosis, or would have been dismissed as 'psychasthenic'" (183). Elisabeth Young-Bruehl (1988) in her biography of Anna Freud presents compelling circumstantial evidence that this fifth patient was in fact Anna Freud, who was struggling with indecision concerning whether to become a psychoanalyst or a teacher. Anna's analysis with her father began in 1918, a year before his essay was published. Her first paper, "Beating phantasies and daydreams," was written for the 1922 International Congress in Berlin, three years after the publication of "A Child Is Being Beaten." Young-Bruehl states further that the beating phantasies that Anna Freud presents in her paper must be autobiographical since the paper was written before she had begun a clinical practice. Furthermore, Young-Bruehl notes, the descriptive framework of Anna Freud's paper is almost identical to that of two of the female cases Freud describes in "A Child Is Being Beaten." It is Freud's central thesis that guilt resulting from incestuous desires toward the father is an inevitable determinant of a beating fantasy; one must wonder how he managed to deal with this assumption in his analysis of Anna.

Freud describes three stages in the evolution of typical beating phantasies in girls. In the first stage, which occurs in a very early period of childhood, the child who is being beaten is not the self but another child, usually a brother or sister. Thus the first phase of the fantasy is influenced by sibling rivalry and jealousy. Inasmuch as the fantasizer is a witness to the sibling's beating, she presumably obtains some sadistic pleasure from the fantasy. The person inflicting the beating is an adult whose identity at first seems vague but who eventually is identified as the little girl's father. In the second stage in the fantasy's evolution, there is a decisive transformation in that the child who is being beaten is now identified as the self. Thus the fantasy has taken a masochistic turn. This is the core or root fantasy. It is frankly incestuous because the (female) child is being beaten by the father; this, in turn, provides a source of sexual arousal and gratification. The fantasy proclaims: *my father's beating stimulates my genitals.* But because of the patently incestuous nature of the fantasy it must be repressed. Not only is the fantasy repressed, but, Freud argues, it has never been conscious: "The second phase is the most important and the most momentous of all. But we may say of it in a certain sense that *it has never had a real existence. It is never remembered, it has never succeeded in becoming conscious*" (185; italics mine). I find this statement puzzling. What did Freud mean when he suggested that this fantasy was never conscious? Was he intimating that this crucial incestuous fantasy of being beaten by the father can be thought of as a "primal fantasy" derived from phylogenesis and therefore never conscious? Because Freud said nothing further on this point, it is a riddle that cannot be solved.

Whether or not we accept his formulation that the second stage was never conscious, it underlines the significance of unconscious fantasy.

In the third phase the fantasy is now again conscious and can be elaborated in a variety of ways, which often extend into daydreams. Typically, the girl who is having the fantasy is a witness to the beating of unidentified boys by a teacher. The teacher may be a father substitute but is not recognized as such. The most important aspect of the third stage is that the fantasy creates unambiguous sexual excitement, which is used for masturbation. Freud says that in boys the unconscious fantasy corresponds to a negative oedipal wish —"I am loved by my father"—that then is transformed into the conscious fantasy "I am being beaten by my mother" (198). Freud explains that the determining factor is the boy's passive feminine wish to be loved by the father. So in both sexes beating phantasies derive from the incestuous tie to the father.

Freud offers several explanations for this puzzling evolution of the fantasy of a child being beaten. Overall, the transformation of the child from witness to victim reflects the transformation of sadism into masochism. He observed this transformation earlier, in *Three Essays,* where he noted that masochism represents the inversion of sadism (1905, 158). Here he offers an important additional explanation: sadism is transformed into masochism because of guilt (1919, 189). The crucial masochistic fantasy in girls that "I am being beaten by my father" remains unconscious, Freud explains, because it is both punishment for the forbidden incestuous wish for genital union with the father and, at the same time, a regressive substitute for that wish. It is regressive because Freud assumes sequential stages of libidinal development, where a beating on the buttocks represents a defensive retreat to anal eroticism. According to Freud's definition of perversion, however, because the second phase of the beating fantasy is unconscious, it is not, strictly speaking, perverse. But inasmuch as it contains regressive (perverse) libidinal desires it may later generate neurotic symptoms or may lead to a perversion. He explains that what remains of the Oedipus complex in the unconscious disposes the individual to neuroses as an adult.

The relation between the second (unconscious) phase of the beating fantasy in girls and the third (conscious and more elaborated) phase, which is used for purposes of masturbation, may be analogized to the relation between the latent dream thought and the manifest dream. The manifest dream, using the day residue, is generated by the unconscious wish. What corresponds in this specimen fantasy to the day residue is witnessing or experiencing a beating on the buttocks by the father or by a teacher at school. We know that in the early part of this century, in Western Europe and probably in North America as well, public beatings in classrooms were part of everyday life in school. Today children no longer suffer such humiliating corporal punishment, and there is some suggestion that beating phantasies in children are today somewhat uncommon (Novick and Novick, 1972).

The wish for sexual union with the father is the root unconscious wish that is stimulated by the day residue of witnessing or experiencing an actual beating. This generative wish is disguised through secondary elaborations such as daydreams. In this sense the daydream is analogous to the manifest dream. The disguised nature of this third phase of the fantasy allows it then to be used for masturbation so that by means of this disguised fantasy, which hides the father, an incestuous wish can be gratified.

In my own clinical practice I have seldom heard an account of the explicit fantasy of being beaten on the buttocks. But what I have observed, and believe to be fairly widespread, is a masturbation fantasy in women in which the person having the fantasy is being humiliated, controlled, and degraded. It is not uncommon to discover that such fantasies are obligatory in order to achieve orgasm, whether in masturbation or with a sexual partner.

An analytic patient reported the following fantasy that accompanied masturbation: she is in diapers and has a bowel movement in her underpants in public.[1] This fantasy undoubtedly has multiple determinants, but one meaning is evident: for the child as well as the adult, losing control of one's bowels is the ultimate source of shame and humiliation. By eroticizing this humiliation in fantasy, she was then able to bring the feeling of humiliation within the sphere of the mastery of the self.

In *Three Essays on the Theory of Sexuality* Freud alludes to the process whereby an instinctual system serving one function is displaced or transferred onto another system serving a very different function. "To begin with," wrote Freud, "sexual activity attaches itself to one of the functions serving the purpose of self-preservation [such as nursing] and does not become independent of them until later" (1905, 182).[2] I would paraphrase Freud's thinking as follows: although nursing and sexuality are separate biologic systems, the affects associated with these systems can be displaced,

1. I report this case in *The Private Self* (Modell, 1993).

2. I discuss this point in greater detail in Some Notes on Object Relations (Modell, 1990).

combined, or substituted one for the other. In the example I have just given, the feelings of humiliation were the source of sexual arousal. This can be viewed as an example of a more general process—the eroticization of painful affects. For example, it is well known that hatred as well as anxiety can be eroticized. Stoller (1975) described perversion as the erotic form of hatred. We also know that for some people the anxiety implicit in the wish to surrender the self to the other is eroticized and can become the core of a sexual perversion. Therefore, the pleasure derived from a beating fantasy cannot be explained only by reference to incestuous desires for the father and libidinal regression to an anal erotogenic zone.

When beating fantasies are obligatory in sexual intercourse, one notes that the fantasy serves an additional function—the subject does not give herself (or himself) over to the experience with the other person insofar as an unshared private world of fantasy is created. This is a way of remaining alone in the presence of the other.[3] This private inner world is captured in a poem Anna Freud wrote during her analysis (quoted by Young-Bruehl, 1988, 83), which includes the following lines:

> In the image of the world
> Where we are living, I would be busily
> Building a little world for myself,
> Made within my own power, a miniature.

It is difficult to draw any general conclusions concerning the prevalence of beating fantasies in our contemporary culture. As I already noted, I have not often observed the paradigmatic beating fantasy that Freud presented in his essay and cannot judge whether such fantasies are as common today as they were in the early part of this century. A contemporary account of such a fantasy appeared recently in the *New Yorker* magazine in a special edition devoted to women's issues, however. The author, Daphne Merkin (1996), described a lifelong preoccupation with the fantasy of being beaten on the buttocks. In her autobiographical article she emphasized the emotional inaccessibility of both parents. She did not recall being spanked herself but was a frequent witness to such a punishment administered to her brother by the family's nanny. She said: "[In] watching my brother being punished, I think I construed those spankings to be a form of love. The humiliation was safely someone else's, but there was something to be envied in all that attention and

---

3. I discuss this theme in *The Private Self* (Modell, 1993).

energy applied to a little boy's round, bare bottom." She adds: "Spankings have a distinct beginning and end, after which life went back to its usual contours. By contrast, my mother's punitive style was much less succinct: she could go for days without talking to me." In Merkin's account, the role of the unresponsive mother seemed to be a more telling explanation for the beating fantasy than her incestuous desires for her father. One may respond that this is a literary production and that Freud explicitly posited that the incestuous desire for the father was unconscious. Nevertheless, this woman's story coincides with my own observations of women who must conjure up humiliating fantasies in order to achieve orgasm. In those fantasies (in women) in which the humiliation is inflicted by a man, I have no doubt that the sexual arousal can be traced to the father, but I strongly suspect that a more salient determinant can be found in the early relationship to the mother, especially in those cases in which fantasies of humiliation are accompanied by what can be described as the pursuit of unpleasure.

As a result of infant observation we have become sensitized to the importance of the early mother-child affective dialogue. Children whose mothers are depressed or for other reasons emotionally unresponsive may experience the mother as an inanimate, "dead" object (Green, 1983). The mother's joylessness fails to animate the child, who in turn experiences the self as dead. From this perspective the excitement and arousal derived from a fantasy of humiliation are both an antidote to the deadness of the self and an expression of self-hatred. In her *New Yorker* article, Merkin reveals the following: "What I actually suspected is that I wanted to be spanked to death—transported out of my sorrow into a state of numbness and permanent unfeeling." I would therefore place the fantasy that a child is being beaten in the broader context of the psychopathology of the self.

Freud was undoubtedly right in assigning to guilt a central role in the genesis of this masochistic fantasy. But I would question whether the content of the guilt is as uniformly incestuous as Freud describes. The wish to be beaten by the father is not the only and probably not the major determinant of this paradigmatic fantasy. Some years ago, I observed a primitive or elemental fantasy that for many people is a source of unconscious guilt (Modell, 1965). The elemental experience is as follows: when something "good" is taken into the body/self, it is "all gone" and not available to other members of the family. For some individuals, having something good—that is, something pleasurable—means that some other person has been deprived or depleted. The other person can ultimately be identified as the mother, who in the fantasy is damaged as a result of the child's obtaining pleasure. The child therefore requires the mother's permission in order to experience pleasure. If, in the mother-child dialogue, the mother is unresponsive or psychologically dead, the child may experience a prohibition in the pursuit of pleasure. Then the specimen fantasy may be thought of as a symptom in which there is a compromise formation—the pursuit of sexual pleasure must be negated by the pain of humiliation.

The phenomenon of the humiliating or masochistic fantasy is therefore more complex and enigmatic than Freud's essay would imply. First, it is not uniform but subject to a wide range of individual variations. Furthermore, as is true of any symptom, one can discern a web of multiple interrelated determinants in addition to the Oedipus complex.

Since the appearance of Young-Bruehl's biography, I cannot read "A Child Is Being Beaten" without thinking of Freud's analysis of his daughter Anna. I strongly suspect that even though his daughter was only one among six patients, it is Freud's experience of his daughter's analysis that permeates this paper and helps to focus his formulations. Freud's central discovery is that the unconscious thought behind the fantasy that a child is being beaten is that "my father is beating me on the buttocks and this stimulates my genitals." How did Freud react when he observed this organizing fantasy in the inner life of his own daughter? Did his puzzling assertion that the second phase of the fantasy was never conscious and hence had little to do with actual experience represent a wish to distance himself from recognizing any seductive involvement with his daughter? What does it mean that Freud published his daughter's masturbation fantasies? This was undoubtedly done with her permission, but then what does her compliance mean? These questions remain unanswerable, but they do suggest that interwoven with Freud's analysis of the beating fantasy are aspects of his conscious and unconscious relationship with Anna. Might it be that his publication of this paper represents a collusive enactment between Freud and his daughter? Freud emphasized the masculine identification (with the father) that is regularly part of the little girl's beating fantasy. For Anna Freud, the presentation of her own paper, "Beating fantasies and daydreams," was the means through which she chose to become a psychoanalyst rather than a teacher. Cementing in this fashion her identification with her father, she also confirmed the theory her father outlined in "A Child Is Being Beaten." Young-Bruehl notes that Freud's response to Anna's paper was fatherly pride not unmixed with anxiety. She reports that when Anna planned to give her paper as a test lecture to the Vienna Psychoanalytic Society, Freud, in a letter to Max Eitingon, compared himself to Junius Brutus, the legendary founder of the Roman republic and chief judge of its tribunals. (Legend has it that Junius Brutus executed his own son by ruling against him.) In thinking of Anna as a son, Freud appears to be mirroring Anna's own masculine identification.

"A Child Is Being Beaten" is an essay that is rich in its ramifications, both in its own right and as a piece of psychoanalytic history.

REFERENCES

Freud, S. 1905. Three essays on the theory of sexuality. *S.E.* 7.
———. 1919. A child is being beaten. *S.E.* 17.
Green, A. 1983. *On private madness*. Madison, Conn.: International Universities Press.
Merkin, D. 1996. Personal history—unlikely obsession. *The New Yorker.* Feb. 26 & Mar. 4:98–115.
Modell, A. 1965. On having the right to a life: An aspect of the superego's development. *Int. J. Psycho-Anal.* 46:323–31.
———. 1990. Some notes on object relations, "classical" theory and the problem of instincts (drives). *Psychoanal. Inquiry* 10:182–96.
———. 1993. *The private self*. Cambridge, Mass.: Harvard University Press.
Novick, J., and Novick, K. K. 1972. Beating fantasies in children. *Int. J. Psycho-Anal.* 53:237–42.
Nunberg, H., and Federn, E., eds. 1967. *Minutes of the Vienna Psychoanalytic Society,* Vol. 2. New York: International Universities Press.
Stoller, R. 1975. *Perversion: The erotic form of hatred*. Washington: American Psychiatric Press.
Young-Bruehl, E. 1988. *Anna Freud: A biography*. New York: Summit.

Comments on Freud's "'A Child Is Being Beaten': A Contribution to the Study of the Origin of Sexual Perversions"

LEONARD SHENGOLD

In this paper, Freud presents conclusions and mysteries that follow from his observations of specific sequences of sadomasochistic phenomena in six patients. The sequences center around beating fantasies, characterized by Freud as "the essence of masochism" (189). His focus on these fantasies raises some questions that challenge ordinary assumptions. Why would anyone want to be beaten? How do the wishes and impulses involved become subject to a compulsion to repeat? How does this become sexual perversion? Perverse sexual masochistic impulses exist in many varieties of conflictual ambiguity. They tend to involve the promise of overwhelming, intense sexual pleasure, featured in fantasy, which in action (if allowed) can transiently overcome the usually concomitant potentially inhibitory "unpleasure"—anxiety, disapproval, and disgust.

In commenting on, reading, and (especially) quoting Freud, one optimally needs the perspective of a historian of ideas, specifically of Freud's and Freudian ideas. We have in recent years endured a flow of papers of unequal merit commenting on and criticizing Freud's case histories. Many of these are without much sense of chronological sequence, prone to condemn the

Freud of the early 1900s not only for not anticipating his own later views but even for not following current psychological trends. Freud published "A Child Is Being Beaten" (written in 1918) in 1919, before many of his major theoretical revisions—of his instinct theory (*Beyond the Pleasure Principle*, 1920); of his model of the mind from the topographical to the structural (*The Ego and the Id*, 1923); of his theory of anxiety ("Inhibitions, Symptoms and Anxiety," 1926). He had not yet arrived at any systematic view of the pre-oedipal phase of libidinal and ego development or begun to modify his views on women and the role of the mother (see Young-Bruehl, 1988). And he had something further to say on masochism (in "The Economic Problem of Masochism," 1924; *An Outline of Psychoanalysis*, 1940; and elsewhere).

In considering the evolution of subsequent Freudian (in contrast to Freud's) ideas, we should remember (to use a metaphorical cliché) that he is the giant on whose shoulders subsequent psychological thinkers stand. Some seem unaware of this, and others are eager to bite those shoulders. The past few years have seen a great acceleration of attacks on Freud's character and ideas ranging from the justified and balanced to the biased and murderous. Harold Bloom has titled one of his books *The Anxiety of Influence* (1973; see also 1994), a phrase epitomizing his description of the conflict in creative intellectual life to absorb and to get rid of the dominant ideas of the previous generation of creative thinkers. This would involve (for psychoanalysts if not for Bloom, whose sophisticated ideas avoid reductive formulae) deeper unconscious wishes derived from parricidal impulses—murderous and cannibalistic, oedipal and pre-oedipal. These are sometimes not well sublimated so that primitive hate-filled passions show. This kind of intense hatred is especially to be found in, but of course is not confined to, former believers in or followers of charismatic intellectual leaders. The passionate emotional road from apostle to apostate has been particularly well traveled in recent decades by followers of Marx and Freud. Freud-bashing is current intellectual fashion, at least in the United States; Freud has become the child who is being beaten as well as the giant who is being bitten. Looking at his 1919 work may supply some perspective on this.

The psychologically afflicted who come for help require the therapist's empathy. This is not always easy to supply. The ideal precept for empathy is Terence's "Nothing human is alien to me" (*Heautontimorumenos*, I.i.25). The greatest difficulties for the would-be helper's attempt to live up to this impossible standard are encountered when the patient's pathology exists in the psychic realm that Freud characterizes as "beyond the pleasure principle" (1920). In that metaphorical place of illogical and self-destructive mystery lie the murky paths to the understanding of human aggressive phenomena—murder and cannibalism, not only aimed at others (where they can sometimes make defensive and adaptive sense) but also turned inward toward the self, in contradiction to our insistent assumptions of being motivated by instinctual self-preservation.

Aggressive impulses become mixed with sexual ones at some time in the course of early psychic development. Sadism—sexual excitement and even delight in wishing, watching, or causing the suffering of others—is puzzling enough. (We all need to cling to the myth of original innocence in paradise.) It is even more difficult to follow the emotional logic of masochism—the admixture of sexual arousal and aggression turned back on oneself. Sadism and masochism always occur together, as a package, with each human being having his individual, dynamically changeable pattern of confluence of both. The sadomasochistic impulses are even further differentiated by the countless individual variations of psychic defenses arrayed against them that are part of everyone's inevitable ambivalence. These infinite varieties produce phenomena formed from the same components, but (as in our common human facial features) no two combinations are exactly alike. The excitement of making fresh discoveries when exploring these specific idiosyncratic differences is one of the incidental benefits of doing psychoanalytic work.

We know about, yet we do not easily accept, the existence of the destructive, evil part of human nature—especially in relation to ourselves. Can such things really be? Here the acceptance of inexorable reality yields only to stupidity or to delusion and denial. Of course we are all prone to, and even sometimes require, such denial (and delusions) and do not easily—and perhaps never completely—give up the promise of Eden, at least in relation to ourselves (see Shengold, 1995). It is perhaps hardest of all to accept aggression as inherent to human (therefore to one's own) biological nature—as part of phylogenesis: inherited instinctual drives. This piece of Freudian doctrine (already incipiently present in the beating fantasies paper but so tellingly and pessimistically spelled out in *Beyond the Pleasure Principle* [1920] and "Civilization and Its Discontents" [1930]) especially has been under siege in recent years. It is obviously more reassuring to emphasize the less tragic, invariably present environmental contribution to aggression:

inevitable frustration, bad parenting, bad social forces, even—for some—
bad supernatural forces. (The devil, or his equivalent as some sort of magi-
cally endowed malignant Adversary[1]—has been a needed figure on which to
project and transfer evil.) There is more hope of at least amelioration
achieved by our will when evil is, or is felt as, coming from without—rather
than having to depend on a miracle or on some dimly possible but certainly
improbable unconscious, biological, rectifying, evolutionary manifestation
(see Trilling, 1955) that mitigates our inherently destructive animal nature.
Narcissism pushes toward some "higher purpose" dedicated to the centrality
and improvement of human beings, oneself in particular—a purpose that
wisdom does not allow one to count on.

Freud's paper begins with a clinical statement that is still valid: "It is surprising how often people who seek analytic treatment . . . confess to having
indulged in the phantasy: 'A child is being beaten'" (179). In his practice
Freud found that the fantasy (which begins in early childhood) at some point
becomes associated with masturbation; as maturation proceeds, the fantasy-
action combination tends to acquire a repetitive, compulsive intensity. Freud
comments on the probable general prevalence of the fantasy and its consequences. He sees the fantasy-masturbation complex as a transient developmental phenomenon in children, part of an "infantile perversion" (p. 181)
that sometimes goes on to pathological chronicity and intensity.[2] The beating
fantasies, although initiated earlier, become reinforced, Freud says, when the
six-year-old goes to school and sees others, generally boys, being beaten
(this was in 1918). The children were rarely beaten themselves at home, and
"It was impossible, on account of the one-sidedness of the material, to confirm the first suspicion that the relation was an inverse one. [The patients]
were very seldom beaten in their childhood, or were at all events not brought
up by the help of the rod" (180). Freud's "suspicion" needs to be questioned
(although not necessarily rejected), especially in light of current knowledge
that Freud's daughter Anna, whom he took into analysis in 1918, shortly
before he started to write "A Child Is Being Beaten," was a principal supplier
of her father's observations on masturbatory beating fantasies (see Young-
Bruehl, 1988). I feel that the "suspicion," based in part on Freud's knowledge

1. *Satan* is Hebrew for "adversary." He appears not in Genesis but later, in 1 Chron-
icles and Job.

2. This idea of developmentally "normal" transiency but pathological fixation in
regard to beating fantasies in childhood is also the current view decisively expressed
by the Novicks (1995).

or at least his wish[3] that his daughter was not beaten at home, is of doubtful general validity. Not being a child analyst, I am on insecure ground here, but certainly I have seen (or heard about in supervising) adult patients with similar beating fantasies who have convincing memories of having been beaten in childhood, at home, or at school—as well as others who produce no such memories in analysis and for whom beating may never have taken place but who have nonetheless registered terrifying and exciting expectations of being beaten similar to those described in Freud's paper. Individuals from both groups can retain beating fantasies that continue into adult life.

Regular home and school beatings in childhood—the free use of the rod and the cane—are familiar from memoirs, biographies, and fiction of the past few centuries, especially by authors from Russia and England (with its public schools). Notable here are accounts by Dickens, Turgenev, Dostoyevsky, Samuel Butler, Swinburne, Chekhov, Kipling, Orwell—among many others. Chekhov and Samuel Butler are two well-known examples of victims and documenters of beatings by their fathers at home. Beating and watching beatings is especially associated with slavery (*Uncle Tom's Cabin,* mentioned by Freud) and serfdom (Turgenev, Dostoyevsky).

I have found that beating fantasies can exist apparently without the actuality of having suffered beatings as a child. It is interesting that Freud describes the acquisition of the "infantile perversion" (fantasy plus masturbation) as an "event" (182).[4] This seems somewhat ambiguous. Is it the masturbatory action that turns the fantasy into an event? Is not the fantasy itself often powerful enough to constitute an event? (As usual when he is writing about pathogenesis, Freud does bring in the always concomitant "congenital constitutional" factor that interacts with what happens to a child: here he identifies it as previous premature sadistic development.) We always have difficulty trying to assess "what really happened" in the past. Freud here touches on another, sometimes seemingly unsolvable, mystery in this paper —that of pathogenesis.

3. Freud has been condemned, quite rightly, for taking his own daughter into analysis. That he was a child-beater does not follow; I am not trying to suggest that unlikely role. Physical punishment of children was frequent enough in Freud's time, and probably some was administered to Anna. But the expectation in fantasy would have been enough to lead to her sadomasochistic wishes and fears.

4. The German word he uses is *Ereignis* (event, incident, happening); I believe the German word has wider connotations than the English *event*—connotations of having lived through something experienced mainly as coming from the outside.

Indeed, the paper contains one of Freud's most forthright statements about recovering memories: "Strictly considered—and why should this question not be considered with all possible strictness?—analytic work deserves to be recognized as genuine psycho-analysis only when it has succeeded in removing the amnesia which conceals from the adult his knowledge of his childhood from its beginning (that is, from about the second to the fifth year)" (183). I feel that Freud's purpose in idealizing memory recovery was to emphasize the genetic principle, the need to trace psychic pathology to its roots in the first five years of life by "recovering" the past, specifically by reviving the Oedipus complex in the analysis. Freud in 1918 had a much more static idea of memories than we have today, and the importance of working on a variety of resistances and on defenses other than repression was not yet appreciated. The roles of ego development and of object relations were not completely grasped.

Freud's prescribed strictness would also no longer seem appropriate in the light of the difficulties of recovering historical truth and of currently accepted ideas in neurology and psychology about the shifting nature of memory. Historical truth should be retained as an impossible goal to aim for in our impossible profession. But it would be better to abandon the concept of fixed memories as well as Freud's archeological metaphors about memory recovery. We should instead stress the study of the patient's current psychic registrations of the first five years of life (as they exist in memory and fantasy), including their vicissitudes, and the failures (and resultant blanknesses) of those registrations.[5]

Freud supplies a study of the developmental "transformations in beating-fantasies" (184). The presentation can at times give the unfortunate impression that these are *the* transformations, which scants the tremendous variety of individual variations that are to be found. I want to illustrate something of these.

Patient C was an intelligent and capable man driven to psychoanalytic

5. The adult mind has "registered" the past in a dynamic state that features (1) patterns compulsively repeated in fantasy, impulses, and actions that are projected and transferred and (2) "memories" (I use the quotation marks to denote unreliability) constantly shifting (in relation to contents and conviction about validity), subject to lifelong transformations as maturation proceeds. Reconstructions, based on (usually distorted) revivals of the past in transference and projection onto the analyst and other important people in the patient's life, are needed to supplement "memories." I view "memories" as an often indecipherable mix of historical and psychological truth.

treatment by anxiety, work inhibition, intermittent low self-esteem, and distress about sexual masochistic impulses (generally not acted out). Owing to a motor accident that hospitalized and disabled both parents for a long time when he was about six, C and his slightly older sister were unable to be cared for by their parents at home. His sister was taken in by relatives, but C was sent away to a boarding school in another state, where he was younger than the other boys in his class. This private school was a kind of military academy with a good reputation for scholarship. The school was vaguely based on the British public school model: it was upper class and Protestant, classical languages were studied, and caning the boys for misconduct was a matter of course. There were daily line-ups of boys waiting to be beaten. (The caning may have been due to the tastes and training of the headmaster, who kept a collection of well-used birches in his office. C had subsequently heard that many years later, when the headmaster had retired, the beating policy was halted.)

C's descriptions evoked Orwell's (1947) recollections of the sadistic atmosphere of the British public school at the beginning of the twentieth century. The headmaster had declared more than once, as do so many parents, "This beating hurts me much more than you," and C remembered feeling guilty. Despite the man's stern and unchanging facial expression, C did have an impression of the headmaster's fierce (later he concluded it had been impassioned) involvement with the beatings, administered to the boy's bare buttocks. C remembered that after being beaten he wanted to be comforted by the headmaster. But this did not occur. "Nothing overtly sexual happened," C added. In the course of telling me about all this, C expressed another unsolicited assertion: he had never been beaten at home by his parents.

C reported having felt confused, despairing, and guilty toward his parents for sending him away, but his rage was suppressed. Later in the session his disclaimer about parental beatings was amended. He was not sure why he had said it—he had believed it while he was saying it. But actually his mother had often threatened to beat him with a leather belt. Although this never occurred, C was left with fantasies of being belt-whipped and some fetishistic excitement about leather. And occasionally, when his usually "nice" mother would lose her temper, C had been spanked by her or by his father, but, he said, "They never made me take my pants down" (in contrast to the headmaster). C did not remember whether these rare spankings had occurred before boarding school. His parents were obviously reluctant to administer the spankings and upset afterwards; the spankings were humiliating but rather gentle. They made him very angry, especially with his mother. (It was easier to be angry with his father than with his mother.) C later in analysis found the idea that she had allowed him to be sent away so painful as to be almost unbearable.

The school experiences, so imbued with the danger of separation and of rage at his parents as well as with sadomasochistic excitement, had clearly scarred C and influenced his fantasy life. He suffered afterwards from a need to be punished, and in adolescence he remembered beginning to have occasional obscure daydreams and dreams of being beaten by anonymous men. But, just as often, the dreams were of administering beatings, usually to younger boys. These fantasies still occasionally occurred to the mature man.

In one session, following my being away on vacation, he reported a dream: "I am punishing a boy but I seem to be only lightly touching his shoulders with a familiar cane. The boy is crying and I feel loving toward him and I want to comfort him, but I don't." The "familiar cane," C said, was a peculiar, heavy stick carried by his headmaster but not used for beating. C repeated his wish for "tenderness" from the headmaster after being beaten. In the dream he had cast himself as a tender version of the headmaster and as the boy who was rather tenderly treated. C said there were no sexual feelings in the dream, just some generalized loving emotion toward the boy. He had, however, awakened with an erection.

This seemingly predominantly heterosexual man had strong homosexual longings that had not been acted out. His sexuality was marred by inhibitions and, aside from sporadic casual contacts with prostitutes and women he looked down on, C had lived a relatively abstinent life, one he called "spartan and measured"; he had avoided lengthy attachments. He had suppressed wishes to beat and be beaten during sexual contacts. His mildly erotic feelings toward men featured the craving for tenderness displayed in his dream. The dream seemed to me to express wishes to be loved by the father (and/or the phallic mother) and now by the analyst, seemingly a predominantly negative oedipal phenomenon, regressively expressed in mild sadomasochistic terms. (This was also evident in fantasies of being punished, often direct or disguised beating fantasies, sometimes accompanied by masturbation.) In general, C was subject to idealization of sadomasochistic excitement (occasionally homosexually tinged in fantasy) that seemed especially to screen out penetration, destruction, and hatred. Instead of wanting to kill or even aggressively to fuck the female or male headmasters of this world or to submit to their aggression (the other side of the predominantly anal coin), he had tried to avoid the destruction by equating punishment with love in masturbatory fantasy. This confirms one of Freud's general conclusions.[6]

C's frequently provocative masochism seemed designed to hold onto parental objects whom he expected to lose—especially to preserve them from the destructive rage associated with such expectations. Novick and Novick (1995) convincingly present a view of pathological masochism mainly as an attempt to counter the danger of losing the mental image of parents, defending them from the child's sadism. I will illustrate this clinically.

Patient D, after my August vacation (which had evoked the same threat of object loss in C), was additionally distressed when I needed to cancel another session, at the end of my first week back, because of a minor illness. In the first session of the next week, D stated that he "thought" he was angry because I had cancelled on the previous Friday, although he had noticed that I was coughing the day before and hadn't been all that surprised by the cancellation. (D was one of those patients who hated surprises and sudden changes, which I have found—frequently but not invariably—to be a residue of childhood traumata.) He had the thought, "I'll pay you back"— meaning that he would further postpone paying July's overdue bill. This "not paying" involved, I felt, an unconscious holding onto the parent as represented by the analyst—the link in unconscious fantasy being the equation of the money owed to the analyst's fecal phallus in D's anus. I did not interpret this. (The resolution to withhold payment seemed to D to be so obviously and irrationally provocative that he started to laugh as he told me about it.) I did remark that he had said he "thought" he was angry, and I wondered if he had felt the anger. "It goes away when I see you," D said. "I must be afraid of it." (It was typical of this bright man that he could permit himself intellectual insight if he used it unconsciously to ward off concomitant, threateningly intense feelings from consciousness.)

On the Friday that I had canceled he had been home alone and, after the transient anger, had felt lonely and anxious. "I did what I do so often when I feel that; I resorted to the beating fantasies." He had talked about these fantasies from the beginning of his analysis, but only in recent months had he begun to reveal their details. The fantasies usually consisted of being beaten by an anonymous woman, "handsome," large, and tough. With great plea-

6. I am trying to show the clinical usefulness of Freud's generalizations in this 1919 paper, whatever modifications or qualifications one might want to add to them, and even when one finds variations from the specific details Freud describes.

sure he submitted to her commands and to her beating him on his bare back-side. Sometimes the roles were reversed and he did the beating—another common variation from Freud's formula. Friday's had been the more typical masturbatory fantasy in which he was beaten by a "dyke-ish" woman. He "thought" that maybe she stood for me. But actually she had reminded him of a much-admired camp counselor from boyhood he had recently dreamt about. This young man had been tall and handsome, with a reputation for seducing all the pretty female counselors. In the dream, D was a boy watching the counselor; it wasn't clear if the latter were a man or a woman. "But," D asserted, "there was no beating in the dream and no submission." (The emphasis was his and I regarded it as an expression of negation, in Freud's sense.) There was little emotion attached to the dream, but it had remained in his mind for some time and had not been mentioned previously in the analysis.

During his early camp years D had admired this young man greatly and had vague "romantic feelings about him—not sexual!" (compare C's de-claratory negations). D went on: "I was a kind of favorite of his. But once he did yell at me and swatted me on the behind, and then I hated him so I wanted to kill him. I had beating fantasies then too, but it was always a woman who beat me, and if I pictured submitting to a real person I felt rage at that person. I guess I felt rage at you. You aren't young and you aren't handsome, but you are tall." (The analysis took place many years ago. I was younger than D and believe that I looked it, but he had the insistent, multi-determined belief that I was of an older generation.) "My counselor stood for you [pause], I guess."

D had been physically punished regularly as a child, spanked with a hair-brush by his "generally cold and disapproving" mother. He remembered these experiences as pleasurable at first; they showed that at least she cared. But eventually it became clearer and clearer to D, as his suppressed rage at her (and at his father for allowing the spankings) emerged, how terrifying the beatings also were. There had not been much pain, but there had been excitement that had become overstimulation, helplessness, rage—and, per-haps most of all, terror, terror of his rage. "The beatings would last too long," he had said earlier in the analysis. As a child, he had felt the rage. He did his best to focus it away from his mother onto the hairbrush. How he had hated that hairbrush!

D found later in the analysis that he was terrified of anger so intense that it made him want to kill the mother he felt he couldn't live without. It was as if the intensity of the feeling itself had magical murderous power. And during the session I am quoting from, D was able to see that he had been afraid of losing me. This was especially true when he had briefly felt—as he finally acknowledged in the session—"murderous" toward me. That had occurred at home, just before the masturbatory fantasy; the submission and "anal" contact in the fantasy preserved me and the relationship to me. Punishment temporarily became "love," or at least a preservation of the hope and need for love.

Genetically, both parents seemed involved in the transference onto me. Freud speaks of the "regressive debasement of the genital organization itself to a lower level. 'My father loves me' was meant in a genital sense; owing to the regression it is turned into 'my father is beating me.' . . . This being beaten is now a convergence of the sense of guilt and sexual love. [The beating] is not only the punishment for the forbidden genital relation, but also the regressive substitute for that relation" (189). But with D (contrary to Freud's assertion elsewhere in his paper that *"in both [boys and girls,] the beating phantasy has its origin in an incestuous attachment to the father"* [198, italics Freud's]), the mother even more than the father was imbricated in unconscious and conscious fantasies in the forbidden genital sexual and anal regressive forms; and both parents—phallic mother and active father as well as, in reversal, passive mother and passive father—had become transferable in all these versions onto the analyst, who was then beginning to appear in D's beating fantasies.

For my patients and Freud's, an even more profound regressive retreat from oedipal conflict than the anal libidinal one can be involved in beating fantasies. Toward the end of this hour, D said: "If I had a beating fantasy about you, in my fantasy you and I would be in it together; I wouldn't be alone. I hate to get up off the couch and walk out the door at the end of my hour. It means showing you my ass. I hate you while I'm telling you this. I feel so ashamed. And yet hate comes with separation. I guess I would hold onto you with the shame and excitement if I let myself put you in the fantasies. I want it, but, you know,[7] that being together also threatens to make

7. I was not surprised by what the patient said, but of course I did not know. The "you know" sounded here as if it were something involuntary. I feel this kind of "you know" was a projection, as it often is for people and therefore for patients. Something D himself would not or could not know was emerging in the second person, in projection onto the analyst—"I know" becoming "you know." This everyday kind of projection does involve a transient and tiny loss of identity, a giving away of "I"—

me lose my identity, as if I'll become part of you. This is not just about sex. There is pleasure in my fantasies, but this is the terrifying part."

It was one of the terrifying parts. On the anal developmental level are predominantly sadistic impulses with their terrifying threat of loss of the parental other, which the concomitant anal passivity and masochistic submission (also full of danger) was meant to counteract. The danger of loss of identity, loss of self, comes from the wish for oral merging. This stems from a time of development earlier than the anal, when the mother is felt as the indispensable "only" other, who starts out, we know today, as part of the self.[8] What is dangerous is also desired—the trap of narcissistic regressive defense (see Shengold, 1988).

This session was one of those sessions that fits Kris's description of "good" (1956, 253), but the insight D had come to took many years to work through emotionally so that he could safely *own* it and use it to liberate himself enough to attenuate the sadomasochistic burden he had carried since he was a child.

The erotization of being beaten and beating features a fixation on and regression to what seem to be predominantly anal feelings and impulses (involving anal erogeneity [body feeling] and sadomasochistic libido [energy]; see Fliess, 1956). Freud stresses regression from oedipal impulses—from passively submitting to the father (or, we would now add, phallic mother).

---

marking in this example with D the ego's momentary retreat from an emerging insight, a miniature shift in the long backwards-and-forwards (dynamic intrapsychic) struggle involved in analysis. This kind of "you know" means that what the person is saying is not "owned" (see Shengold, 1995).

8. The contact and merging on both the anal and the oral levels were both gratifying and terrifying, representing the ubiquitous psychic compromise between impulse and defense stressed by Brenner. A current developmental view is that the earliest mental representative of the parent starts out, according to Freud (1941), as "The breast is part of me; I am the breast" (299), and in the course of development the mothering figure gradually is separated out as a whole person. The father becomes important later on, at first in displacement from the mother and then in his own right. But the earliest mental impressions are never erased, and the mothering figure as primal parent retains a basic importance for both men and women. (Dying people tend to call for the mother, or for God unconsciously perceived as the primal parent.) This view grants a complex perspective that modifies Freud's insistence on the father as primary in beating fantasies.

Anna Freud, in her 1922 paper, "Beating Fantasies and Daydreams," presents a case history according to the "stages" outlined in her father's paper (it seems undoubtedly her own story) and restates his insight that the beating fits are regressive "substitutes for an incestuous love scene" (1922, 152).

Swinburne, in his life and writings (not so overtly in his poetry, but in his letters and novels), provides an example. The first of his two novels, *Love's Cross Currents,* was published in 1877 under a pseudonym; his letters and the second novel, *Lesbia Brandon,* were not published in Swinburne's life-time. Wilson (1962) says:

> One's enjoyment of the splendor and wit of these novels is, however . . . likely to be somewhat disturbed by an element which seems bizarre and repellent, and this element appears in [Swinburne's] correspondence in an even more repellent form. As a result of his experience as a boy at Eton, Swinburne had made a cult of the traditional British practice of flogging, and this had become for him inseparable from his capacity for sexual gratification, which seems to have been exclusively masochistic. The pleasure and importance of being flogged are made to figure in . . . these family fictions. . . . In *Lesbia Brandon* Swinburne pulls out all the stops, and howls of pain become cries of ecstasy. (28–29)

Swinburne never married. As a young man, he had what appeared to be an incestuous attachment (apparently never enacted) to a female cousin who was like a sister to him. She married another. (Brother-sister incest is abundant in his writings.) Swinburne lived most of his adult life with another bachelor, Theodore Watts-Dunton, toward whom he had a characteristic submissive attitude. In his letters he calls Watts-Dunton "Major" and himself "Minor"; there was an unconscious parent-child identification. Swinburne gave Watts-Dunton the manuscript of *Lesbia Brandon* to read, and "Major" refused to return it, prohibiting and preventing its publication. In Swinburne's letters to Watts-Dunton he often falls into a schoolboy persona, with frequent allusions to birchings. It is not known what, if anything, was acted out between the two men in this regard, but most commentators agree that there probably was no overt sexual contact.

Wilson cites Edmund Gosse's suppressed postscript to his memoir about the poet in which "he says that Swinburne found a brothel in London which specialized in flagellation" (Wilson, 29), apparently administered by women. Wilson observes that Swinburne was fond of swimming and would swim in the ocean "in dangerous waters. [His] letters confirm explicitly that Swinburne's love of swimming, besides providing ordeals, afforded him masochistic gratification. He liked to be pounded and slapped about by the inexorable 'great sweet mother'" (34).

Freud was thinking about masochists such as Swinburne when he insisted that such men always have fantasies of being beaten by women. Freud at this time was still insisting on the father as the object of such men, unconsciously hidden behind the female beater, who stood for the mother. Today we would see a much greater variety of multilayerings — with both father and mother involved, in individual varieties disguised by censorship.

In regard to fantasies of being beaten, Freud views the girls as wanting to be boys and the boys as wanting to be girls. Today we recognize that analsadomasochistic phenomena can aim at the denial of the differences between the sexes and the generations (see Chasseguet-Smirgel, 1978). These beating fantasies, which Freud regarded as almost universal, at least in their transient forms, are for me a confirmation of the assumption that in relation to sex we all basically want to be and to have everything — mother *and* father, girls *and* boys, women *and* men.

Freud feels that the ubiquity of beating fantasies establishes that "the perversion is no longer an isolated fact in the child's sexual life, but falls into its place among the typical, not to say normal, processes of development which are familiar to us" (192). Freud sees the generic childhood perversion as incestuously founded in relation to the "child's incestuous love-*object*" (192). (This should be *objects* — Freud is still thinking too much of father *or* mother.) The parents are inevitably the first others and so become the object of the drives as they develop. This is, we would now say, the pre-oedipal road to the Oedipus complex: pre-oedipal incestuous objects become incestuous oedipal objects. Alongside this, and continuing with the travel metaphor, one can also accept Freud's statement about "the origin of infantile perversions from the Oedipus complex" (192) if we take it to mean that defensive regression from the complex largely or partly traverses the road back to established and never completely abandoned pre-oedipal perverse positions.

In "A Child Is Being Beaten" Freud tends to contradict himself in an uncharacteristically clumsy way. On one hand he outlines rather fixed general rules, formulae, and sequences for beating fantasy formation and for the causation of perversion; on the other, he makes it clear that many of his conclusions are based on limited observation and that much is unknown, speculative, and indefinite. (We would now feel strongly that sadomaso-chistic tendencies are multidetermined and can follow a variety of paths and form a variety of patterns.) A hard-to-attain *balance* between what is known and unknown, certain and uncertain, is necessary and even optimal for psychoanalytic clinical and theoretical work. This is another impossible part of our profession that cannot be avoided. In the psychic realm in which we labor, one needs a mind that, like Freud's, is capable of containing contradictions. He is a fine model. But in this paper the balance seems off; the contradictions jar. The paper features a comparatively rare overuse of the unqualified (that is, not slightly modified or negative) terms *always* and *never*[9] as expressions of too much certainty in his generalizations. Most of the words and phrases expressing invariability pertain to the beating fantasies of girls, which are central to Freud's clinical material. The paper also contains many instances of Freud's more characteristic balance[10] of uncertainty along with assertion; for example, he says that, in contrast to what he declares about girls, "I have not been able to get so far in my knowledge of beating-phantasies in boys" (196).

Freud's paper is based on analytic study of four women and two men. He mentions the diagnosis of five of them (four obsessional, one hysterical), but the sixth is neither diagnosed nor mentioned further. I wonder (with Young-Bruehl) if the sixth is his daughter Anna, Freud's "Antigone," whose analysis was a major impetus for Freud to write this paper. Six cases are an inadequate base for a theory of masochism or of perversion, but of course Freud brings his entire prior experience to bear on his generalizations (most of which follow from his *Three Essays on Sexuality* which he published first in 1905 but kept changing and adding to). Jones calls the beating-fantasies paper "a purely clinical study" (1955, 305), but it contains notable contribu-

9. The concordance lists 1,053 instances of the use of *always,* but most of these either do not express invariable generalizations or are qualified ("almost always," "almost never"). There are also alternative ways of saying these absolutist words. In this paper Freud uses "certainly," "invariably," "cannot fail to," "almost invariable," "precisely the same," "no less a necessity," "it is not with," "as a rule," and other phrases to the same purpose. Strangely enough, the *nevers* are omitted from the concordance listings, which skip from *neutral* to *nevertheless*—an unexplainable "slip" of the editors or printers.

10. There are many phrases stressing how much is not known, including "impossible to say," "perhaps," "most probably," "doubt remains," "seems to be," and "not uncommon."

tions to Freud's changing theoretical views, especially those on instinct theory, sadomasochism, and perversion.

Mahony points out "Freud's extensive use of the present tense" in this paper (1987, 140). This, he says, is a characteristic, although intermittently used, aspect of Freud's style, one that provides immediate "impact" and conveys dramatic and emotional intensity—especially obvious when Freud writes about dreams and clinical narratives. Freud's use of the present tense gives a sense of "imminence" (128), says Mahony.[11] If there is unusual emotional intensity in this paper, it could again be (speculatively) attributed to the centrality of Anna Freud's contribution to it as Freud's patient.[12]

So some of Freud's failings in this important paper can be ascribed to his personal version of the oedipal and pre-oedipal family complexes that affect us all—he had *revenants* from his own infantile and racial past. Freud's strength is that, despite his awareness of inevitable failings—his own and others'—he tried and demanded that his followers try to take account of the cannibalism, murder, and incest within. The guilt that is part of the human condition does not lessen Freud's own deficiencies or sins. But he reminds us at the end of his paper of the inexorability of our own and our parents' burdens of evil and relative helplessness—we all have to face in our own way what Hamlet and Oedipus faced. In my comments, I have stressed the conflicted and inhibitory consequences of the reverse form of these murderous impulses, directed from the parent toward the child (my modernizing modifications are italicized): "Infantile sexuality [*and aggression*], which [*are*] held under repression, [*act*] as the chief motive force[*s*] in the formation of symptoms; and the essential part of [*their*] content, the Oedipus complex [*together with its pre-oedipal antecedents,*[13] *transformed but not eliminated*

11. Mahony points out that the instances of present tense in Freud's German are not always so translated by Strachey in the *Collected Works,* but he specifically cites the beating fantasies paper as an example of Freud's use of the first person that is retained in its English translation.

12. "Anna Freud several times protected her privacy by declaring that the clinical material for 'Beating Fantasies and Daydreams' came from her own analytic practice. But the paper was actually written some six months before Anna Freud saw her first patient" (Young-Bruehl, 1988, 103).

13. A statement from Freud's paper is relevant: "The emphasis which is laid here upon the importance of the earliest experiences does not imply any underestimation of the influence of later ones" (183). The statement could be repeated with the "earliest" and "later" reversed.

by it], is the nuclear complex of neuroses" (204). The Oedipus complex and its pre-oedipal antecedents of course involve murder as well as sex.

This is too much for some of Freud's self-righteous critics. Accepting our individual immersion in cannibalism, murder, and incest is both a narcissistic blow and a source of terror, but, alas, it is all too easy to demonstrate the universality of this dark side of human nature. Our need for denial, another necessary part of our humanity that is hard to transcend for long, makes it inevitable that Freud's role as a disturber of the peace of the world (maintained in the Freudian analyst's role as a mirror of the patient's mind and impulses in every analysis) will continue to foster anxiety and hostility toward Freud and psychoanalysis.

POSTSCRIPT

I want to connect patient C, a child who was beaten, and Anna Freud as Freud's patient; the bridge is that both of them had dreams that featured tenderness.

Anna Freud wrote in 1942, three years after her father's death:

About Losing and Being Lost/Concerning last night's dream: I dream, as I have often done, that he is here again. All of these recent dreams have the same character: the main role is played not by my longing for him but rather by his longing for me. The main scenes in the dreams are always of his tenderness to me, which always takes the form of my own, earlier tenderness. In reality he never showed [tenderness] with the exception of one or two times, which always remained in my memory. The reversal can be simply the fulfillment of my wish [for tenderness], but it is probably also something else. In the first dream of this kind he openly said: "I have always longed for you so." The main feeling in yesterday's dream is that he is wandering about (on top of mountains, hills) while I am doing other things. . . . [I] feel that I should stop whatever I am doing and go walking with him. Eventually he calls me to him and demands this himself. I am very relieved and lean myself against him, crying in a way that is very familiar to both of us. Tenderness. My thoughts are troubled; he should not have called me, it is as if a renunciation or a form of progress had been undone because he called. (1942, 296–97)

This is very moving, not least because of her obvious but gentle reproaches toward her father. The reproaches are not only for the rarity of his
expressions of tenderness. They also refer to his demands for a damaging or
at least inhibiting too-closeness, and, muted and not directly spelled out, I
feel, is a complaint against her father for having "called" her to be his
analysand.

The notes finish with a retreat from anger and reproach toward longing,
love, guilt, and denial: "Sympathy and bad conscience. Associations: The
poem by Albrecht Schaeffer, 'You strong and dear wayfarer . . . I was with
you at each step of the way — / there was no victory I did not also win — / no
sorrow I did not suffer beside you, / you strong and you dear wanderer'"
(297).

These dreams of Anna Freud's bring her dead father back to life. I feel
they demonstrate the masochistic child's need to suppress hostility toward
the parent and direct it toward the self, to avert or try to undo the loss of the
parent. To suffer ill-treatment is to keep a connection with the parent without
whom the child feels life is not possible. This need is then sexualized. There
is a compulsive craving for the beating, emotional or physical, to turn to tenderness and love.

REFERENCES

Bloom, H. 1973. *The anxiety of influence*. New York: Oxford University Press.
———. 1994. *The Western canon: The books and school of the ages*. New York: Harcourt, Brace.
Brenner, C. 1994. The mind as conflict and compromise formation. *J. Clin. Psychoan.*
3:473–88.
Chasseguet-Smirgel, J. 1978. Reflections on the connexions between perversion and
sadism. *Int. J. Psycho-Anal.* 59:37–48.
Fliess, R. 1956. *Erogeneity and libido*. New York: International Universities Press.
Freud, A. [1922]. Beating fantasies in daydreams. *The Writings of Anna Freud*. New
York: International Universities Press, 1:137–57 (1974).
———. 1942. Notes toward the essay "About losing and being lost." In *Anna Freud
in her own words*, comp. R. Rosen. *Bull. Anna Freud Centre* 18:293–305 (1995).
Freud, S. 1905. *Three essays on the theory of sexuality. S.E. 7*.
———. 1919. A child is being beaten. *S.E. 17*.
———. 1920. *Beyond the pleasure principle. S.E. 8*.
———. 1923. *The ego and the id. S.E. 19*.

—————. 1924. The economic problem of masochism. *S.E.* 19.

—————. 1926. *Inhibitions, symptoms and anxiety. S.E.* 20.

—————. 1930. Civilization and its discontents. *S.E.* 21.

—————. 1940. *An outline of psychoanalysis. S.E.* 23.

—————. 1941. Findings, ideas, problems. *S.E.* 23

Jones, E. 1955. *The life and work of Sigmund Freud, 1901–1921.* Vol. 2. New York: Basic Books.

Kris, E. [1956]. On some vicissitudes of insight in psychoanalysis. In *The selected papers of Ernst Kris,* 252–71. New Haven, Conn.: Yale University Press (1975).

Mahony, P. 1987. *Freud as a Writer.* New Haven, Conn.: Yale Univeristy Press (paperback).

Novick, J., and Novick, K. K. 1995. *Fearful symmetry. The development and treatment of sadomasochism.* Northvale, N.J.: Jason Aronson.

Orwell, G. 1947. Such, such were the joys. In *A collection of essays.* New York: Harcourt Brace Jovanovich.

Shengold, L. 1988. *Halo in the sky.* New Haven, Conn.: Yale University Press, 1992.

—————. 1995. *Delusions of everyday life.* New Haven, Conn.: Yale University Press.

Trilling, L. 1955. Freud: Within and beyond culture. In *Beyond Culture,* 89–119. New York: Viking (1965).

Wilson, E. 1962. Introduction, *The novels of A. C. Swinburne,* 3–37. New York: Farrar, Straus & Cudahy.

Young-Bruehl, E. 1988. *Anna Freud: A biography.* New York: Summit.

The Scene and

Its Reverse

Considerations on a
Chain of Associations
in Freud

MARCIO DE F. GIOVANNETTI

Writing about any of Freud's texts is inevitably not only a frightening experience but also a presumptuous venture because, just as in working with an
analysand, our task from the beginning entails elements of impossibility,
deficiency, and inadequacy. After all, when we read Freud or any other great
writer, we are immediately confronted with the question of knowledge and
truth, or of the truth about knowledge; in either case, we are transported into
the realm of the half-said, the forbidden, and the void (André, 1994).
Whether it is taken as a whole or line by line, the Freudian text is in effect a
mimesis of its own subject—the human being—in that it never ceases to
speak about what actually cannot be said. It presents itself in a constant state
of flux, like a word forever in search of another word, like a word in a dialogue, which records the dialogue while at the same time bearing witness to
the impossibility of dialogue as an entity. Like the unconscious, it is never
whole, but always a part, showing by its very structure that there can be no
word from the unconscious that does not break through and exceed the limits
of every word that can be uttered, transforming it even at its birth into a half-

Translated by Philip Slotkin, MA MITI.

word, something half-said and thus not complete in itself that, even while being uttered, calls for a new, interpreting word, one that will in turn demand yet another new word.

Acting as a metalinguistic word for the human word itself, the Freudian text is born and dies simultaneously as it constantly refashions itself, as if drawing attention to the symbolic and metaphorical nature of all language. Since it is always in flux, the text constitutes only a starting point and never a point of arrival; in the course of its constant refashioning of itself and its object, and through its displacements, condensations, reformulations, and negations of itself, it resists synthesis, even when it so lends itself on the manifest level, and that is the source of original character (see Giovannetti, 1994).

From the beginning of Freud's writing career (*On aphasia;* "A project for a scientific psychology") to the end (*New introductory lectures on psycho-analysis;* "Analysis terminable and interminable"; *An outline of psycho-analysis*), the titles of his works emphasize the impossibility of finding words to supply more than an outline or project, words that are more than mere interpretative introductions to the living nature of their object, man. Neither terminable nor interminable, Freud's text simply points toward the *Deutung,* indicating the direction of a necessary further text—the basic condition for the constitution of any human discourse and for that discourse to have a historicizing justification.

Freud's method is based on free association and its counterpart, evenly suspended attention in listening. If his own method is applied to his oeuvre, the various associative flows that pervade it are revealed. Although the beginning of *The Interpretation of Dreams* resembles a scientific treatise in its structure, the break with the positivists that the work represents emerges clearly from the second chapter on. Freud's approach becomes increasingly essayistic: in demonstrating how his own work was produced, he assumes the position of a subject who relates to the object of his study in a number of ways.

Whereas it took Freud three long years to write *The Interpretation of Dreams,* all his later texts, except for *Moses and Monotheism,* were produced over very short periods, in effect testifying to his allegiance to the method of free association: he would make notes, set down everything that came into his mind in each chain of associations, and follow every strand until he came up against the irresistible force of the censorship, which would inevitably punctuate his utterance. But only for a moment. For when he resumed his argument in a new text, the previous chain of associations would be taken up again, albeit transformed and disguised—but the successor chain would retain a close relationship to its predecessor, whether of continuity, opposition, or mental imagery. Examples are the footnotes and postscripts that Freud added over the years to most of his texts and the prefaces and notes accompanying Strachey's translation of his oeuvre—the former placing each contribution within a specific context and the latter constantly referring us to another text, whether earlier or later than the one in which they are included. The excellent biographies by Jones, Anzieu, and Gay, to mention only a few, adopt a similar approach.

It is therefore impossible to read a text by Freud without also referring to his previous and subsequent writings. Similarly, there is no obvious gateway to his oeuvre, because each text is both a gateway to other work and part of the foundation of the entire building. Equally, there is no exit.

Meltzer (1978) notes that there were two main bursts of genius in Freud's writing: from 1899 to 1904 and from 1919 to 1922. To my mind, this idea is interesting more for its implicit content than in terms of the manifest statement, because latent in the second burst is the fact that the original chain of associations succeeded in overcoming its maximum point of resistance. From then on, as with an analysand who recovers a traumatic memory and can thus achieve a reorganization on a different level of his history, Freud's works were structured on a different plane. The new plane was neither better nor worse than the previous one but, as the Sandlers (1987) point out in connection with the first and second topographical theories, would refer to but never replace it, recasting it by making some of its latent aspects explicit.

It is commonly held that the transition from Freud's first topography to the structural theory involved a radical change of direction. Similarly, the antithesis between the sex instinct and the ego instinct has traditionally been contrasted with that between the life and the death instincts. My own approach, however, focuses more on the idea that Freud overcame a resistance that had been holding up the original chain of associations, resulting in a new associative flow. Anticipating somewhat, I can say that this resistance has to do with mortality.

It is this new associative flow that gave rise to "A Child Is Being Beaten," one of the most stimulating, disconcerting, and difficult works in the entire Freudian canon. It actually belongs in a line of writing that begins—if indeed the word *begin* is appropriate here—in 1914 with "From the History of an Infantile Neurosis" (1918 [1914]) and continuing with "On Transformations of Instinct as Exemplified in Anal Erotism" (1917a) and with "A Childhood Recollection from *Dichtung und Wahrheit*" (1917b), immediate predecessors of the three contributions written between January and May 1919: "A Child Is Being Beaten," *Beyond the Pleasure Principle,* and "The 'Uncanny,'" with their rich network of signifiers.

Being at the same time new and old, this strange conceptual fabric is woven from the threads of infantile memories, infantile sexual theories, the primal scene, the Oedipus complex, the castration complex, the phallus, and pleasure—with pleasure here showing its darkest face.

The tag "*homo homini lupus,*" quoted by Freud in "Civilization and Its Discontents" (133), could be connected with the dream of an exiled expatriate in which a window is suddenly opened, revealing a tree from which five motionless wolves are watching the dreamer. (Although Freud refers to six or seven wolves, there are in fact five in the Wolf Man's drawing.) Freud was concerned from the beginning with the idea of infantile curiosity and its connection with sexuality. This particular line of inquiry commences with *Three Essays on the Theory of Sexuality* (1905a) and continues with "On the Sexual Theories of Children" (1908), the case history of Little Hans (1909a), "Leonardo da Vinci and a Memory of His Childhood" (1910a), "Contributions to the Psychology of Love" I and II (1910b, 1912), "Psycho-analytic Notes on an Autobiographical Account of a Case of Paranoia (Dementia Paranoides)" (1911 [1910]), *Totem and Taboo* (1912–13), and "On Narcissism: An Introduction" (1914). All these works deal in one way or another with the problems of curiosity, knowledge, and sexuality as Freud gradually worked his way toward what was to become explicit as the primal scene in "From the History of an Infantile Neurosis" (1918 [1914]).

Although the concept of the Oedipus complex appears in his writings from the beginning, in the works just mentioned it is always connected with the same question: "What is it that distinguishes males and females if there is only one libido?" This question is inevitably associated with that of Little Hans about where babies come from. Or, as reformulated by Oedipus, "Who am I?" It can be answered only by recourse to history. Hence the need to take it to a past time and place, showing that there must have been a beginning or origin, thereby transforming the question into "Where did I come from?"

Freud too indulged in speculation, putting the same question in a much wider context, that of the species; where, he wonders in *Totem and Taboo,* did man come from? His speculation is incidentally brilliant; it transcends the polemic concerning the reliability of its foundations and argument, because, together with Schreber's delusional speculations about the creation of the world, it was to provide him with the foundations of his new concept, that of narcissism.

On the level of identification, then, we now have a combination of curiosity, the Oedipus complex, sexual gender, and narcissism. If curiosity is exercised from a narcissistic position, the answer to the question "Who am I?" is "The world." In the case of oedipal curiosity, however, the answer is much more complex. It is "I do not know for certain": the knowledge concerned is deficient and incomplete and, far from exhausting curiosity, stimulates it. The answer is transformed into something like: "The world exists and I exist; therefore I must get to know this world in order to know something of myself."

This knowledge of the world coupled with knowledge of oneself is one of the fundamental structuring components of the Oedipus myth: the roads leading from one city to the other, the fateful crossroads, and the coming and going of people from one city to another are all intimately connected with the search for identity and represent the background to the scene in which the Sphinx presents its riddle.

This connection between self and world had in a way already been hinted at by Hans, the little boy who looked out of his window and saw trains moving back and forth on the railway line and horses trotting up and down the street, as a result of which he refused to leave his house. It had also been indicated by the Rat Man through his detailed accounts of the maneuvers of the Austro-Hungarian troops on border alert and his descriptions of the route a particular letter would have to take in order to reach its addressee. Now, with the Wolf Man, an exile—representing separation from the house of one's birth and a road already traveled—a new window opens, revealing the primal scene.

Curiosity is fateful because it introduces the subject to temporality. The time of the Wolf Man's conception, five o'clock in the afternoon, is symbolized by the five motionless wolves in the branches of a tree, a fine allegory of inclusion in a genealogy. What the Wolf Man sees is a genealogical tree in which he is a link in the chain that began long before him and would continue after him. The motionlessness of the wolves may be an image of his own mortality. The subject then sustains a powerful blow to his narcissism, because he has been abruptly displaced from his central position: his curiosity, which is structured oedipally, causes him to take a fundamental step toward his primal objects. In ceasing to be the creator of his parents, he learns that it was the parents, a man and a woman, who came together to create him. His world is henceforth no longer the same. It is bigger—indeed, endless. What does end, being finite, is human life. This is the dark side, that which is beyond pleasure: the uncanny.

"[My birth] took place on 28 August 1749, at mid-day on the stroke of twelve." So begins Goethe's account of his life, which he started writing at the age of sixty. Freud tells us this in "A childhood recollection from *Dichtung und Wahrheit*" (1917b), in which he interprets a childhood memory of Goethe in the light of clinical material from one of his own patients. The recollection in question is of hurling all of the household crockery out of the window. In his interpretative construction, Freud rearranges the sequence presented in Goethe's autobiography: "I was a child of fortune: destiny preserved my life, although I came into the world as though dead. Even more, destiny removed my brother, so that I did not have to share my mother's love with him."

The words "at mid-day on the stroke of twelve" arouse echoes of another clock, the one that told the Wolf Man that it was five in the afternoon. In the same way, we cannot fail to notice that the window is an especially important signifier for Little Hans, as it was in the dream of the young Russian and was again for Goethe. Through the window Hans observed the world; through the window the Russian nobleman tore away the veil concealing his finitude; and through the window the young Goethe got rid of his rage and jealousy at the birth of his brother—a theme also present in both Little Hans and the Wolf Man.

The marking of time and the opening of the window are the components of Freud's text that denote the point of maximum resistance to the flow of associations, but they return until the resistance is overcome.

The themes of curiosity, birth, oedipal rivalry, possessiveness, and jealousy thus featured more and more prominently in Freud's oeuvre until he was finally able, in 1919, to overcome the resistance. Then emerged the three works that stress the dark side of sexuality: perversion and death.

These themes had previously been treated only by their reverse—perversions having been seen as the negative of neuroses—and had therefore constituted a resistance to the flow of associations, but from now on they are confronted head on, the images hitherto contemplated in the negative, so to speak, being gradually revealed. Freud thus returns to dreams, not now only as hallucinatory wish fulfillments but in terms of their traumatic virtuality and of the working through of trauma. We are "beyond the pleasure principle." Death comes out of hiding and takes its place at the front of the stage. The psychic world has become larger; it is no longer *heimlich* but has become *unheimlich*—and different. From now on, sexuality will be dealt with in the light of this difference.

The essay "A Child Is Being Beaten" is subtitled "A Contribution to the Study of the Origin of Sexual Perversions" (1919a). Freud here shows us that what is involved is no longer the polymorphous perversion of the child but an act that is being performed in the present, as the tense of the verb ("is being") informs us; it is a recurrence or repetition of the perverse act. But who is the child? The text does not tell us.

Hitherto we have had names or nicknames specifying a subject—Dora, Hans, Leonardo, Schreber, Rat Man, Wolf Man. The subject was defined. "A Child Is Being Beaten," however, introduces an unnamed subject who exists only with reference to an action undergone (or performed). Whereas the first topography was established in relation to a specific subject, namely Freud himself, through the analysis of his own dreams or, as noted in chapter 1 of *The Psychopathology of Everyday Life* (1901), through the recovery of the forgotten proper name Signorelli, the new order—the structural theory—is based on a nonspecified subject. The one is thus the counterpoint of the other, its reverse or mirror image. The subject of "The Psychogenesis of a Case of Homosexuality in a Woman" (1920a) is surely the counterpoint of Dora. And the displacement of the oedipal focus from man to woman, the "dark continent," cannot but indicate that the theories of sexuality and identity are now being tackled through the exploration of woman, not man.

This new vision of sexuality, and hence of identity, ushers in the new chain of associations that starts with the issue of castration and stresses the complexity of the differences between the male and female Oedipus complexes, with implications for the structuring of the concept of the ego. Although it was initially identified with consciousness, the ego will take on a dark and obscure side whereby it merges into the unconscious. Moreover, with the dissolution of the Oedipus complex, it divides into two agencies, the newer of which is the superego. Once these two aspects of the ego have been recognized, it gradually becomes possible to distinguish neurotic, psychotic, and perverse mechanisms. This new chain of associations runs from 1919 to 1937 and is punctuated by the works on masochism, fetishism, femininity, and the splitting of the ego.

Freud states explicitly in "A Child Is Being Beaten" that his aim is to explain the genesis of the perversions in general and masochism in particular, as well as to evaluate the role of the difference between the sexes in the neurotic dynamic; he makes it clear once again that his investigation is based on the structuring of the Oedipus complex, "the actual nucleus of neuroses" (193). He goes on to say that "the beating-phantasy" and analogous perverse fixations are also precipitates of the Oedipus complex, scars, so to say, left behind after the process has ended, just as the notorious "sense of inferiority" corresponds to a comparable scar.

It is interesting to see how he links investigation, the Oedipus complex, the narcissistic scar, fantasy, the perverse act, and finally the difference between the sexes. I shall base my analysis of Freud's text on this combination, because it brings together the components of the primal scene, in which the subject looks with curiosity upon his own origin—in my view a nodal point for the structuring of perversion.

Freud writes that "analytic work deserves to be recognized as genuine psycho-analysis only when it has succeeded in removing the amnesia which conceals from the adult his knowledge of his childhood from its beginning" and that "anyone who neglects childhood analysis is bound to fall into the most disastrous errors" (183). A little earlier, he notes: "The present state of our knowledge would allow us to make our way so far and no further towards the comprehension of beating-phantasies. In the mind of the analytic physician, it is true, there remains an uneasy suspicion that this is not a final solution of the problem. He is obliged to admit to himself that to a great extent these phantasies subsist apart from the rest of the content of a neurosis, and find no proper place in its structure. *But impressions of this kind, as I know from my own experience, are only too willingly put on one side*" (italics mine).

An attentive reading of this passage clearly shows that Freud is referring to the constant struggle in everyone, at every moment of development, between the search for knowledge and its rejection and that not only is he investigating the fantasy "a child is being beaten" on this battlefield but that the battlefield is actually the basis of the structure of the fantasy in itself. He writes: "It is only with hesitation that this phantasy is confessed to" (179). And his patients say: "I know nothing more about it" (181).

Shame and a sense of guilt accompany the hesitant words of analysands confessing to the fantasy—and more strongly so than in the case of similar accounts of memories of the beginning of sexual life, according to Freud.

What, then, is this entity that so surprises the analyst by its frequency, provokes such emotion and reticence on the part of the analysand, and dates from a time "certainly before school age, and not later than in the fifth or sixth year" (179)? Or, put differently, what is this entity that is beyond sexual life?

Freud's answer is that the fantasy-riddle is remodeled at school by education and by books for young people such as *Uncle Tom's Cabin* and *Les Malheurs de Sophie*. The fantasy therefore lies at the root of knowledge itself—as a construction that subsists "apart from the rest" and makes the structuring of knowledge possible in the first place. It is the quantity of pleasure required to confront the misfortunes (*malheurs*) brought about by the knowledge (*sophia*) afforded by the father's "cabin." And it is, so to speak, the quantity of ignorance, or of refusal of knowledge, necessary for having some knowledge. When Freud inquired as to the sex of the child being beaten, the answer was sometimes "always boys," sometimes "only girls," but more often "I don't know" or "It doesn't matter which."

The other question implicit in the text is: "Why should a quantity of pleasure—specifically, masturbatory pleasure—be necessary for the acquisition of knowledge of the differences that make it possible to enjoy sexuality?" Freud's reply is that "man, probably alone among all animals, [is compelled] to begin his sexual life twice over, first like all other creatures in his early childhood, and then after a long interruption once more at the age of puberty" (193). This answer characterizes the quality of being human as lying in the register of separation, discontinuity, suspension, and solitude. Hence the reconstitution of his history, the task of the analytic couple, is a matter of recognizing this discontinuity and these disjunctions and differences.

Freud writes in his final chapter, "[It] would have been quite impossible to give a clear survey of infantile beating-phantasies if I had not limited it, except in one or two connections, to the state of things in females" (195). He means by this that even the limit has its limits (he had limited himself, except . . .). In a mea culpa of which few would be capable, he here makes it clear that the difference, which he has hitherto rejected, is of fundamental importance. The differences between men and women are not merely anatomical. Whereas he had until then argued that the male and female Oedipus complexes were totally parallel, he has here bowed to the evidence. The wish for and expectation of seamless complementarity are wrong. Sexual desire is one thing, but the act is another. This is one of the scars left behind by the

Oedipus complex, one of the three blows inflicted on the child by knowledge: the child must abandon his primary sexual object in order, only later, to seek to obtain satisfaction with others on the basis of difference.

Another blow resulting from the confrontation with the primal scene, "a spectacle the sight of which cannot be avoided," occurs when children are "cast down from all the heavens of their imaginary omnipotence" (187) by the discovery of the genital organs. Whereas the narcissistic child hitherto created the parents and world in its image, it now discovers that the mystery of creation is connected with the genitals: "The child seems to be convinced that the genitals have something to do with the matter [babies], even though in its constant brooding it may look for the essence of the presumed intimacy between its parents in relations of another sort, such as in their sleeping together, micturating in each other's presence, etc." (188). Whereas the infantile sexual theories hitherto had it that feces were the same as babies, both parts of the body, henceforth the perception of another, different body forces itself upon the child. Once again it wishes to create, but for this purpose it now needs the body of the other. A new time is instituted, bringing to a close the time when the child was the creator of the world, so that there are two times, namely, the present, the time of potency, and the past, that of omnipotence.

A third blow to infantile narcissism follows naturally from the other two: if the child is no longer omnipotent and needs another who is different from itself to create a baby, it naturally encounters the idea of its own conception. It therefore knows itself to have been created by its parents, with the radical implication that it belongs within a genealogical temporality, since there was a time in which it did not yet exist but its parents did. This places the child in a new relation to its limitations. Since there are differences between the generations, not only does the child discover the succession of the generations, with the implication that it does not belong to the same generation as its parents, but also, and in particular, it has to confront the mortality of the individual. All it can do is wait for its turn, both to procreate and—the dark side—to die. Unless . . .

Unless—and this is why the masturbatory beating fantasy is observed so often—the child rejects this knowledge, at least in part; unless time does not pass. . . . Freud's keen ear noticed that the fantasy was structured in the present continuous: "is being" is the tense of desire, the tense of the unconscious, the nonexistence of a past and a future.

"It is surprising how often" stands for the present continuous tense, the tense of fantasy as opposed to knowledge, which, for its part, is embedded in a genealogical temporality. The masturbatory character of the fantasy arises from the rejection of this genealogy or from omnipotent triumph over it. This is yet another fantasy. Surely this is why, as Freud puts it, neurotics "make masturbation the central point of their sense of guilt" (194 f.).

Six years after "A Child Is Being Beaten," Freud took up the subject of the beating fantasy again in "Some Psychical Consequences of the Anatomical Distinction Between the Sexes" (1925):

> While I was still unaware of this source of jealousy [penis envy] and was considering the phantasy " 'a child is being beaten,' " which occurs so commonly in girls, I constructed a first phase for it in which its meaning was that another child, a rival of whom the subject was jealous, was to be beaten. This phantasy seems to be a relic of the phallic period in girls. The peculiar rigidity which struck me so much in the monotonous formula "a child is being beaten" can probably be interpreted in a special way. The child which is being beaten (or caressed) may ultimately be nothing more nor less than the clitoris itself, so that at its very lowest level the statement will contain a confession of masturbation, which has remained attached to the content of the formula from its beginning in the phallic phase till later life. (254)

Hence the fantasy "a child is being beaten" points to the masturbatory context of the phallic phase, combining the Oedipus complex, the castration complex, the primal scene, the difference between the sexes, and the phallus. This context provides a clear watershed between masturbatory activities and sexual activities proper. This is why the fantasy can be confessed to only with hesitation and with much more anxiety than accounts of the beginnings of the subject's sexual life: it is above all a confession of rejection of the oedipal law, at least in part, insofar as that law places the individual within the chain of the species and of genealogies. The subject is in effect confessing: "I am outside the law." In order for this to be said, however, there must first be a knowledge of the law.

But what is the law? Freud's answer is that it is the castration complex ("The Dissolution of the Oedipus Complex" 1924b; "Some Psychical Consequences of the Anatomical Distinction Between the Sexes" 1925; "Fetishism" 1927; "Female Sexuality" 1931); the law is the father's prohibition against the child's possession of the mother as a sexual object and the prohibition against possession of the object in general. The law permits enjoyment of the object as a sexual object, but not its possession. The law is what places both the ego and its object in the human dialectic, that of sexuality and of difference. Hence there is an I and an other that is different from this I. Where rights are concerned, there must be a dialogue: both the individual and the object of the individual have rights. In principle, the word of neither can prevail over that of the other; all are subject to the same law.

The field of masturbation, by contrast, presupposes not only the possession but also the very creation of the object by the ego. Sexual enjoyment of the object and its possession are confused, just as the object is still confused with the ego, there being no clear distinction between ego and object, between I and the outside world, between I and the other, between father and mother. All the components that will in the future join together to make up the Oedipus complex can already be found here in some form, but they are scattered, colored by projections of all kinds, and practically extensions of a still-primitive ego that is predominantly omnipotent and narcissistic, self-generating and the creator of the world. This is the breeding ground of infantile sexual theories, which paves the way for the experience and knowledge of genital sexuality insofar as this places the individual within a genealogical chain. Surely genitality serves the propagation of the species more than the satisfaction of the individual. This must be the area "beyond the pleasure principle," which shows that sexuality makes sense only in the same context as mortality and transience.

The transition from pregenitality to genitality takes place by the reconfiguration of the various components of what Freud called the primal scene, which, by excluding the child from the act of generation, strikes a blow at his narcissism, the foundation of his fantasies of self-generation and creation of the world, and places it in the dialectic of differences, incompleteness, lack, and deficiency.

Although the internal affective and fantasy constellation, through the image of the parental sexual act, carries with it the apprehension of the notion of the primal scene—namely, conception—it contains implicitly, as it were, on its reverse side, the notion of finality, of the end, but this is a notion without an image, for no mental image of death is possible.

In consequence, the penis, as the entity that appears most and also disappears most in the sexual act, and as the most conspicuous token of differences, undergoes affective hypercathexis. It becomes, so to speak, the image of the scene itself, the object in the full glare of the spotlights, the object that shines, the object that will contain every notion. It becomes the phallus, the signifier of life and also of death. The life-death duality of its nature means that it is constantly under threat. Hence castration anxiety, which is inherent in the very nature of the phallus. It is the *Glanz,* the shine, and at the same time the "glance" mentioned by Freud in "Fetishism" (1927).

Freud tells us (1925, 256) that the castration complex leads to the Oedipus complex in girls, whereas it destroys it in boys. In my view, however, the primal scene introduces castration for both. When the girl discovers that neither she nor her mother possesses a penis, she begins to desire one intensely: she wants a son and therefore requires another body that possesses the phallus. When the boy discovers that, like his father, he possesses a penis, he conceives an intense wish to use it. Implicit in both attitudes is the father's word, which conveys the first lesson, the first carnal knowledge, that reality is the mortality of the individual and the preservation of the species. To comply with the law, the boy, the possessor of the penis, must actively use it. The girl, who does not possess it, must actively desire it so that she can recover it through a son, thereby also complying with the law. In both cases this presupposes a detachment from the mother as a sexual object and as the embodiment of pregenital sexuality.

In other words, on the basis of the distinction between the sexes, the primal-scene constellation sets in train the symbolic dialectic of differences: between fantasy and knowledge, between omnipotence and creative potency, between pleasure object and sexual object, between I and other, between animate and inanimate, and between life and death—that is, ultimately, the human dialectic.

It is against this dialectic that the perverse structure rebels. The pervert is not unaware of the law but rebels against and repudiates it (by disavowal). The law he recognizes is the law of his desire.

However, once glimpsed, even if only "glanced at," the primal scene leaves its mark, so that no other course is open to the pervert than to split his consciousness, as Freud shows in "Fetishism" (1927) and "Splitting of the Ego in the Process of Defence" (1940b [1938]). This mark is manifested in his sexuality. The pervert is not really ignorant of the difference between the sexes; on the contrary, the difference he experiences is a radical one, unlike that observed in psychotic structures, where the combined figure predominates. The pervert is unique in his fundamental rejection of *mortality.* He spends his life compulsively trying to derive pleasure from nonsubmission to the primary law, the law of the father, which places him in the genealogical chain, involving mortality. Thus he exacerbates the radical difference still further.

The homosexual perverse structure uses acknowledgment of differences for the purpose of separation rather than of union; the repudiation here basically concerns procreation and the propagation of the species, and it is in this respect that the homosexual triumphs over the law.[1]

The fetishist subjects his sexual pleasure to the possession of the fetish object, which offers him reassurance as to the reality of the phallus, thereby making him the master of life and death.

In sadism and masochism, the mortality and hence the humanity of the partner and of the subject himself are considered only as limits to pleasure— that is to say, by making sexual pleasure conditional upon coming within an inch of taking the life of the object or of the subject himself, both partners triumph in fantasy over death. The arsenal of leather, steel, and whips typically accompanying the sadist's act is a concrete symbol of the first law, over which he triumphs as the possessor of the whip and to which he subjects the other. The sadomasochistic couple is thus the most obvious, because the most concrete, image of the splitting of the ego.

The other perverse couple, the voyeur and the exhibitionist, constantly repeat the primal scene, but actively, as if staging a play, and the triumph in this case lies in the belief that the subject is the instigator of the action.

Finally there is necrophilia, the most radical image of the triumph over mortality and the most obvious rejection of the limit set by the law.

All these are radical manifestations of the masturbatory field, hinted at by the beating fantasies. The beating fantasy is masturbatory because it rejects sexuality in the sense of joining, of incorporating the individual in a genealogy, and of expressing incompleteness and transience. It is also masturbatory because it rejects the field of the other as a sexual partner only to be enjoyed and never to be possessed, instead transforming the other into an object for possession, a piece of the subject himself.

This is why it is so difficult to confess it to the analyst—to the other.

My intention here is not, of course, to discuss all the possible interpretations of a text so complex as "A Child Is Being Beaten," let alone to undertake a critical review of the literature spawned by it. Concentrating on the text itself would be more consistent with the purpose of this monograph series.

1. I do not believe, however, that all homosexuals are perverse.

Again, I believe that none of Freud's writings is complete in itself: each needs to be read in the context of the whole of the oeuvre, because each is but a mooring on the long voyage represented by the chain of associations of one of mankind's great thinkers. I therefore believe that the best way of presenting it is to immerse myself in a dialogue with Freud's text, without claiming to find answers or final solutions to the range of questions it poses.

On the other hand, psychoanalysis differs from the conventional sciences with their characteristic linear development; its own development is more like a genealogy, in which each advance is neither better nor more correct than its predecessor, but an heir capable of presenting a different viewpoint on what it has inherited.

I should therefore like to mention some authors from the past who are enshrined in our literature, as well as some contemporary authors, who have provided a new vision of questions raised by "A Child Is Being Beaten" or derived new ideas from these questions, in particular those concerning the ego, the Oedipus complex, and the genesis of thought, fantasies, psychosis, and the perversions. The former group includes Klein, Horney, Bion, Winnicott, Kohut, and Aulagnier; the latter, Chasseguet-Smirgel, McDougall, Green, and Kernberg. My reading has been influenced to a great extent by my agreement or disagreement with their contributions.

I have been concerned here mainly to emphasize what I consider to lie at the root of the perverse structure, namely, the difficulties and pain associated with knowledge or the rejection of the knowledge as a result of which the human being discovers what constitutes both his greatness and his most drastic limitation—the erogenous and mortal body.

This question of knowledge and its limitations is a constant challenge to every practicing psychoanalyst. As we approach the end of the twentieth century, it is unfortunately not difficult to observe the perverse logic and aesthetic that permeate our culture: the image of the human being is becoming more and more dehumanized, as every advertising poster, film, and television program shows. Male and female models, actors and actresses, the ideal images presented to us, are practically devoid of human attributes and the marks of life. They resemble human, or "neo-human," clones, a reversal of the picture of Dorian Gray, held up as examples to ourselves, our children, and our patients.

What can we psychoanalysts do with these new forms of beating?

REFERENCES

André, S. 1994. *O que quer uma mulher?* São Paulo: Jorge Zahar.

Anzieu, D. 1959. *Freud's self-analysis,* trans. P. Graham. London: Hogarth, 1986.

Aulagnier, P. 1990. Observaçoes sôbre a feminidade e suas transformaçoes. In *O desejo e a perversão,* 67–96. Campinas, Brazil: Papirus.

Chasseguet-Smirgel, J. 1976. Freud and female sexuality: The consideration of some blind spots in the dark continent. *Int. J. Psycho-Anal.* 57(3):275–86.

———. 1984. *Creativity and perversion.* New York: Norton.

Dadoun, R. 1982. *Freud.* Lisbon: Publicaçoes D. Quixote.

Freud, S. 1901. *The psychopathology of everyday life. S.E.* 6.

———. 1905a. *Three essays on the theory of sexuality. S.E.* 7.

———. 1905b [1901]. Fragment of an analysis of a case of hysteria. *S.E.* 7.

———. 1908. On the sexual theories of children. *S.E.* 9.

———. 1909a. Analysis of a phobia in a five-year-old boy. *S.E.* 10.

———. 1909b. Notes upon a case of obsessional neurosis. *S.E.* 10.

———. 1910a. Leonardo da Vinci and a memory of his childhood. *S.E.* 9.

———. 1910b. A special type of object choice made by men. Contributions to the psychology of love I. *S.E.* 11.

———. 1911 [1910]. Psycho-analytic notes on an autobiographical account of a case of paranoia (dementia paranoides). *S.E.* 12.

———. 1912. On the universal tendency to debasement in the sphere of love. Contributions to the psychology of love II. *S.E.* 11.

———. 1912–13. *Totem and taboo. S.E.* 13.

———. 1914. On narcissism: An introduction. *S.E.* 14.

———. 1917a. On transformations of instinct as exemplified in anal erotism. *S.E.* 17.

———. 1917b. A childhood recollection from *Dichtung und Wahrheit. S.E.* 17.

———. 1918 [1914]. From the history of an infantile neurosis. *S.E.* 17.

———. 1919a. A child is being beaten. *S.E.* 17.

———. 1919b. The "uncanny." *S.E.* 17.

———. 1920a. The psychogenesis of a case of homosexuality in a woman. *S.E.* 18.

———. 1920b. *Beyond the pleasure principle. S.E.* 18.

———. 1923a. *The ego and the id. S.E.* 19.

———. 1923b. The infantile genital organization. *S.E.* 19.

———. 1924a. The economic problem of masochism. *S.E.* 19.

———. 1924b. The dissolution of the Oedipus complex. *S.E.* 19.

———. 1925. Some psychical consequences of the anatomical distinction between the sexes. *S.E.* 19.

———. 1927. Fetishism. *S.E.* 21.

———. 1930. Civilization and its discontents. *S.E.* 21.

———. 1931. Female sexuality. *S.E.* 21.

————. 1940a [1938]. *An outline of psycho-analysis. S.E.* 23.

————. 1940b [1938]. Splitting of the ego in the process of defence. *S.E.* 23.

Gay, P. 1989. *Freud: A life for our time.* New York: Norton.

Giovannetti, M. de F. 1994. A voz do ausente. *Jornal de psicanálise* 27(52):21–27.

Horney, K. 1968. El temor a la mujer. In Klein, M., Horney, K., Boehm, F., Ferenczi, S., Fenichel, O., Alexander, F. *La sexualidad en el hombre contemporáneo,* 116–37. Buenos Aires: Paidos.

————. 1978. La peur de la femme. In *Le complexe de castration: Un fantasme originaire,* B. Grunberger and J. Chasseguet-Smirgel, 219–36. Malesherbes: Tehou (Les Grandes Découvertes de la Psychanalyse).

Jones, E. 1953–1957. *Sigmund Freud: Life and work.* 3 vols. London: Hogarth.

Kernberg, O. F. 1991a. A contemporary reading of "On narcissism." In *Freud's "On narcissism: An introduction,"* ed. Joseph Sandler, 131–48. New Haven, Conn.: Yale University Press.

————. 1991b. Sadomasochism, sexual excitement and perversion. *J. Am. Psychoanal. Assn.* 39(2):333–62.

Kohut, H. 1984. A reexamination of castration anxiety. In *How does analysis cure?* ed. H. Kohut and A. Goldberg, 13–33. Chicago: University of Chicago Press.

————. 1991. The analysis of the self: A systematic approach to the psychoanalytic treatment of narcissistic personality disorders. New York: International Universities Press, 1982.

Lacan, J. 1964. A relação de objeto. *O seminário,* IV. Rio de Janeiro: Zahar, 1995.

Meltzer, D. 1978. *The Kleinian Development.* Perthshire: Clunie.

Sandler, J., and Sandler, A.-M. 1987. Past unconscious, present unconscious, and vicissitudes of guilt. *Int. J. Psycho-Anal.* 68:331–42.

Winnicott, D. W. 1985. *The maturational processes and the facilitating environment: Studies in the theory of emotional development.* London: Hogarth.

"A Child Is Being Beaten"

A Seminar with Candidates from the Perspective of Contemporary Psychoanalysis

JEAN-MICHEL QUINODOZ

Preliminary note

In her letter of invitation, Ethel Person not only stressed that contributors to this monograph should both express "their own views" and be "didactic," "exactly as if he (or she) were teaching a seminar," but she also required them to discuss the important points in the text without giving a detailed account of the literature. It is in just this spirit that I have for several years run seminars enabling candidates to study Freud's works in chronological order. I have therefore drawn up my contribution as if it were a seminar devoted to "A Child Is Being Beaten" and attended by candidates for membership in our Society at the Centre de Psychanalyse Raymond de Saussure in Geneva.

In general, each of my seminars has three stages: a presentation stage, a discussion stage, and a stage devoted to contemporary clinical studies. In our actual (rather than virtual) seminars, at the end of the seminar each participant receives for his records a copy of each of the texts prepared by the participants, each text being a maximum of one page long, and a brief account of the final seminar.

I. THE PRESENTATION STAGE

Seminar members are asked to study and present texts from various points of view. One will place the text biographically, another will present a résumé of the contents, a third will highlight the new psychoanalytic concepts appearing there. I follow this course in the case of "A Child Is Being Beaten."

A. At What Stage in His Life and in What Circumstances Did Freud Write "A Child Is Being Beaten"?

When he wrote this paper, in 1919, Freud was coming out of the "dark years" he had experienced during World War I. He was still short of clients and money, and he was worried about two of his sons, who had been called up for military service, but he had recovered his creativity, and he wrote to Ferenczi that he was getting "some very good ideas about masochism."

It is also important to think of "A Child Is Being Beaten" in the context of his analysis of his daughter Anna. Anna herself suffered from beating fantasies, and they were one of the symptoms leading her to start her first analysis, which she undertook between 1918 and 1922 with her own father, a practice that was not unusual at that time. According to biographers, there is little doubt that the case of Anna should be numbered among those Freud speaks of in the article (Young-Bruehl, 1988, 104).

In 1922, at the end of this analysis, Anna Freud presented to the Vienna Psycho-Analytical Society as part of its requirements for applicants a clinical thesis describing beating fantasies in a fifteen-year-old girl. She then published it under the title "The Relation of Beating-Phantasies to a Day-dream" (1923). According to her, beating fantasies develop in three stages: first the beating fantasy appears, accompanied by masturbatory pleasure as a substitute for a scene of incestuous love between father and daughter; in the second stage, the girl tells herself "nice stories" that take the place of the beating fantasies; last comes the stage of "cure" as a result of sublimation — such as writing — which replaces the fantasies and the daydreams. I personally find this thesis merely descriptive and rather shallow, which makes sense when one remembers that in 1922 Anna had not yet seen a patient in psychoanalysis and that she had in all likelihood described her own case. But this was not the end of beating fantasies for Anna. Indeed, in 1924 the redevelopment of these fantasies led her to undergo a second period of analysis, again with her father. She wrote to Lou Andreas-Salomé on May 5, 1924:

"The reason for continuing was . . . the occasional and unseemly intrusions of the daydreams combined with an increasing intolerance—sometimes physical as well as mental—of the beating fantasies and of their consequences (i.e., masturbation), which I could not do without" (quoted in Young-Bruehl, 1988, 122).

Question: Could the fact that Freud analyzed his own daughter have had any effect on his ideas, particularly those on femininity?

It cannot be denied that Freud's analysis of Anna profoundly influenced his way of thinking about women's sexuality. Thus Young-Bruehl points out that just as Anna's first analysis was closely linked to Freud's publication of "A Child Is Being Beaten," so her second analysis seems to have been linked to the contents of "Some Psychical Consequences of the Anatomical Distinction Between the Sexes" (1925b), even though there is no documentary evidence in support of this latter contention (1988, 125). In the 1925 text, Freud makes penis envy the central element in the girl's development and notes that if giving up the penis normally leads to a wish for a child, when she is subsequently obliged to give up her father as well the result may be "an identification with him and the girl may thus return to her masculinity complex and perhaps remain fixated in it" (Freud, 1925b, 256). There is a clear connection between this falling back to identification with the father and the conclusions reached in Freud's "A Child Is Being Beaten" and Anna Freud's "The Relation of Beating-Phantasies to a Day-dream." Reparative father identification also seems to connect with Anna's own strong masculine identification, asceticism, renunciation of an active sexual life as a woman, and difficulties in relationships with men.

According to Pragier and Faure-Pragier (1993), in reintroducing the real, the anatomical, and making penis envy the major factor in women's libidinal development, Freud was defending himself against unresolved oedipal feelings toward his daughter during her two analyses and thereby denying his guilt as a father (and simultaneously introducing the concept of denial into his theory in his paper "Negation" [1925a]). But that does not explain everything.

Personally, I think that Anna's analysis certainly reinforced Freud's particular conception of feminine sexuality, for him more a question of pregenital infantile sexuality than of genitally mature sexuality; probably the experience of analyzing Anna, when linked to that acquired from other women analysands, also led him to begin to ask questions about a daughter's precocious attachment to her mother, as we shall see.

Table 6.1

Phases in the case of girls	Phases in the case of boys
1. Cs 'A child is being beaten' daydream —indeterminate—without sexual character	1. [No equivalent]
2. Ucs 'I am being beaten by my father' —unconscious masochistic fantasy —strictly speaking direct Oedipus complex—'normal Oedipus attitude'	2. Ucs 'I am being beaten by my father' —unconscious masochistic fantasy —strictly speaking inverted Oedipus complex—boy's 'feminine attitude'
3. Cs 'A child is being beaten by a substitute for the father (teacher)' —masturbation—the girl becomes the spectator of a masochistic sexual scene where she becomes a boy in her fantasy —renounces her sex	3. Cs 'I am being beaten by my mother (or by a substitute for her)' —masturbation —masochistic sexual relations —passive fantasy—boy's 'feminine attitude' —no change of sex (apparently)

B. A Résumé of the Phases of Beating
Fantasies According to Freud

Table 6.1 is designed to set out the phases of beating fantasies described by Freud in the case of girls and boys on the basis of the six cases he studied, four women and two men. Its sole purpose is to serve as a basis for discussion; Freud himself was at pains to say that the interpretations proposed in this article were far from exhaustive.

Let us begin by discussing the *girl's* beating fantasies, which, according to Freud, have three stages:

(1) In the first stage the fantasy is *conscious* and appears as a daydream, a sort of infantile memory with undefined participants: "My father is beating a child." The first phase does not have a sexual character. The child who is being beaten is not the fantasizer but usually a brother or sister. Under the effect of jealousy or sibling rivalry, the fantasy comes to mean "My father is beating a child whom I hate"; in other words, "My father does not love this other child, he loves only me."

(2) The second phase is "I am being beaten by my father." In this transformation of the fantasy, the person producing the fantasy has become the child who is being beaten, and her father remains the person doing the beating. Unlike the first phase, which is often a memory attached to an actual scene, the second phase has never had a real existence; it is an unconscious

fantasy that must be reconstructed in analysis. The pleasure accompanying the beating gives the fantasy a masochistic quality, in which being beaten by the father leads both to oedipal guilt and to eroticism; *the fantasy* "is not only the punishment for the forbidden genital relation, but also the regressive substitute for that relation" (Freud, 1919, 189).

(3) Finally, the fantasy becomes "A child [generally a boy] is being beaten by a substitute for the father." Here the person producing the fantasy is no longer being beaten herself but has become a spectator of the scene, and the person beating is no longer the father. What makes this phase different from the others is the presence of strong sexual excitement leading to masturbatory satisfaction. In this last phase, the girl has "renounced her sex" and "since she has herself become a boy, it is principally boys whom she causes to be beaten" (200).

Let us now come to the *boy's* beating fantasies. Freud was surprised not to discover a parallel with the three phases he had described in girls. First he notes that with the boys there was no first stage equivalent to that found in girls, at least not in his clinical material. Then he discovered that the boy's conscious fantasy was "I am being beaten by my mother"; he had expected to find that fantasy to be unconscious and to be equivalent to the girl's second-phase fantasy, namely, "I am being beaten by my father." In addition, Freud notes that the boy's conscious fantasy was regularly preceded by the unconscious fantasy "I am being beaten by my father," exactly the same unconscious fantasy as the girl's. So, according to Freud, beating fantasies in both sexes have their origin in an oedipal attachment to the father; the parallel he anticipated did not exist.

He tries to explain these unanticipated observations in the following way: if beating fantasies in both sexes start from the Oedipus complex, in a girl the fantasy issues from a "direct" or "positive" complex, whereas in a boy it issues from an "inverted" or "negative" complex. Freud stresses that with a boy, in both phases the fantasy is regularly passive, "derived from a feminine attitude towards his father" (198), and this in spite of change in the sex of the person performing the beating (father in the unconscious fantasy, mother in the conscious fantasy). On the other hand, the boy, unlike the girl, experiences no change in his own sexual designation between the second and third phases.

His findings convinced Freud that perversions, notably masochism, originate in childhood and find their source in the Oedipus complex. Freud considers that masochism "originates from sadism that has been turned round upon the self" under the influence of "the sense of guilt" (194). He assigns the sense of guilt, closely linked to infantile masturbation, to the critical moral conscience, an agency that he was later to call the superego. I should point out that in this paper, Freud emphasizes the guilt attached to pleasure as the motive force behind the feminine attitude of the boy; later he will argue that fear of castration plays an even more important role.

C. New Psychoanalytical Concepts Appearing in "A Child Is Being Beaten"

This is a brief list, without commentary, of the new psychoanalytical ideas appearing in the 1919 text.

(1) In "A Child Is Being Beaten" Freud shows that the sexual pleasure to be found in pain—characteristic of masochism—is closely linked to the eroticization of incestuous objects. He argues that the Oedipus complex plays a central role in perversions, just as it does in neuroses.

(2) Freud claims that perversions, like neuroses, originate in infantile neurosis.

(3) According to Freud, masochism is the result of a turning round of sadism upon the self under the influence of a sense of guilt; it is not (contrary to what he is to say later) of primary origin.

(4) Analyzing different aspects of beating fantasies, Freud shows the importance of psychic bisexuality—that is to say, of the masculine and feminine elements that go to make up any individual.

Question: Freud sometimes seems to use the term fantasy *to express very different notions. What exactly does he mean when he talks of fantasies in this paper?*
In this text, Freud uses the word *fantasy* in various senses. First, *fantasy* describes the consciously imagined scenarios of a child being beaten that the patient would recite to himself in a waking state. In this sense, the word *fantasy* corresponds to a conscious daydream, as Schafer (1968), among others, has noted. Freud also uses the word, however, to describe unconscious fantasies—that is, scenarios that have been repressed and are therefore situated in the unconscious, where they form defining structures for the psychic organization. Whether what is being described is conscious or unconscious, whether its content is manifest or latent, the same term, *fantasy,* is used.

Question: The adult beating fantasies Freud speaks of may be perverse. How about children? Is it not true that all children have sadistic and masochistic fantasies and episodes of acting out in which they beat brothers, sisters, or friends or are beaten by them, and that these are not considered in any way perverse?

Expressing and acting out sadistic and masochistic fantasies of beating or being beaten by brothers, sisters, or friends are part of the "polymorphous perverse" aspect of infantile sexuality (Freud, 1905), and thus we do not consider as perverse all children who express or act out these fantasies.

Sadistic or masochistic fantasies or behavior can, however, be distinguished from a polymorphously perverse infantile organization in children. Indeed, there can be perverse organizations in the child resulting in characteristically perverse fantasies or behaviors. They appear mainly as pathological disorders of identity, when for example a boy needs to dress up as a girl, or as sadomasochistic behavior, but not as psychosexual disorders as in adults. The most serious cases are those in which the perversion is acted out without the subject's being able to fantasize it.

Question: Does actually having been mistreated or beaten as a child influence the appearance of masochistic fantasies in adult life?

Certainly, having actually been mistreated often results in the creation of a regression or traumatic fixation and a blasting of the psyche that makes the later work of representation and elaboration difficult. To this must be added the eroticization of the pain linked to regression or unconscious fixation on incestuous oedipal objects, which will be all the more marked when the perpetrators are people close to the child and to whom the child is particularly attached. But it is often difficult to establish any correlation between actual events and fantasy.

II. DISCUSSION

We will deal now with the second stage of the seminar: questions prepared by the seminar members.

Question: In "A Child Is Being Beaten" Freud argues that there is no parallel between the unconscious beating fantasies of boys and girls. Is it possible that, to support his theory, he has stressed certain types of fantasy and placed less emphasis on others? For example, I sometimes wonder whether he has not purposely emphasized the role of the girl's attachment to her

father (positive Oedipus complex) and underestimated the role of her preco-
cious attachment to the mother (inverted Oedipus complex).

Commentators, male and female, have been quick to point out that there were precursor fantasies to the beating fantasies, notably those concerning the girl's precocious attachment to the mother. Thus, Bonaparte, among others, noted that a phallic mother could replace the father in a girl's beating fantasies (1957, 77). It might also be argued that in some beating fantasies there is a combined object, father and mother at the same time, rather than a clearly differentiated father or mother.

For the moment, however, let us stay with Freud's 1919 theories concerning the psychosexual development of boys and girls. Until then, Freud had considered the child's development in essentially masculine terms and had stressed the role of love for the father in the child's development in the case of both boys and girls. This is why, for the girl in "A Child Is Being Beaten," it is essentially desire for the father that, for Freud, causes repression of the beating fantasy. According to him, everything happens within the context of the girl's "normal" or "direct" Oedipus complex—both the tender fixation on the father and the hatred for the mother.

According to the Freudian ideas of the time, if a daughter takes her mother for a love object and prefers her to the father, it is because she has been disappointed by the father and has turned away from him. In "A Child Is Being Beaten," Freud does not for a moment consider the alternative possibility that this is a regression on the girl's part or a pre-oedipal fixation on the mother; he even goes so far as to exclude any role for the girl's attachment to the mother: "It is not with the girl's relation to her mother that the beating-phantasy is concerned" (186). If it should happen that the girl's unconscious homosexual tendencies are reinforced and she comes to engage in "an excessive reaction of devotion to her" (186), this can only be—again according to Freud—because she is disappointed in her oedipal love for her father. He defends a similar point of view in an article written in the same period, "Psychogenesis of a case of homosexuality in a woman" (1920a).

Question: How did Freud's conception of femininity develop?

In general terms, Freud's ideas on the development of women's sexuality followed two main lines. In one, dating particularly from the time of the 1925 article "Some Psychical Consequences of the Anatomical Distinction Between the Sexes," he gave central importance to penis envy. In the other, developed later in "New Introductory Lectures on Psycho-Analysis" (1933), he became increasingly aware of the girl's pre-oedipal relationship with her mother and her difficulty in changing objects in order to direct herself toward her father. But one can already see an evolution in his thinking in the note he added to Dora's case in 1923, when he realized, after twenty years, that he had interpreted the paternal transference only and had minimized Dora's "homosexual love" for Madame K., which, he said, "was the strongest unconscious current in her mental life." He added: "Before I had learnt the importance of the homosexual current of feelings in psychoneurotics, I was often brought to a standstill in treatment of my cases or found myself in complete perplexity."

Question: If one considers Freud's second-stage unconscious fantasy, it is possible to argue that there is no parallel between what happens in girls and in boys. But if one compares their final stages, could it be argued that, contrary to what Freud thought, there is a parallel between the "masculinization" of the girl and the "feminization" of the boy?

On the basis of the third stage of the beating fantasy, it appears that there is a parallel between the girl and the boy, because in both sexes the situation has elements of an inverted Oedipus complex. But for this conclusion it is necessary to disregard the unconscious fantasies put in evidence by Freud and to base the argument on other elements.

We can certainly follow Freud in thinking that the boy's "masochistic attitude coincides with a feminine one" (197) and therefore that the boy's masochism derives from an inverted Oedipus complex and corresponds to an unconscious homosexuality. The reinforcement of the boy's unconscious homosexual tendencies is accompanied by a diminution of heterosexual tendencies, and in the cases described by Freud various sexual troubles, such as excessive masturbation and impotence, make their appearance.

On the girl's side, Freud notes that by changing the sex of the protagonist between the fantasy's second and third stages and turning herself into a boy in her fantasies (196) she "escapes from the demands of the erotic side of her life" (199); that is to say, she has "renounced her sex" (200). If, however, we look at this from a modern viewpoint, we can say that the girl's masochism and her masculinization derive from her inverted Oedipus complex—that is, from the persistence of her unconscious desire to be the husband of her mother and to be her father's rival, which corresponds to an unconscious homosexuality. Thus it is the girl's inverted Oedipus complex, and not the normal Oedipus complex, as Freud thought, which stokes her unconscious homosexual tendencies and necessarily entails a corresponding diminution of heterosexual tendencies.

There are two other points I would like to make. At the time, Freud could not imagine a situation in which the girl, identified with her father, or rather with her father's penis as part object, would be a rival to the father for possession of her mother. Indeed, it was only because he believed that a daughter was not competing with her father for such possession that he could justify a father's treating his own daughter in analysis. On the other hand, as far as the boy is concerned, Freud expected him to show feelings of hostility and jealousy toward his father, and for this reason he recommended that fathers not take their own sons for analysis. For example, Freud wrote to E. Weiss: "Concerning the analysis of your hopeful son, that is certainly a ticklish business. . . . With one's own daughter I succeeded well. There are special difficulties and doubts with a son" (letter of 1 November 1935 [Weiss, 1970]).

The second point is this. As far as homosexual tendencies are concerned, I have noticed that when a girl "loves" her mother, it is not the genital mother she loves but the pregenital mother, whom she envies and wants to possess exclusively for herself, eliminating the father—the mother's husband—whom she feels to be a dangerous rival. In fact, such a girl experiences unconscious hatred for the genital mother, the genital father, and the couple they make (Quinodoz, 1989).

Question: When Freud discusses the characteristics of masochism in men, he talks of the boy's "feminine attitude." Can we therefore assume that the "feminine attitude" in a woman—that is to say, her femininity—is also masochistic?

This question was to be the center of a controversy that started in the 1920s and is not yet completely resolved. In "A Child Is Being Beaten" Freud describes a "feminine attitude" in boys, and in "The Economic Problem of Masochism" (1924) he speaks of "feminine masochism" in men, connecting it with infantile masochism. But in the latter article, Freud speaks specifically of masochism "as an expression of the woman's nature" (161), and this phrase has given rise to misunderstandings. A few psychoanalysts have followed in Freud's footsteps; for example, Bonaparte writes that "all masochism is essentially female" (1957, 71). Others, however, such as Jones (1935), Klein (1932), and Horney (1932), have stressed the specificity of feminine identity.

Even if, as Laplanche and Pontalis point out (1988, 245), Freud intended to describe "what constitutes the essence of masochistic perversion" when he spoke of "feminine attitude" and "feminine masochism" in men, it cannot be denied that he often claimed that masochism was a feminine characteristic.

Question: Freud turns beating fantasies in all directions. Does he to some extent lose direction in his repeated attempts to explain them?

It does sometimes seem so. On one hand, Freud's perspicacity and tenacity are admirable when, with an acute clinical sense, he carries his analysis of the fantasy into its most secret places. And it is one of his strengths that he sets out the development of his thoughts and is never fully satisfied with his conclusions. But it has to be recognized that these endless reformulations do make it difficult to read him. Even Freud seemed to throw in the towel at the end when he declared, "In the last resort we can only see that both in male and female individuals masculine as well as feminine instinctual impulses are found, and that each can equally well undergo repression and so become unconscious" (202).

On the other hand, the "overwhelming multiplicity" of the symbolic meanings of such a fantasy has been described as a specific property of perverse mechanisms. Observing the infinite variety of scenes of flagellation fantasized by one of her patients in psychoanalysis, D. Quinodoz (1992) has stressed its "demoniac" character: "No sooner had one of the patient's perverse manifestations seemed to acquire meaning and be on the point of disappearing than we would have to become disillusioned, it would reappear with increased strength, sustained by a new mechanism, and as soon as that was made clear, yet another would take its place" (1693). She attributes this "breaking into pieces" like a jigsaw puzzle to the extreme condensation and splitting typical of perversion. As a result, interpretation is very difficult unless the analyst can get a grasp of the whole. She likens the phenomenon to the theme of S. A. Steeman's 1939 story "L'assassin habite au 21" ("The Murderer Lives at No. 21"), adapted for the cinema by H. G. Clouzot. In this story there is a series of crimes, but each time the police think they have put the perpetrator in prison, a new crime is committed, and the person thought to be guilty has to be released. This continues until the police realize that they are facing not a single criminal but a group of three who substitute for one another and that all three must be arrested at once.

According to D. Quinodoz, it is the same with these patients: "One may accurately find particular significations of a perverse manifestation, but unless the essence of the whole is attacked, the patient is unlikely to overcome his perversion" (1699).

Question: From the cases Freud has described, it can be seen that more or less serious masochistic perversions are involved. But from his explanation of the origin of perversion, I am not clear on what basis he specifically distinguishes perversion and neurosis, particularly from the point of view of the psychic structure.

The distinction between perversion and neurosis as set out in "A Child Is Being Beaten" is far from satisfying. Let us, as an example, consider the boy's "feminine attitude" as described by Freud in 1919, where he considers it to be specifically characteristic of masochistic perversion. Nowadays, we would no doubt say that an inverted Oedipus complex and a regression to the anal stage can be found in both perversion and neurosis. But in perversion, such an attitude would imply the feeling of omnipotence, of being able to possess both sexes at the same time, what has been called ambisexuality or "hermaphrodite narcissism" (de Saussure, 1929) to distinguish it from psychic bisexuality strictly speaking. When psychic bisexuality is integrated, an individual can assume his own sex because he has renounced the one he does not have, integrating in fantasy aspects of himself as male and female, father and mother.

As to the specific question of the distinction made between perversion and neurosis in "A Child Is Being Beaten," Freud himself was avowedly dissatisfied with his explanations. During the same period, he was trying to make sense of the destructiveness manifested by certain patients in analysis, contradicting the pleasure principle, which constituted his first theory of instincts. In his first theory, avoiding unpleasure and procuring pleasure were the aim of all psychic activity. In "Beyond the Pleasure Principle" (1920b) he introduced a new hypothesis postulating the existence of two instincts, one the creative "life instinct," the other the destructive "death instinct." Bound together, they work in the service of life; if they are pulling apart, the destructive tendencies dominate, and this can lead the subject to psychic disorganization and even death. From then on, it was on the basis of this revolutionary new theory that Freud distinguished what is observed in neurosis from what is observed in perversions, psychoses, and depressive states (the so-called melancholic states). I do not propose to say more here of Freud's views on the conflict between life instinct and death instinct, but it should be added that in 1924 he was to consider the phenomenon of masochism in light of his new ideas on the death instinct, so that "The Economic Problem of Masochism" and "A Child Is Being Beaten" are complementary and should be read together.

By no means do all psychoanalysts accept Freud's newer theory of instincts. One may agree or disagree with his hypothesis, but it seems that if one does not take it into account, one tends to view perverse phenomena such as masochism as though they were neurotic phenomena, and therefore to use the same technical approach in dealing with them. As a result, perverse manifestations—which have their root in psychic mechanisms that are not neurotic—will continue to be denied and split off, making the life instinct's task of binding the death instinct more difficult, so that the death instinct tends to remain free.

Question: It is said that masochists prefer a bad object that mistreats them to no object at all. Does fear of losing the object have any relation to masochism?

Masochism is indeed closely linked to separation anxiety and fear of object loss. Thus, in pathological mourning, a significant object loss can install in the intrapsychic world a perverse sadomasochistic relation between the "critical agency" (superego) and the ego transformed as a result of identification with the lost object, as Freud showed in "Mourning and Melancholia" (1917). Thus, there are many points of similarity between the masochism described in melancholic depression and that described in beating fantasies—for example, regression to narcissism, the turning round of sadism onto the subject's own person, and unconscious guilt, hypotheses that Freud later elaborated in light of his concept of the death instinct.

Both introjection of the lost object in melancholic depression (1917) and the "regression from an object to the ego" (1919, 194) in beating fantasies are explained by masochistic patients' attachment to their torturer and their difficulty in separating themselves and facing the anxiety of solitude. With these analysands, a lot of work has to be done on differentiation and separation from the object before they can move from a predominantly narcissistic relationship to a more object-related one. Working through separation anxieties and object loss within the transference plays an essential role in this process (J. M. Quinodoz, 1991).

Question: Speaking of beating fantasies, Freud writes: "These phantasies subsist apart from the rest of the content of a neurosis, and find no proper place in its structure" (183). Is this a way of imagining that perverse fantasies may have a different nature from neurotic fantasies?

In my opinion, when Freud stresses that beating fantasies "find no proper place in the structure [*of the neurosis*]" he is implicitly introducing the notion of *splitting,* which he distinguishes from repression. It must be noted that Freud expressed doubts about the role played by repression in beating fantasies. Only in 1927, in "Fetishism," was he able to develop the notion of splitting of the ego, which is another element characterizing psychic functioning in perversion—notably masochistic perversion—and distinguishing it from neurosis.

III. CONTEMPORARY PERSPECTIVES

I have chosen two clinical papers to discuss "A Child Is Being Beaten" in the light of contemporary psychoanalytic contributions. The first, by Ruth Lax (1992), enables us to consider superego differences in neuroses and perversions. The second, by Ruth Riesenberg Malcolm (1988, 1995), offers a detailed account of the complex mechanisms involved in masochistic perversions and so enables the analyst to improve his approach to such patients.

A. The Neurotic Superego and the Perverse Superego

Although some modern psychoanalysts claim that they have never come across a "child-is-being-beaten" fantasy in their patients, others, among them R. Lax, have observed it as it was described by Freud. In her paper "A Variation on Freud's Theme in 'A Child Is Being Beaten'—Mother's Role: Some Implications for Superego Development in Women" (1992), Lax presents the beating fantasy in four women patients, in whom the unconscious fantasy "I am being beaten by my father" corresponds to Freud's second phase. Unlike Freud, however, Lax found that feelings of guilt toward the mother played a much more important role than feelings of guilt toward the father. The mother was felt by these patients to be a harsh judge, forbidding the girl's incestuous desire for her father and threatening her with loss of her female genital organs. At certain moments, this "hostile and accusatory" maternal superego (460) would suddenly be projected onto the analyst, who was then experienced as a strict and forbidding mother. For the author, this strict maternal superego, carrier of the "oedipal law," would play the same role for the girl as that played by a paternal superego threatening castration for the boy.

This very vivid article shows the structuring role of the maternal superego throughout the range of beating fantasies, but, according to Lax, all seems to be played out in the context of a positive Oedipus complex and an oedipal superego. "In the context of the intense *positive* oedipal feelings which characterized this stage of my patients' psychoanalytical process it was clear that they experienced mother as judge and punisher who forbade the transgression of the incestuous father taboo" (471).

The author observes that as the treatment progressed, the patient's masochistic fantasies and masturbatory activity became less intense, and at the same time the positive oedipal feelings became stronger. Lax went so far as to wonder whether the daughter's more regressive incestuous desires for the mother, part of the inverted Oedipus complex, might be involved. But she admits that her patients did not provide any material in support of that argument.

Although Lax describes the four cases as examples of masochism, it seems to me that she presents them as cases of neurotic organization with masochistic aspects based on a positive Oedipus complex involving a superego whose severity is that of the "oedipal law" rather than as perverse organizations of pregenital origin. I do not believe, however, that there are any perversions organized on a purely neurotic base; rather, all perversions must involve primitive defenses, different from those at work in neurosis.

Looking at Lax's article (1992) from this point of view, I notice that she has considered her cases only in the light of masochism as conceived by Freud in 1919 in "A Child Is Being Beaten"—that is, before he introduced his second theory of instincts. In order to discuss perversion fully, it is important to be able to refer to Freud's later ideas, particularly the splitting of the ego and the death instinct, both of which enabled him to better conceptualize destructiveness. This is particularly so in sadomasochism, where the superego shows a sadism that Freud described as a "pure culture of the death instinct" (1923, 53). Although Lax does not address these issues, her patients appear to possess the destructiveness characteristic of the perverse superego, which can be seen bursting out when they project a "hostile and accusatory" maternal superego onto the analyst (460). In addition to the projection of a maternal superego linked to the direct Oedipus complex (Lax's view), there appears to be a re-emergence in the transference of a sadomasochistic conflict situated in a split-off part of the ego, from which sadism is projected onto the analyst, who is experienced as attacking the patient. The patient herself unconsciously plays the role of the victim.

In my experience with similar cases of masochism, I have come to distinguish the transference projection of a strict superego of an oedipal type from that of a precocious superego linked to perverse intrapsychic sadomasochistic elements. One of my analysands would often project onto me the image of a strict and forbidding superego, and it was not always easy to decide which mechanism was at play. At one moment in the transference, this patient might project a strict superego feeling like that of a father threatening to castrate his son but nevertheless protecting and loving him. In this case hate remains linked with love. At another moment, this patient experienced me as an early superego, being felt as a part object and as a terribly sadistic father totally devoid of love. In that case hate was split from love. In the latter situation, for example, he would feel that my interpretations were no longer hypotheses to understand him but ways of humiliating or crushing him in order to show my power over him. I thought this image had little to do with that of a forbidding oedipal superego, whether paternal or maternal, but showed an unconscious need to be punished within the context of transference projections of a destructive sadomasochistic relationship. The sadistic, ego-crushing superego that had suddenly burst out of the fantasy had no connection with neurotic transference but corresponded rather to the bursting through of an unconscious sadomasochism belonging to a part of a split-off ego.

B. Perversion, Projective Identification, and Voyeurism

Finally, I would like to discuss a patient with a serious masochistic perversion, published by R. Riesenberg Malcolm under the title "The Mirror: A Perverse Sexual Phantasy in a Woman Seen as a Defence Against a Psychotic Breakdown" (1988). The clinical tableau presented by this patient differs somewhat from that found in patients who report a beating fantasy, but it does present many similarities. The pathological aspects characteristic of the beating fantasy can still be seen, particularly the central role of projective identification and also the role played by voyeurism, a type of fantasy in which the subject is at the same time taking part in the scene and watching it. The admirably detailed analysis of this patient's internal world and the painstaking study of the complex mechanisms involved in this form of perversion provide a model for the analysis of patients presenting with beating fantasies. This patient developed favorably in a long analysis, and we can therefore examine, as a final question, the factors that were relevant in effecting change.

1. The Fantasy of Identification with Another, Projective Identification and Omnipotence. In this case the patient's sexual life had been dominated since the age of twenty by perverse sadomasochistic fantasies, compulsive masturbation, sometimes lasting for hours, and a constant need for new male partners. She had frequently been admitted to the hospital because of psychotic breakdowns before she began what turned out to be a long analysis.

In analysis, the patient did not mention either her perverse fantasies or her masturbatory activity for several years. It was the analyst who discovered these elements through the countertransference. The patient would often describe scenes of daily life in a way that fascinated the analyst and excited her curiosity to the point where she found herself wanting to take part. Becoming slowly aware of the intense curiosity that was gripping her, the analyst interpreted it one day as the result of the patient's desire to excite that curiosity. This interpretation made the patient think of her own curiosity, which was particularly vivid during the weekend separations from the analyst. She then admitted with shame that she spent considerable time masturbating, feeling excluded from the parental couple represented by the analyst, and then, for the first time, she told the analyst of her mirror fantasy.

In this fantasy, the patient sees a mirror in which violently sadistic and humiliating sexual scenes are taking place. The participants are incestuous homosexual and heterosexual couples, and their bouts last for hours. The patient imagines that she is in turn one or another of the partners in these brutal scenes. While the mirror fantasy is going on, there are spectators watching the scene, fighting their own excitement, for if they give in, they will fall into the mirror.

The interpretation the analyst made about curiosity was effective in mobilizing and transforming the situation so that instead of being acted out unconsciously in the transference it could be put into words. Over the course of the analysis, it emerged that the patient's psychic life was carried out on two main levels. On one level, she was intensely involved in the perverse activities taking place in the mirror and so could avoid feeling excluded or overwhelmed by the feelings of despair and hatred that she might have felt in front of the parental couple. On another, more developed level, the patient was equally identified with the spectators outside the mirror. These were less regressed than the people inside the mirror, but nevertheless they could only watch and try not to fall in. Reproducing this scene in the transference relationship, the patient had projected her spectator side onto the analyst while she herself played the scenes designed to excite transference curiosity.

During the analysis it came to be seen that the mirror fantasy prevented her both from going forward to work through the oedipal situation and from regressing further and breaking down psychotically, as had been the case before analysis.

Riesenberg Malcolm describes two striking elements in the psychic structure of the mirror patient: first, the importance of psychic fragmentation
resulting from multiple splitting, and second, the role played by omnipotence
in the intensity of projective identification. This patient presents in greatly
exaggerated form the primitive defense mechanisms found in all perverse
organizations. Omnipotently, the patient feels both projected into the mirror
and outside it, both man and woman, both spectator and actress, both
masochistic and sadistic, and these various mechanisms combine to produce
multiple scenarios with endless variations.

Freud had already noted that these processes of fantasized identification
with another are particularly evident in perverse organizations. He did not
use the current term *projective identification,* but as far back as 1915, in
"Instincts and Their Vicissitudes," he wrote that "the masochist shares in the
enjoyment of the assault upon himself" (127). As for the sadist, "while these
pains are being inflicted on other people, they are enjoyed masochistically by
the subject through his identification of himself with the suffering object"
(129). In "A Child Is Being Beaten" Freud takes up this point again, saying
that "the boy, who has tried to escape from a homosexual object-choice, and
who has not changed his sex, nevertheless feels like a woman in his conscious phantasies, and endows the women who are beating him with masculine attributes and characteristics" (200). Similarly, the girl "has even
renounced her sex . . . and since she has herself become a boy, it is principally boys whom she causes to be beaten" (200). At this stage, however,
Freud has not differentiated this primitive form of "hermaphrodite" bisexuality, based on omnipotence, splitting, narcissistic identification with the
object by projection, and a fantasy of the "combined parents" (M. Klein,
1932), from the integrated form of psychic bisexuality, the elements of which
appear when he introduces the concept of the direct Oedipus complex and
the inverted Oedipus complex as applicable to boys and girls (Freud, 1923).

2. From Voyeurism to the Desire to Know. Hanna Segal recently (1995) discussed the factors allowing Riesenberg Malcolm's mirror patient to develop
favorably. Her comments throw light not only on that case, but also on many
of the aspects touched on by Freud in "A Child Is Being Beaten."

The first point Segal raises concerns the factors likely to reverse the course
of pathological projective identification and thereby to facilitate the process
of introjection and identification. For Segal, constructive introjection demands that the patient be capable to some extent of recognizing that what he

is projecting is separate and different from the object receiving and containing his projections. "I think the differentiation and the capacity to differentiate must have existed from the start, otherwise projection would lead to a vicious circle. And of course the crucial battlefield for this differentiation is the depressive position" (4).

In a second point, in which her comments apply equally to the patients Freud described as "spectators" and "observers" of beating scenes, Segal points out that the "spectators" of beating scenes are "voyeurs." Such a scenario, she says, "is no ordinary curiosity. It is the classic voyeuristic scenario" because "the voyeur is not animated by the wish to know" (2). It is as if, without really seeing the scene, the voyeur is watching it unfold on a screen that is at the same time both a support for projections and an obstacle to curiosity. This situation reminds me of the rules set up in nudist camps, where everybody is obliged to be naked but strictly forbidden to look.

Segal adds that it is essential for the analyst to help the patient change his perverse voyeurism into normal infantile curiosity. This change became possible for the mirror patient as soon as the analyst managed to change her own countertransference voyeurism into curiosity about her patient, so that the patient could introject an analyst showing curiosity about her patient and catalyze a process of identification forming the base of a better-integrated psychic bisexuality.

In a similar case of masochism involving a young woman whose beating fantasy was associated with compulsive masturbation, I was myself able to note the role played by pathological projective identification. My patient was particularly disturbed at the level of her psychic life, which was dominated by a tendency to project herself endlessly into other people rather than remaining herself, to the point that she no longer knew if it was she who was thinking or someone else in her place. This resulted in an almost permanent state of confusion.

It was a dream that gave her the chance to picture this internal situation. She dreamed that she was at the theater, at the same time standing on the stage taking part in the action with the actors and in her seat watching. Thus, in her dream, my patient was both actor and audience, like Riesenberg Malcolm's patient, who was simultaneously participant in and spectator of the bouts taking place in the mirror. Interpreting this dream allowed me to help her understand the source of her state of confusion and to see that by being both actress and audience she was in fact neither one nor the other, and that this situation would last until she chose her place. She must either be the actress and take the risk of seriously exposing herself in her role or be part of the audience, making a serious effort to understand the play. No one can be both on stage and in the audience without losing his identity.

Although my patient was relieved to escape from her confusion, it took her a long time to give up her massive use of projective identification because that would mean giving up her feeling of omnipotence. Each time she made a gesture toward remaining comfortably in her seat and not at the same time getting up on stage, she would be confronted by a feeling of sadness and intolerable solitude and seized by anxiety. Gradually, however, as she worked through the depressive position, which, as Segal stressed, remains the only way to abandon pathological projective identification in favor of introjective processes, she succeeded in transforming her voyeurism into curiosity.

IV. CONCLUSIONS

Study of "A Child Is Being Beaten" has shown us that the pathological state described by Freud in 1919 is just as relevant today, as confirmed by two recent contributions. Moreover, these works also show us that we must pay increased attention to the role played by this type of unconscious masochistic fantasy in our analysands, because often they will not confess to it, and the symptoms remain difficult to detect. But if the analyst is particularly attentive and gives the analysand the opportunity to overcome his shame and reveal his secret, the latter feels obvious relief and can begin to give meaning to his fantasy.

REFERENCES

Bonaparte, M. 1957. *La sexualité féminine*. Paris: Presses Universitaires de France.
Deutsch, H. 1944. *The psychology of women: Psychoanalytic interpretation*. New York: Grune and Stratton.
Freud, A. 1923. The relation of beating-phantasies to a day-dream. *Int. J. Psycho-Anal.* 4:89–92.
Freud, S. 1905 [1901]. Fragment of an analysis of a case of hysteria. *S.E.* 7.
———. 1915. Instincts and their vicissitudes. *S.E.* 14.
———. 1917. Mourning and melancholia. *S.E.* 14.
———. 1919. A child is being beaten. *S.E.* 17.
———. 1920a. The psychogenesis of a case of homosexuality in a woman. *S.E.* 18.
———. 1920b. Beyond the pleasure principle. *S.E.* 18.

132 / Jean-Michel Quinodoz

———. 1923. The ego and the id. *S.E.* 19.

———. 1924. The economic problem of masochism. *S.E.* 19.

———. 1925a. Negation. *S.E.* 19.

———. 1925b. Some psychical consequences of the anatomical distinction between the sexes. *S.E.* 19.

———. 1927. Fetishism. *S.E.* 21.

———. 1933 [1932]. New introductory lectures on psycho-analysis. *S.E.* 22.

———. 1940 [1938]. Splitting of the ego in the process of defence. *S.E.* 23.

Horney, K. 1932. The flight from womanhood. In *Feminine Psychology,* ed. K. Horney. London: Routledge & Kegan Paul (1967).

Jones, E. 1935. The early development of female sexuality. *Int. J. Psycho-Anal.* 8:459–72.

Klein, M. 1932. The effect of the early anxiety-situations on the sexual development of the girl. In M. Klein, *The psycho-analysis of children.* London: Hogarth (1980).

Laplanche, J., and Pontalis, J.-B. 1988. *The language of psychoanalysis.* London: Karnac Books and the Institute of Psycho-Analysis.

Lax, R. 1992. A variation on Freud's theme in "A child is being beaten"—Mother's role: Some implications for superego development in women. *J. Amer. Psychoanal. Assn.* 40, 455–73.

Pragier, G., and Faure-Pragier, S. 1993. Une fille est analysée: Anna Freud. *Revue Franç. Psychanal.* 447–57.

Quinodoz, D. 1992. Les alibis de la perversion, ou "L'assassin habite au 21." *Rev. Franç. Psychanal.* 56:1693–1701.

Quinodoz, J. M. 1989. Female homosexual patients in psychoanalysis. *Int. J. Psycho-Anal.* 70:57–63.

———. 1991. *La solitude apprivoisée: L'angoisse de séparation en psychanalyse.* Paris: Presses Universitaires de France. (*The Taming of Solitude: Separation Anxiety in Psychoanalysis.* 1993. London: Routledge.)

Riesenberg Malcolm, R. 1988. The mirror: A perverse sexual phantasy in a woman seen as a defence against a psychotic breakdown. In *Melanie Klein Today,* ed. E. Bott Spillius. London: Routledge.

———. 1995. Introjection: The undoing of projective identification. University College London Conference on Projective Identification, London, October 1995 (unpublished).

Saussure, R. de. 1929. Les fixations homosexuelles chez les femmes névrosées. *Rev. Franç. Psychanal.* 3:50–61.

Schafer, R. 1968. *Aspects of internalization.* New York: International Universities Press.

Segal, H. 1995. Comments on Ruth Riesenberg Malcolm's paper. University College London Conference on Projective Identification, London, October 1995 (unpublished).

Steeman, S. A. 1939. *L'assassin habite au 21.* Paris: Librairie des Champs Elysées.

Young-Bruehl, E. 1988. *Anna Freud: A biography.* New York: Summit.

Weiss, E. 1970. *Sigmund Freud as a consultant.* New York: Intercontinental Medical Book Corporation.

"A Child Is Being Beaten" and the Battered Child

ISIDORO BERENSTEIN

This essay is structured as follows:

Part 1. 1919: Freud's position in regard to both his personal circumstances and psychoanalysis

Part 2. A section-by-section commentary on Freud's original contribution

Part 3. A clinical vignette as the basis for a discussion of masochism and its clinical manifestations

Part 4. The increasingly disquieting real-world situation in which the scenario is analogous to the fantasy of the child being beaten—that of the battered child who is ill-treated most often by the father, but occasionally by the mother

Part 5. The fantasy structure and the reality structure; similarities and differences

Translated by Philip Slotkin, MA MITI.

134 / Isidoro Berenstein

FREUD AND PSYCHOANALYSIS IN 1919

In 1919 Freud was sixty-three years old. World War I had ended the year before, and 1919 began with the Versailles peace conference. The Allies imposed severe terms on Germany and Austria. The end of the war did not signal the end of the belief in violence as a quick solution to Europe's political, social, and economic problems. Vienna was experiencing the repercussions of social change, an upsurge of nationalism, the uprooting of large sections of the population, and increasing disappointment and resentment at the Treaty of Versailles and the economic and financial crisis. It was a time of great political turbulence, which would eventually culminate in the harsh European dictatorships of the 1930s (Kinder and Hilgemann, 1973).

Freud was profoundly ambivalent about Vienna, although he lived there until 1938. The Austro-Hungarian Empire was on the verge of breaking up, and in consequence Austria and Germany were impoverished, their citizenry imbued with a sense of social humiliation; these conditions would prove a fertile breeding ground for National Socialism, which was to arise in the 1920s and continue to develop in the 1930s.

Freud and his family were living virtually at subsistence level, as letters and comments from this period testify (Gay, 1988). Despite the deteriorating social situation, Freud had a large number of patients, but his income remained meager (Jones, 1957).

The precariousness of his position was not Freud's only concern. Throughout his career, he was dissatisfied with psychoanalytic theory: although its underlying concepts were innovative and original, some of them proved to have shortcomings when applied to a new range of clinical problems; as a result he realized that the theory was incomplete. Natural as such a situation may appear in the development of any great theory—as Freud already knew psychoanalysis to be—it left him feeling restless. The theory of the unconscious, which dated back to 1899, the time of *The Interpretation of Dreams,* was giving way to a topographical theory with an ego and an ego ideal—that is, a different psychic structure. In 1919, psychoanalytic concepts were being put to the test in their applicability to the psychoses and to the challenging phenomenon of the perversions, of which Freud had given an initial account in 1905 in *Three Essays on the Theory of Sexuality.* "From the History of an Infantile Neurosis" (1918 [1914]) had just been published. (The treatment reported in that article, begun some years earlier, had ended in

1914.) The metapsychological papers of 1915 had been followed by "A Metapsychological Supplement to the Theory of Dreams" (1917b [1915]) and "Mourning and Melancholia" (1917c [1915]). After "The 'Uncanny'" (1919b) came *Beyond the Pleasure Principle* (1920b), with Freud's new conception of both the drives and the psychic structure.

Freud announced the composition of "A Child Is Being Beaten" in a letter to Ferenczi dated January 24, 1919. The paper was published in the summer. (The Versailles peace conference had begun on January 18.) At about the same time (in March 1919), he began what would become *Beyond the Pleasure Principle*. He informed Ferenczi in a letter of May 12, 1919, of the writing of "The 'Uncanny,'" which was published in the autumn.

Several interrelated themes are addressed in "A Child Is Being Beaten." Masochism had been treated in the metapsychological works as a process secondary to sadism; it was seen as the result of sadism being turned back on the subject—the transformation of sadism into its opposite, the mechanisms considered to be more primitive defenses than repression and sublimation. Freud now returned to this subject with a variation on this 1915 theme; "A Child Is Being Beaten" in fact anticipates the reformulation of masochism in 1924, the importance of which ranks alongside the formulation of the duality of the drives and the new psychic topography.

Freud's paper also sets out his views on female sexuality; he gives a particularly subtle description of the child-being-beaten fantasy in girls, of the phases and phrases in which it is embodied, and of how it differs in girls and boys. "The Psychogenesis of a Case of Female Homosexuality" (1920a), which was completed in January 1920 and published that March, dates from about the same time. It anticipates his works on femininity of the following decade. Another theme contained in "A Child Is Being Beaten" concerns the Oedipus complex, particularly that of the woman, in the context of the complex and controversial area of female sexuality.

A further subject addressed in the 1919 paper dates from the very origins of psychoanalysis: the role of the father, developed in connection with the elaboration of Freud's dreams after the death of Jacob, his own father. The subject pervades all the case histories (Little Hans is treated through his father) and is considered in depth in *Totem and Taboo;* it also figures prominently in the work that is the subject of this discussion.

The vicissitudes of that mental activity—fantasy—in relation to the component drives are a central topic in this work. Fantasy was coming to be seen as an important entity in its own right—indeed, more so than real traumatic events—and was seen as lying at the root of "psychic reality." Fantasy has the character of a scene highly specific to the subject, with a generally visual content, in which the unconscious wish is fulfilled. Yet its configuration also presents great similarities in different subjects, and this led Freud to the idea of "primal fantasies," in which the reality of the event was reinscribed, albeit transferred back to a prehistoric time.

The reality principle entails the constant rejection of fantasy. Almost a century of psychoanalysis has unraveled the complexities of internal reality, but much still remains to be explored. The real world has not received the same attention and has generally been regarded as an obstacle or hindrance to analysis. With regard to the fantasy "a child is being beaten," the real situation of the battered child, which is similar in format, presents us with a theoretical challenge.

Freud's inclusion of so many fundamental themes in "A Child Is Being Beaten" shows that, at the time of its composition, he was in the midst of a reformulation of psychoanalytic concepts that began in 1919–20 and continued over the ensuing years.

SECTION-BY-SECTION COMMENTARY ON "A CHILD IS BEING BEATEN"

Familiar as the paper's six sections are, it should be borne in mind that any transcription inevitably imposes a new order on the original and transforms it in a way that bears the stamp of its transcriber.

In section I Freud presents his "fantasy-representation." The fantasy appears to be frequent and pleasurable; its confession is associated with shame and guilt as tokens of resistance; its culmination is masturbatory (autoerotic); and its initial onset is lost to memory. Physical punishment at school calls up the fantasy and reinforces it but does not lie at its origin. It may be regarded as the displacement of an earlier experience to a later age. For Freud, "early" means the period from two to five or six years of age, before school. Later, during latency or after, the fantasy is linked, if not to beatings inflicted on other children, to books in which children are punished for bad behavior. (Here we already see the conscious cathexis that keeps the pleasurable connection with masturbation repressed.) Freud rejects any relation between this fantasy and actual physical punishment, which, in any case, he had not observed in his patients' accounts. This is reasonable, because it was important to describe the structure of the fantasy, its unconscious functioning, its specific reality, and the laws governing its working, which differ from those of external reality. Here the fantasy "a child is being beaten" is connected with pleasure, whereas the actual experience of beating is accompanied by intolerable feelings. Freud must have been very concerned to make this distinction, which he attempted to specify in detail many times throughout his essay. A disparity is noted between the external reality of actual punishment undergone by the child and psychic reality, with the strength of the emotions attached to the psychic reality of the fantasy. Hence the locations of the fantasy-representation and the characters who will figure in it are particularly relevant.

Freud adds that the beating is inflicted on the "naked bottom." Although he does not specifically say so, it is understood that this means not the anorectal area but the buttocks, which may become autonomous in terms of skin erogenicity and its alternating registers of pleasure and pain. The buttocks are distinguished from the anorectal region, which has the functions of expulsion, control, and incorporation, and from feces and their meaning.

In section 2 Freud discusses the relation between the infantile characteristic of perversion and its persistence into adult life. "Perversion" here is equivalent to a component drive not subjected to the hegemonic or unifying aim of genitality that then evolves as a separate, autonomous tendency. The component drives have several possible fates: they may undergo repression, in which case they disappear from conscious life; or they may be incorporated in a reaction formation, as in obsessional neurosis or sublimation. A perversion in adult life arises when repression or sublimation has not been achieved; in such a case something like fixation will presumably have occurred. If a repression takes place, this will give rise to a predisposition that, in the case of sadism, will be to obsessional neurosis. When the chance episode of witnessing a punishment becomes associated with the sexual tendency, a congenital constitution may be involved. What is this congenital constitution? It is an obscure concept that explains little but merely gives a provisional name to what we do not yet understand.

In section 3 Freud sets forth his position on theoretical knowledge and therapeutic success. Psychoanalysis is stated to be the method of lifting infantile amnesia, enabling the adult to become acquainted with his infantile life from its beginnings, which Freud at this juncture places between the ages of two and four or five. Perhaps he chooses the age of two because it is then that the child ceases to be merely a subject spoken of by others and begins to be a speaker himself—that is, to have a preconscious register that is becoming separate from the unconscious. At the same time the child acquires mastery and control over the anal sphincter and attempts to stand firmly on his own feet and walk, thereby acquiring the notion of an external and internal supporting basis. This knowledge of infantile life, however, stemming as it does from the position of repression that governs the adult psyche, is registered as theoretical insofar as therapeutic success is deemed to be the disappearance of symptoms, a criterion that is important and obvious only from the standpoint of adult life. On the other hand, it is the patient who speaks about later events and the analyst who speaks to him, through interpretation, about childhood matters. To the patient, the unconscious comes from the analyst; it is experienced as foreign, as if of external origin, although it provides him with a firmly based experience of what is truly his own.

Freud now illustrates the phases of the beating fantasy in girls, each of which can be expressed in a phrase.

The first phase and the first phrase is: "*My father is beating the child* [of as yet unspecified sex] *(whom I hate)*" (186; italics original). This phase can also be expressed as follows: "My father does not love this child, *he loves only me,* because he is beating the other child." What is involved may be recollections, wishes originating in various circumstances, or a fantasy. It has a sadistic character, which is projected by the girl onto the father.

The second phase and the second phrase is: "*I am being beaten by my father*" (186; italics original). This never had a real existence and will never be remembered or become conscious. It may be a production prior to the constitution of repression; it is a construction of the analysis and perhaps of the subject. As an unequivocally masochistic phase, it must not have undergone the process of repression. But what, then, is this phase-phrase? What makes the infantile—and perhaps that is what the unconscious is—intelligible and comprehensible is not only the discovery of a memory or the deduction of an experience but the construction of a meaning that assigned sense to this type of emotional experience. That experience must pass through the ego, however incipient its structure may be, in order to be subsequently transferable to others; hence masochism and narcissism are bound up early on with the very constitution of the ego.

The third phase is once again conscious. The person inflicting the beating has been displaced from the father to a substitute, such as the teacher; the fantasying girl does not appear in the scene but now is looking on. The phrase might be: "*An adult (teacher) is beating children*." It is like the dream situation in which the dreamer is often not included in the action, although he may be said to be represented in all the characters who appear in the dream. In the fantasy, the children being beaten are boys. The third phase gives rise to intense sexual excitement and leads to masturbation.

Later, in "Some Psychical Consequences of the Anatomical Distinction Between the Sexes" (1925), Freud returns to the argument presented in "A Child Is Being Beaten" and states unequivocally that the child being beaten is a personified transformation of the clitoris and that the beating is a transformed caress, associated with the girl's infantile masturbation. Freud had already pointed out in "From the History of an Infantile Neurosis" (1918 [1914]) that the masochistic reversal had taken the form of chastisement and beating and that, in boys, "especially being beaten on the penis," in this way the sense of guilt associated with masturbatory satisfaction was assuaged. At this time Freud still regarded masochism as sadism turned against the subject himself.

The fantasy takes the form of a mental scene with interchangeable positions and characters. The second and perhaps most profound phrase makes the girl's ego the subject of the passive action of the verb *to beat* (*I am being beaten*), the agent the father inflicting this punishment (*I am being beaten by my father*). Its basis is the wish to be desired, expressed regressively as being beaten by the father. This is the position that is transformed into sadism because the subject changes, the ego yielding place to the father as the subject of the action of beating, which takes the child as its indirect object. This is the first phase-phrase. The beater is then displaced from the father to a substitute for the purpose of adaptation to more recent circumstances, such as school and other experiences with adults. This is the third phrase.

The second and most unconscious phrase is of fundamental importance. Here the subject (I am) is initially presented as the mental space in which the wish (to be beaten) is located, but always as indicated by an other (the father). This function of indication by an other is the basis of the initially masochistic sexual tendency. Here masochism and narcissism are superimposed, as stated earlier, and so are the subject (the place and agency in which the wish originates) and the agent (who performs the specific action of the verb). These may be and appear to be the same until the establishment of the passive voice allows the wish to be beaten (the subject that is the girl) to be distinguished from the object inflicting the beating (the father).

These unconscious operations take us back to "Instincts and Their Vicissitudes" (1915), in which Freud returns to the problem of masochism in connection with the vicissitudes of the drive prior to repression and sublimation; here he invokes reversal into the opposite and turning round upon the subject's own self. The reversal has to do with the change from activity to passivity. What comes first is the activity involved in the child's muscular action on the object toward whom this power of torture is directed, with variations such as humiliation or subjugation. At this time masochism was seen as sadism turned back on the ego itself: the object toward whom the action is directed changes from the other to the ego, and activity is exchanged for passivity. If the ego receives the passive action, another subject must take charge of its performance.

The masochistic position calls for the presence of the other as the person who performs the action on the ego. Perhaps the model of specific action shows that the ego's need comes first and is then followed by the wish, thus indicating the hegemonic place of the other. Subsequently, the ego, by identification, adopts the position of the other and addresses itself to him, albeit now transformed into an entity like itself; here the other is an object on whom the ego performs the sadistic action. For this reason, masochism always requires the other in order to fulfill the ego's wish, and sadism is exercised with an object of the ego that is necessarily located in another.

It is in this reciprocal motion between ego and object that the ego centers and decenters itself as a subject. The ego takes the other as subject or object. In the former case it is the father or the parents prior to sexual differentiation (Freud, 1921). In the latter case, the mother is chosen as the object, especially by boys. In this way the subject begins to negotiate the Oedipus complex. It seems to be a law of mental functioning that, by way of identification, the subject cathects himself as he does the other and that this operation in fact gives rise to what we call the subject. This movement involves a process of centering and decentering extending from masochism to sadism. It is hardly surprising that, once armed with the conceptual tool of the death drive, Freud ultimately established the priority of masochism.

He returns in section 4 to the first phase, which depends on infantile jealousy and also the child's egoistic interests. He offers a consummate description of a link (Berenstein, 1995): the girl is tenderly attached to the father, who may have done everything possible to obtain her love and therefore colludes in her hatred of and competition with her mother. Each depends on the other. The girl's ego is molded by the father's love, as is the latter by the girl's wish. Neither could create the link alone. If the link is inscribed in the mind, this occurs in a different place from that of the representation of the father as an internal object subject to the vicissitudes of unconscious fantasy. In this case the father would be almost entirely a creation of the ego, but this is not true of the father of the link, who "does everything possible to obtain her love." He performs significant acts and does not merely accept the meanings stemming from the girl.

There are clues here to the idea of hate as older than love, put forward in "Instincts and Their Vicissitudes." This is due to the narcissistic ego's rejection of the external world, which supplies unwanted stimuli, including the presence of younger siblings. The wish then extends to the mother and is represented in the boy as the wish to have a child with her and in the girl as the wish to receive a child from the father. These loves undergo repression or, rather, are destined to be buried. Burial is not the same as repression but involves destructuring: never again will they find expression, nor will it ever be possible to remember them. Perhaps the situation resembles the burial of the Oedipus complex, whose meanings persist, but in the form of an inheritance: the heir to the buried Oedipus complex is thus the superego. The heir to the infantile bonds of love is the constitution of two psychic kingdoms or worlds, one of which calls for the presence of the other in order for the mental life of links to unfold, while the other kingdom demands the absence of the other so that the world of fantasy can develop. The former might be called "the link with the other" and the latter the "object relationship" (Berenstein and Puget, 1995). Admittedly, this distinction becomes more blurred the closer we approach to the origins.

The persistence of incestuous wishes, by contrast, gives rise to repression, with its consequence of the consciousness of guilt. Its fulfillment as a punishment leads to the second phase of the fantasy: *"He does not love you, because he beats you."* It is not only repression, however, that changes the sense of love and turns it into aggression; here we have the "essence of masochism" for the Freud of 1919. A further vicissitude of the aim of the drive—regression—is now added, in which satisfaction is attained in the form of being beaten by the father. Because this is so difficult to bring into consciousness, its inscription presumably predates the acquisition of language, the separation of preconscious and unconscious, and hence its constitution.

Since fantasy is a space in which the characters can change both their positions and their costumes, in the case of boys the person inflicting the punishment is the mother, and this gives rise to the masochistic structure that can be displaced to other women. In the case of Freud's female patients, the victims of the beating represent younger siblings. To return to the third phase, which is sadistic in form, the aim is the masochistic satisfaction connected with the sense of guilt. The indeterminate children are representatives of the same person.

Section 5 deals with the genesis of the perversions and the role of the difference between the sexes. The origin of the perversions is bound up with the components of normal sexuality that are molded by the Oedipus complex, or rather by a particular vicissitude of that complex, favored by some obscure constitutional element or impelled not to go under, so that the unusual component persists. This places perversion within the logical chain of sexuality, from which it is not isolated. Fantasies of being beaten and other perverse fixations result from what Freud calls "scars" left behind by the process in which the Oedipus complex ends. They are the precipitate of the wounds sustained before and during the contradictory unfolding of the Oedipus complex such as the birth or death of a younger sibling or other family events—for instance, the death of the father—or the results of these or other losses, such as depression in the mother (Green, 1980), hidden infidelities or unhappiness in the parental couple, or concealment of family swindling, especially on the part of members of the mother's family in relation to the father (Berenstein, 1989).

The scars of traumatic experiences persist in the young boy or girl and are recathected in fantasy in transfigured or rearranged form.

Concerning the genesis of masochism, passivity is distinguished from its unpleasant character. The latter proves to be connected with the consciousness of guilt (as regards both the ego's sadism in ill-treating the object and the incestuous choice of object), as a result of which the ego is accused by the agency that was soon to be called the superego, which includes conscience and self-observation. Masochism is what is expressed by the second unconscious phrase: "I am being beaten by my father." It may perhaps not be capable of becoming conscious because it arises so early, prior to repression. It is manifested in problems with persons who represent the father.

Freud turns in section 6 to the masochism-related vicissitudes of the fantasy in the light of the difference between the sexes. He compares the beating fantasies of girls and boys, noting that, in the latter, the fantasy is associated more with the masochism whereby men assume a feminine attitude. Owing to the compromise with consciousness, those being punished appear as young boys and the administrator of the beating is always a woman.

In boys, the first phase is "*I am being beaten by my father.*" This is unconscious and is equivalent to the second phase in girls. As in the latter, the underlying meaning is "*I am loved by my father*"—a passive, feminine position. This is later transformed into "*I am being beaten by my mother.*" In girls and boys alike, the erotic, incestuous attachment is to the father. In view of her oedipal position, however, the girl makes a heterosexual choice, taking her father as a love object, whereas the boy's choice is homosexual, although the chastisement is transferred from the father into the mother. This must be important in terms of not yielding to the homosexual choice, but the situation is betrayed by the masculine character assumed by the women cast in the role of the beaters. In girls the administrator of the beating is the father, so that the form of the heterosexual link is retained, although, by adopting the position of an observer, the girl evades the experience of erotic life represented by the contact of the father beating other children.

If the operative mechanism is repression, the content is expelled from consciousness but the unconscious structure is preserved. If regression holds sway, the unconscious structure itself changes, so that what is retained is the masochistic fantasy of being beaten by the father. The unconscious is stable but not immutable, and its contents can be changed.

A CLINICAL VIGNETTE

Continuing this consideration of the child being beaten in relation to masochism and its connection with perversion, the role of the father, the infantile scene, the present-day visual staging of the drama, and the wish as interlaced with death, I shall now present some of the clinical material of a patient with perverse and homosexual pathology superimposed upon a masochistic unconscious foundation. His masochistic structure culminated in the apparent carelessness whereby he contracted HIV, eventually leading to his death after enormous suffering. This was no doubt due to so-called opportunistic germs, active on account of the immunodepression resulting from the viral infection. Although from the medical point of view this is an efficient cause in almost all AIDS patients, in the case of Mr. A. the unconscious fantasies connected with his childhood history and the structure of his internal world lent a particular meaning to his physical suffering.[1] Sadism had become displaced onto "life" as embodied in different persons who took pleasure in ill-treating him and in his suffering. These persons formed a series that included the mother of infancy, the father of infancy, and a variation on the latter represented by the "baker," as we shall see later, who initiated him homosexually. There followed a series of colleagues who inevitably "stole his ideas"; then, when he became clinically ill with the virus, he was delivered up to "the doctors" who subjected him to numerous painful tests and interventions, which he underwent passively. His apparent passivity concealed disproportionate activity in seeking out these persons. Inevitably, the analyst was incorporated into this series because he was in charge of this "therapeutic" ill-treatment, but at other times the positions were reversed and the analyst found himself ill-treated by the patient. When attempting to work through this situation, in close proximity to its masochistic foundation, he wanted to break off the analysis a few weeks before his death.

Mr. A. (more of whose clinical history can be found in Berenstein, 1995) commenced treatment with me when he learned that he was HIV-positive, at the age of forty. After two previous marriages, he had remarried fifteen years earlier. In his adolescence and early youth, he had indulged first in homosexual, then in heterosexual, and finally in bisexual activities. He had lately been impotent in any type of sexual relationship. An only child, he had the infantile memory of having been his mother's executive arm in actions directed against his father: for example, she had asked him to take money out of his cash register without his knowledge. As he put it, he had to "take money from him behind his back." This phrase condensed the structure of both his infantile and his more recent situation, which involved entering the

1. This is the justification for taking a patient with clinical manifestations of HIV, currently deemed terminal, into psychoanalytic treatment. The fact of the illness is included in psychic reality as an "accident" or "catastrophe" that, owing to the difficulty of assigning meaning to it, is experienced repeatedly as a real fact external to the ego, thus blocking any possibility of insight. The superego appropriates the accusation to itself and holds the ego guilty of not having prevented the impossible: the future. The so-called carelessness is a way of thinking that the future can be avoided; this is not the same as the masochistic determination to seek a punishment for the ego. But for the infection this subject's life would have taken a different course from that reported here. The decision whether to give analytic treatment to a person with HIV involves the above and many other ethical considerations. In my view, however, the overriding criterion for us is relief of the other's suffering.

father anally; as we shall see, this was transformed into being possessed (sexually) by a representative of the father. This may have been a defense against, or equally an association to, the fantasy of being the mother's hand-phallus and may have resonated with what was to become his most significant and painful physical symptom when he contracted HIV, namely, diarrhea.

The theft featuring in the infantile account emerged in material connected with the later kleptomania of his mother, who would surreptitiously—"behind his back"—remove objects or money from her son's house, to his profound irritation. His mother had died a few years earlier, and it still upset him deeply to talk about this in his sessions. In the transference, this fantasy was activated by having me sit behind him in the analytic situation, giving rise to distrust and a chronic state of alertness in the patient. The same symptom subsequently arose in his own son, who would take money from the house and from his mother's handbag. Thus he was confronted by his son's repetition of his own infantile situation.

When in the hospital during an acute phase of his illness, one of the treatments he needed was kinesitherapy. Having been treated first by a male masseur and then by a masseuse, he decided that he wanted to continue the treatment with the latter. This choice was based on the fact that she "kneaded" his body, which gave him pleasure and also calmed him. The Spanish word *amasar* (to knead) aroused a set of childhood recollections spanning the period from age six to age ten, including the beginning of his passive homosexual activities. The scene evoked in memory was set in the rear of a bakery where bread was kneaded (*amasaba*) and where, as a child, he had been fascinated to see how flour and water were mixed to form a paste that could be molded into a variety of shapes. He later learned that this paste was called dough (*masa* in Spanish) and the action was kneading (*amasar*). In the scene he was possessed sexually by one of the bakers, who was wearing a big white apron with nothing underneath it. He must have liked it, he thought, as he had no other explanation for the fact that this situation was repeated a number of times at his own instigation.

His fascination with fecal matter and his infantile curiosity about its formation were connected with his anal activity, in which he was able to distinguish feces from the anus and from the buttocks and invoked those different considerations. The first had to do with the formation or gestation of bodily and, later, mental products, signifying the first questionings about what was produced inside the body—feces and babies being intuited as the result of a relationship between two elements, represented by the flour and water or by his anus and the father's penis. The second concerned control and expulsion, the sphincter constituting a gateway for exit (feces) or entry (penis) when the control broke down. The third implicated the anus as the locus of reception of contact with the father, imagined not as penetration but as caressing or— its equivalent after regression—chastisement and ill-treatment.

At this stage in his present illness, he was undergoing physiotherapy with a woman who was treating his body "to help him stand firmly on his feet"— something he found difficult because of his increasing weakness—and "to restore anal sphincter control," with which he was having problems due to his constant and copious diarrhea.

These women were the present-day representations of the men who in the childhood situation had "worked" on his anus, an idea that had to do with kneading (*amasar*) as a particular form of *ama(sa)r* (*amar* meaning "to love"), in its passive form, loved (*amado*)—being "kneaded" (*amasado*)— by a father substitute working "behind his back," as he had done in obeying his mother's orders. "Behind his back" was the anal zone and its surroundings as the locus of the initial masochistic fixation and of its subsequent unfolding. The wish to be "possessed" by the father assumed the infantile form of possessing the father behind his back, in his cash register, where the money was, not only in the sense of feces but in order to take possession of the penis so as to satisfy the mother of infancy.

The diarrhea became his principal tormenting symptom as his condition worsened. Its significance is hinted at by the following dream.

It was a Monday in the first year of his analysis. In the dream he saw himself going into a toilet—perhaps a public toilet. He saw a "guy" urinating with a big, erect penis, who then left. A girl came into the toilet and looked down at the floor as if searching for something. She went out again. He himself then bent down to tie his shoelaces and looked through a hole in the door of another cubicle. The "occupant" came out, looking tough and aggressive. The dreamer moved aside and hid. He left the toilet and saw the tough guy taking the girl by the shoulder, whereupon they both left. They said something about the police—either that they were police officers or that they were going to call the police. He thought that, if they asked, he would say that he was in the toilet because he had diarrhea. He would use it as an excuse.

In the days leading up to the dream, he had prolonged attacks of diarrhea. The comings and goings of these characters in the public toilet represented movements in a space whose model was the rectum and the anus, the location of the father of infancy-baker who had penetrated him while he was watching the process of *ama(sa)r* (kneading-lovemaking). Here he was looking and hiding; with the onset of persecution feelings, he would tell a lie: that he was here because he had exactly what he was suffering from when he was awake—diarrhea. He would say that it was an excuse in order to evade an increasing sense of persecution. He would tell as a lie what was in fact the truth.

One activity in the dream was to watch how others did what they were doing. He associated the persecution with a letter from W., who had been his partner many years before and had then had an operation for testicular cancer. Having committed a crime, he was now in prison, where Mr. A. imagined that he was constantly being raped and otherwise ill-treated.

He saw the erect penis as an instrument of aggression (displaced onto the tough guy) or of exhibition. The gaze of the eye observing through the hole in the door was penetrating. The aggressive penis was then joined with the girl searching for something she did not have. He himself was seeking part of his identity in the toilet. He had felt better that weekend, however, and that was the context in which the dream had arisen. The fact that he felt better and more vital seemed also to reinforce his perverse functioning, where he observed penises in order to combat the solitude of confronting the primal scene. To allay the persecution, his excuse was diarrhea. At this point the wish took shape: if only the diarrhea were an excuse and not a threat of death! At the same time, however, he was wondering which was the most persecutory: the physical illness, the diarrhea, or his internal situation. The diarrhea confronted him with an experience of voiding. But it arose as a pretext in the face of an internal situation that aroused more fear. The wish connected with the destructive was in itself a masochistic formation that had to do with punishment for possession of the penis and of the father through theft and plunder. The toilet stood for the "rear," where this criminal act whose object was the father took place.

At this point in the analysis, the fantasy scenario was represented by the pornographic videocassettes he used for the purpose of turning on both himself and his partner of the day, a young boy. The latter had telephoned him to say that, as it so happened, "he could not do anything from the front" but "it was OK to use the rear." This was a coded message that acted as a password to unleash a series of fantasies and acts from which he was unable to restrain himself. This impossibility of abstention and self-restraint was connected with the addictive component of his homosexuality. When they actually met and the young man offered himself to him, all he was able to do, on account of his impotence, was to lie on top of his back. Unable to achieve penile penetration, he did it digitally instead. This anal masturbation enabled him to enter possessively into the young man, in whom he installed his infantile part, and to identify aggressively with the father; this aggressive identification lay at the root of his genital impotence. By putting himself inside the young partner, he may have been transforming him into the impotent, castrated father, rendered passive as an externalization of his masochistic structure: being punished, castrated, and rendered passive as a way of being turned into a woman. Feeling unable to satisfy his partner, he then telephoned another young man, whom he asked to come over so that they could develop the sexual scene further; the aim was to satisfy ostensibly his partner but in fact mainly himself, watching, becoming director of the action instead of an actor in it, determining the actions to be performed and the roles to be played by each. This is where the videos watched by the young men came in, as well as himself watching the young men watching. The films contained the infantile situation, possibly altered by the failure of repression, the recourse to regression, and the perverse transformation. One video was about a seminary attended by young men. In one scene, equivalent to a phase-phrase-fantasy, an adolescent was robbing a butcher's shop and the owner, catching him in the act, raped him as punishment. The young man's face apparently showed an expression of pain. The punishment was a sadomasochistic form of love and of the wish to possess the penis of the owner-father through theft. Another scene showed young men involved in sexual games and intercourse, in this case tender and loving.

At this point the patient's young partner, who may have been feeling frustrated, began "zapping" alternately between the video and live television programs, searching for some impossible scene. Running the video backwards and forwards indiscriminately, he suffered a mental disintegration, had hallucinations, and heard noises through the wall; his activity became uncontrollable. At this point A. wanted to get rid of him; unable to tell him to go, he himself went off, leaving the young man in his apartment. On his return a few days later, he found everything "damaged" and in a state of "disaster" (terms that came up in the analysis to describe the evidence of destructive activity): the television set and video recorder were broken, the furniture was damaged, perfumes had been spilt, and broken bottles and cigarette butts littered the place. That was the condition of his world after these exploits in contact with his perverse part, which subsequently also proved to be psychotic.

The wish for annihilation arose in the form of "killing the non-life." That was his term for states of mind in which he felt extremely dejected, his thoughts made up of repetitive images and phrases, immobilized in time and space, interminably invaded by the same situation of illness and of there being no way out. He was in a place where the loss of an internal support made him feel most defenseless, and that was where the analysis had become established, as the following dream showed (Berenstein, 1995).

He dreamed that he had to do some shopping in a supermarket, and to get there he turned into the access road, but the wrong way (*de contramano*). Realizing this, he left the car there. On his return he found that the car, a Mercedes, had been stolen. Then the insurance assessor arrived and was filling in a form. He asked A.: "What kind of car is it?" A. answered: "A Mercedes." He assumed that the insurance company would replace it with a similar car. The assessor said: "Ah, it's a jeep." The patient, surprised and irritated, said: "What do you mean, a jeep?" "Yes, a jeep," insisted the assessor, who was an unpleasant, aggressive fellow. The patient would have none of this and said: "How can it be a jeep if it is a Mercedes?" The assessor did not reply and went on writing.

The patient's associations showed that a Mercedes was the car he wanted to have and to which he had always aspired so as to consolidate his position. He also associated to what he called "another theft of ideas" connected with his work and a competition. He mentioned a series of events that had to do with his homosexuality (*contramano* in Spanish [the wrong way] can refer both to a one-way street and to a contrary sexual orientation), the theft as an aggressive plundering of his mental possibilities, the loss of something greatly desired, Mercedes as a woman's name, and so on. There were associations to the origin of his homosexual relations and to the aggression that featured in them. Despite the analytic work on the dream in this session, I remained unsatisfied, still searching, although the patient seemed pleased with his work and mine. In what was perhaps a routine interpretation, I said "Mercedes," and to my surprise A. replied that he thought I had said "*a merced de*" (at the mercy of).

This was in effect a key to the representation of the present moment and of the situation of infancy. Being "at the mercy of" described his position with respect to the ubiquitous and uncontrollable persecutor that A. now called "the virus," which his life had characterized in other ways, sometimes abating and at other times occupying him almost completely. He also felt at the mercy of the analysis and in contact with the experience of destructiveness and physical and mental damage connected with his mad, perverse, or addicted part. At other times in his life he had been at the mercy of the representation of social status as a form of identificatory belonging that seemingly provided him with a sense of (self-)valuation and also of (self-) sufficiency. As an emblematic element, however, it was far inferior to the kind of highly intimate and personal emotional experience that would have afforded ego solidity and support. Perhaps the analyst was the insurance assessor in the dream who questioned this belonging. All the same, the fact that he had dreamed at all showed that he had a mental and representational world.

Like the dream about the toilet, this dream began with an entry, in this case into the supermarket. The theft of the car was a representation of the infantile situation of stealing from the father behind his back; he identified with this "behind," whereby he laid himself open to the theft of his life, another way of representing the state of being at the mercy of that Mercedes for which he longed so much but which was lost. Masochistic pleasure assumes this quality of being longed for but lost, so that it has to be recovered through repetition.

The infantile situation apparently exalted masochism, which he had tried to resolve first through homosexuality and then through bisexuality, on a foundation of perversion. He found himself trapped in a spiral, however, in which each new exploit reinforced the masochistic structure, with the ultimate climax of HIV.

THE BATTERED CHILD

It is curious to note how the fantasy "a child is being beaten" coincides with its fulfillment, that of a father beating a child. This situation has even been systematized into the clinical syndrome of the battered child. It has become an important concern of educators, lawyers, psychologists, and those involved in children's rights. Goldberg (1995, 20–21) gives the following monstrous statistics on ill-treatment: "The number of cases recorded in the United States in 1983 and 1984 was 1,007,658. There were 1,700,000 reported cases of ill-treatment in 1985; the perpetrator was one of the parents in 92% of cases and the type of abuse was deprivation or negligence in 58% and physical abuse in 25 to 40% of cases (in 1983). Some 2% of cases were of sexual abuse. . . . According to Department of Education statistics, physical punishment was administered more than a million times in schools from kindergarten up to secondary level."

Whereas Freud's paper shows us the subject in the internal space of fantasy, the irruption of the real external world through a beating adult—usually the father, the mother, or another significant person—puts us in touch with another world. Whereas the act of beating seemingly resembles the scene of the fantasy, it is actually implemented in another scene, albeit with people connected with the characters in the fantasy, because it often involves the father figure, who is encountered as someone real. Instead of being the fantasizer, the child becomes the victim, and the father is no longer a figure desired in an internal scene but now the person who inflicts punishment on the victim. The person inflicting the punishment does so out of an excess of excitation; the violence sustained either exceeds or falls short of the child's capacity to assign meaning to it. It bursts into and becomes established in his psyche as a thing in itself to which no meaning can be assigned and which cannot readily be transformed. The child cannot bind it, so that, rather than constituting a meaningful event, it often gives rise to a memory in the form of an act. As a result, the child in turn becomes the perpetrator of violence against other children or waits until he has a child of his own on whom to repeat this unbound excess. Many fathers who beat their children were themselves battered children. The determination changes: whereas the fantasy that is the subject of this book concerns the subject's masochistic wish, the real situation in which a child is being beaten involves both the father's wish to be free of stimuli and his relationship with a mother who watches this scene without watching it. In this way the father transfers onto the son the ill-treatment characteristic of such families and people, inflicted both by his own father and by a culture that transmits signifiers of violence.

Being beaten by an adult may come to constitute a representation when cathected secondarily as masochism, in which the wish is directed toward the father as the ultimate expression of survival; this necessarily entails a failure of repression. Real beating is a motor act performed by a parent, generally the father, who does not know that he is the transmitter of a particular relationship with his own father, by whom he himself was as a rule beaten. Here we have a transgenerational model of identification that gives rise to a command in the father's mind that operates against the child. This may to some extent be regarded as the infantile part of the father identified in the beaten child.

STRUCTURE OF THE FANTASY "A CHILD IS BEING BEATEN" AND OF THE REALITY OF THE BATTERED CHILD

Every link comes into being on the basis of an I-other relationship with characteristics of externality, with what is unlike, foreign to, and impossible to equate with the subject's own ego or with the ego that is equatable with the other; meaning has to be assigned to this by both parties (Berenstein, 1995). Beating comes about as an attempt to turn the child into something similar to the beater himself, just as the father becomes similar to his own father. In this case the link regresses; the child is not accepted as other, and the father tries to transform him into an extension of an inner object relationship. If the child cries or does not behave as the father wishes, he hits him, with a view to silencing him and suppressing him as an intolerable stimulus, an intolerable other. That, however, is precisely the quality of what we call an object, so that we are once again in the world of fantasy and not of the link with the other. Yet the child continues to search for the father as other.

The following postulate seems to hold good: the link has to be preserved come what may, at any price, even that of the ego itself. The link with the other in this situation cannot be forgone even though the punishment and lesions stem from that link, because beyond it lies the experience of the void and then death. That is presumably why it is difficult to abandon the link in spite of the enormous unhappiness and suffering involved in remaining in it. Whereas the pleasure principle—or, beyond the pleasure principle, repetition—reigns in the internal world, what holds sway in the world of links is the paradox of the imposition of the other in his non-likeness and at the same time the impossibility of not accepting that imposition if the subject is involved in the link with the other; hence the possibility of violence. This is related to the act of entering the body of the other through an orifice, which may take two forms, according to the level of regression. The first is through a natural orifice, as in a range of phenomena extending from the entry of the nipple into the mouth, or of the image of the mother or father into the eyes, to the entry of the penis into the vagina or anus. Here the imposition still respects a limit in fantasy and its correlate in reality. The other form, connected with violence, is penetration through a non-natural orifice, and here there are two subforms: predestined orifices that, however, constitute closed doors that are violated by the act of penetration, or surfaces in which an orifice is opened up, as in wounding or, in the extreme case, murder. Here the ego has been unable to contain the object relationship and it was in turn impossible to tolerate the link with the other, who is annihilated. In the case of an adult and a child confused with an entity like the subject, the result is what we call sexual abuse. It is equivalent to making an orifice where none exists, in the anus, vagina, or skin, and it is the child's skin that bears the marks of the punishment, beating, or battering, as the imposition of a motor act that the child neither wants nor asks for, since the punishment is never equated with the ego. The situation could be described as one of expulsion of an adult's pleasure and its introduction into a child, but this would come closer to a secondary sexualization of the punishment. It could be confused with the child's search for this parent, which he continues in spite of everything, because his survival depends on him. It may be incorporated in this search in the form of a command—"I have to put up with being beaten"— but this leads rather in the direction of death and away from that of libidinal cathexis. The beating may be erotized in the internal space and become associated with the pleasure derived from primal masochism, now transformed so as to cathect the punishment and blows. The phrase expressing the wish would be: "He is beating me because he loves me." Here the ego is committing an error of judgment, in particular as to attribution: "He loves me when he punishes me" and "I incorporate him because I believe that the bad is good." The ego mistakenly sees the bad as itself (not that which is foreign to the subject) and the bad as what is internal (not what is outside) as identical. This leads to an error in the judgment of existence: this good father, a representation wished for or needed, is not to be found in the real external world and is therefore not avoided. The sadistic father is not only an internal fantasy subsequently to be modified by the "good" external father. This results in a blurring of the boundaries between inside and outside and an incipient failure in the definitive reality-ego.

In the father, the punishment results from intolerance of the otherness of the son, a radical intolerance that makes him transform the son from something different from to something similar to himself on the infantile level. The cathexis assumes the form of possessiveness: "He is my son and I can do whatever I like or whatever it occurs to me to do with him" or "He is mine and therefore my wish is power." Because he cannot do without him and he has to do something, he decides to obliterate or suppress him as other. The child is punished when he cries, demands, asks for something, or is disobedient—that is, when he declares himself as other. Does this beating father know that he is beating? Is he violating a cultural prohibition, a "thou shalt not"? Or, conversely, is he transforming cultural signifiers into violence as a result of an alteration in the definitive reality-ego? Perhaps, as in other fields, the culture conveys two conflicting commands: on one hand it lays down a law, while on the other it urges its contravention. Some feel that the message is "that is the way to do it," to bring up and teach a child. Two contradictory injunctions are here at work: "thou shalt not" and, at the same time, "everybody does it."

It is an unconscious misunderstanding that is responsible for the superimposition of the cultural injunction on an unconscious act that places the ego in the position of being unable not to perform it, as if it were imposed from within. It is impossible not to perform these actions, and the ego knows nothing of this "injunction"; for the ego, that is simply the way things are. The beating father is also passing on an asymmetrical situation when he is ill-treated by his own external environment and cannot respond in kind because that would be a criminal offense.

The beating father may be deemed to be exposed to a series of scenes comprising a number of phases and phrases. First: "I see how 'the situation' (as he calls what goes on in the external world) ill-treats others who are like me." Then follows a phrase resulting from a transformation: "This ill-treatment leaves me impotent and helpless, as if I were a child confronted by an adult." "My father used to beat me and told me that that was how he was bringing me up; since he says he loves me, I have to put up with it." Next: "I am dependent on my father just as I am on my social environment." Now comes the most conscious phase: "The father beats the child on his body"— because he is disobedient or asks for something for himself and ignores the father's demands. This series of phases shows that the link with the others regresses to the object relationship, from which it derives the components needed to make up this type of relationship. There is a transformation from "different" to "like," what belongs to the subject being put onto the other. The feeling and sight of social and other forms of ill-treatment—and it is impossible not to feel and see these—is incorporated and transformed in some subjects by turning against the other and reproduced as the act of beating a child. Social ill-treatment is incorporated in the ego by the mechanism of imposition; it has to be accepted or rejected because the ego has no other way of dealing with it. As a mechanism that derives from the fact of belonging in a link, it is for the ego a form of relationship with another who cannot be equated or transformed or identified with the ego and with which the ego cannot identify. Yet the link has to be preserved at all costs. What is imposed is inscribed in the mental apparatus as "the given," that which is not questioned anymore.

Why is the imposition of the other accepted? It is because the constitution of the ego depends on it, by way of the feeling of belonging that must never be abandoned owing to the threat of ceasing to exist, of unbinding of the subject and of ego disintegration. In the infantile sexual world, the boy, faced with the threat of castration, abandons the erotic link with the mother, turning her into an internal object and thereby saving his own penis, which is what was threatened. In the external world, he renounces part of his own ego, saving the rest from annihilation by accepting the imposition of the other, as a result of which he engages in the link.

The Oedipus complex is the inaugural moment with effect from which one sector of the mind operates by object relations, with the logic of internal processes and the construction of fantasies, while another sector works by means of links with others, whom it places in the external world. Henceforth it will be possible to move from one to the other.

REFERENCES

Berenstein, I. 1989. New ideas about the unconscious family structure. *Brit. J. Psychother.* 5(3).
———. 1991. Reconsideración del concepto de vínculo. *Psicoanálisis XII* 2:219–35.
———. 1995. Psychic reality and clinical technique. *Int. J. Psycho-Anal.* 76:3–7.
Berenstein, I., and Puget, J. 1995. *Estar con uno y estar con otro: Psicoanálisis de lo vincular.* Buenos Aires: Editorial Paidos.
Freud, S. 1905. *Three essays on the theory of sexuality. S.E.* 7.
———. 1909. Notes upon a case of obsessional neurosis. *S.E.* 10.
———. 1912–13. *Totem and taboo. S.E.* 13.
———. 1914. On narcissism: An introduction. *S.E.* 14.
———. 1915. Instincts and their vicissitudes. *S.E.* 14.
———. 1917a. On transformations of instinct as exemplified in anal erotism. *S.E.* 17.
———. 1917b [1915]. A metapsychological supplement to the theory of dreams. *S.E.* 14.

———. 1917c [1915]. Mourning and melancholia. *S.E.* 14.

———. 1918 [1914]. From the history of an infantile neurosis. *S.E.* 17.

———. 1919a. A child is being beaten. *S.E.* 17.

———. 1919b. The "uncanny." *S.E.* 17.

———. 1920a. The psychogenesis of a case of female homosexuality. *S.E.* 18.

———. 1920b. *Beyond the pleasure principle. S.E.* 18.

———. 1921. *Group psychology and the analysis of the ego. S.E.* 18.

———. 1924. The economic problem of masochism. *S.E.* 19.

———. 1925a. Negation. *S.E.* 19.

———. 1925b. Some psychical consequences of the anatomical distinction between the sexes. *S.E.* 19.

Gay, P. 1988. *Freud: A life for our time.* London: Dent.

Green, A. 1980. La mère morte. In Green, *Narcissisme de vie, narcissisme de mort.* Paris: Editions de Minuit, 1983.

Goldberg, D. 1995. *Maltrato infantil. Una deuda con la niñez.* Argentina: Editor Urbano.

Jones, E. 1957. *Sigmund Freud: Life and work.* Vol. 3. London: Hogarth.

Kinder, H., and Hilgemann, W. 1973. *Atlas histórico-mundial.* Madrid: Ediciones Istmo.

Puget, J. 1995. Vínculo—relación objetal en su significado instrumental y epistemológico. *Psicoanálisis XVII* 2:415–27.

The Exceptional Position of "A Child Is Being Beaten" in the Learning and Teaching of Freud

RIVKA R. EIFERMANN

In what follows, I show how, in preparing for a seminar on Freud's paper, I eventually turned to viewing that paper from a specific, perhaps idiosyncratic perspective. From this perspective, I then examine the relation between Freud's 1919 paper and Anna Freud's related 1922 paper—both dealing with the same themes and written in the years of Anna Freud's analysis with her father. I argue that this relation, as well as what is expressed in and through it, places Freud's paper in an exceptional position in the corpus of his writings. Finally, I comment briefly—with reference to the above-mentioned examination—on some of the complex processes involved in teaching seminars at our psychoanalytic institutes, where, moreover, analysands-trainees interact with analysts-teachers.

This paper is dedicated to the memory of Regine Haesler, M.D., an exceptional friend.

PREPARATION

The Circumstances, Setting, and Participants

Analysts participating in this volume were invited "to write [on Freud's 'A Child Is Being Beaten'] as if they were presenting a teaching seminar of the work in question." In the following response to this invitation I write the first part of this paper from the position suggested in that letter, beginning at the point of being invited to give the proposed seminar at my institute.[1] In so doing I assume that I shall describe a situation that is not unfamiliar, perhaps quite common.

I receive the invitation with mixed feelings since, although I like teaching and am pleased to be invited, I have doubts about getting involved with this particular task. In fact, having written about Anna Freud's paper "Beating Fantasies and Daydreams,"[2] I should be familiar with S. Freud's paper, yet I feel that I do not recall it in any detail. I reread the paper and remain uninspired. Other matters that interest me more are on my mind, and I have other commitments that demand my attention. Besides, I don't know the people in the class I am asked to teach. Yet, for various reasons I don't refuse right away, then, under considerable (and friendly) pressure, accept. Having accepted, I feel burdened with yet another commitment. I read through the paper once again, and now feel rather stuck with the added task. I am reluctant to step into it.

I try nonetheless. Careful reading leads to an uncomfortable feeling that the paper is not easy to follow. I encounter inconsistencies and circularities in Freud's line of theoretical argumentation (regarding the role of constitution in the formation of perversions, for example) and in his struggle to define his concepts (for instance, sadism and masochism); I need to re-orient myself when he fails to follow his declared plan (for example, to confine his examination to his female cases; nonetheless he later discusses his male sample as well), and feel burdened with details that I am expected to retain in memory until some pages further into the paper, where Freud finally "makes sense" of them (for instance, the sequence and content of the three

1. That is, in fact, somewhat far-fetched, since it is not the tradition at our institute to earmark specific papers as required reading for a particular teaching course (unless it is a course on, say, Freud's clinical papers).

2. See Eifermann, 1996a; Eifermann and Blass, 1992. Anna Freud regards her paper as "a small contribution" to Freud's 1919 paper.

phases of the beating phantasies). I feel that the paper could do with considerable editing: it is hardly a Goethe Prize piece.

The more I work on the paper the more I question the necessity, even the appropriateness, of letting psychoanalytical trainees read it: surely, in any list of readings from Freud, "A Child Is Being Beaten" could hardly claim high priority. Moreover, inquiries with both colleagues and students at our institute regarding their familiarity with the paper reinforce this view from yet another perspective: I doubt that I reveal an unusual lack of command of Freud among people at my institute when I divulge that although the title of the paper was familiar to all, few of those asked could recall its contents. Considering the inevitably tight schedule of studies at our institute and the "essential readings" competing for attention, it seems that it would make more sense to be satisfied with letting students read an adequate summary of Freud's paper within a broader context than to devote precious time to reading the original.

Meanwhile—the approaching date of the seminar nagging—I do read and reread the paper and explore (with the aid of the *Standard Edition's* index) earlier and later writings of Freud's along various themes that the paper is concerned with or that it evokes in my mind. In addition, I read the papers that Freud wrote just before and just following "A Child Is Being Beaten"; I try to identify his immediate preoccupations and current struggles and clarify for myself Freud's position and thoughts on various issues when he wrote this paper and to identify similar concerns in other papers, both thematic and theoretical. I read, or reread, a lot that has been written since Freud on masochism, sadism and sadomasochism, perversions, repression, childhood amnesia, sibling relations, unconscious fantasies, and, of course, beating fantasies; all this activity stimulates rethinking various issues of theory and practice, not least regarding my own past and present patients and even my own analysis and self-analysis.

As always, I find learning for the purpose of teaching to be an excellent motor for intensive, productive work. Indeed, I am aware all along that I was partly motivated to accept this teaching task for that reason. And for another reason, too: on the whole I enjoy teaching a great deal, and I find it of interest to explore questions regarding what of our experience as analysts is applicable to the teaching situation and how this experience may be applied (Eifermann, 1993). The fact that the invitation to present the seminar emphasized that the seminar should be done in the spirit of "presentations which are *didactic*" is an encouraging, only-too-rare expression of interest in that direction.

I said above that I don't know the class. All I can have in mind in preparing for the seminar is the "typical" class of psychoanalytical trainees as I have known them, not excluding myself as candidate. I assume that although participants read the assigned paper for the oncoming seminar, full of good intentions but greatly overburdened, they do not study it in any depth. Some of the participants in the seminar may nonetheless be inspired by the paper. It may connect for them to matters that concern them personally or that are related to one of their patients; or they may be fascinated, from a historical perspective, by developments in Freud's thinking that are discernible in the paper—for example, early signs of the later conceptualization of a "superego."

Opening

Keeping in mind, however, that most participants have but a general command of the paper and that they are not likely to be overenthusiastic about it, I may open the seminar with a question that invites general participation related to their own experience as clinicians, namely, whether they have encountered beating fantasies in their own clinical work. Whereas Freud was surprised to discover "how often people who seek analytic treatment for hysteria or obsessional neurosis confess to having indulged in the phantasy" (179)—a fantasy that in its climax leads to masturbatory satisfaction—I should be surprised if people in the seminar can report a similar trend. My own experience, as well as that of colleagues with whom I have inquired, and reports in the literature, lead me to anticipate that most participants in the seminar will only infrequently have met with such fantasies among their patients. My question may lead some participants to turn our attention to Freud's paper and point to Freud's general *observations* concerning the experience of *conscious* beating fantasies as presented in the first section, as distinct from the clinical elaborations. These he presents in later sections in which he specifies the phases of beating fantasies that he had discovered in analysis, especially the second phase—"a construction of analysis"—the most important for Freud's theorizing.

The meeting thus begins with an examination of the facts regarding beating fantasies, and in that it follows Freud's empirical stand, which is that the theory of psychoanalysis is "a theory based on observation" (203). I may at this point contribute to the discussion by offering information from post-Freudian literature on beating fantasies in order to bring the participants up to date. I find it particularly instructive to begin by drawing attention to Novick and Novick's (1972) first study of beating fantasies in *children* treated at the Hampstead Clinic and recorded in its Psychoanalytic Index:

> We found that beating fantasies rarely played a significant role in the analytic material of children. For example, only six out of 111 indexed cases were said to have beating fantasies. This does not preclude their being universal but it does indicate that beating fantasies play a significant or visible role in only a minority of cases. No beating fantasies were reported in pre-latency children and the later incidence was about evenly divided between pre- and post-pubertal children" (238). They say, furthermore: "With some resolution of the Oedipus complex and the formation of the superego, these children moved into latency and it was only at this point that what we would call the beating fantasy proper emerged in a few of the girls. . . . Gradually sexual excitement and masturbation are divorced from the fantasy and the wishes appeared in increasingly distanced forms" (239).

I shall further point out in this connection that the Novicks limit the definition of fantasy to conscious daydreams but argue that their findings show that "the wish to be beaten, standing for the oedipal wish, *is or can be made conscious*" (239, italics mine) after the oedipal phase and that that is when the beating fantasy per se arises—in contrast to Freud's far earlier timing. The more I dwell on currently available data, obtained through child observation as well as clinical findings on children and adults, the more complex the picture becomes. What, then, I may ask, makes Freud's paper of such historical value as to recommend it as the centerpiece of reading for the seminar?

EXPLORING A "HIDDEN" TRACK

Turning Point

At this point, I leave my imaginary seminar. I realize that such planning will not work for me in practice. Being open to surprise by what participants say, and trying to take whatever they say into account, is of the essence in my preferred manner of teaching, and any attempt to continue spinning out the imaginary seminar in detail here is therefore bound to fail in presenting any seminar as I would actually teach it. Later I shall return to this didactic aspect.

The more immediate though related reason, however, for stopping the task with which I have begun is that I have become aware that, perhaps not surprisingly, I have come full circle in my imaginary seminar, returning, almost in spite of myself, to the question of the importance of studying this paper today, and that in quoting from the Novicks I have in fact already begun unfolding my own idiosyncratic answer to the question, which remains for me the paper's major drawing power, when close reading is called for.[3] For the Novicks' paper leads me back to my thoughts regarding Anna Freud's very first paper—her 1922 candidacy paper. Although Freud's 1919 paper on beating fantasies may be regarded as a landmark in his thinking concerning the perversions, or sadomasochism, for me its claim to special, detailed attention lies primarily in its relation to Anna Freud's first paper. The complex relation between these two papers and what is expressed in and through it, its possible implications for analytic practice in general, and its ramifications for the teaching practices at our institutes are the issues involved. I now choose to no longer dismiss my particular interest as being "irrelevant," to no longer let the issues involved remain for me "hidden questions" (Gardner, 1994); and, at the risk of sidetracking from the task I have undertaken, I now opt to give center stage to their exploration. In what follows, I attempt no more than a preliminary, illustrative discussion regarding these questions.

A Missing Reference

I begin where I left off above, with the Novicks' 1972 paper. The paper is based on their study of all clinical material that was available and indexed at Anna Freud's Hampstead Clinic (just as Freud's 1919 paper was based on all the data that were available to him from his own consulting room), and, in addition, it refers to other studies in the field. It seems remarkable, therefore, that no reference appears in this paper to Anna Freud's 1922 paper, a most detailed study of beating fantasies and daydreams—the central themes in an analysis of "the girl" presented in Anna Freud's paper. This omission stands out since Anna Freud was actively involved in the formation of the Novicks' paper, as the authors acknowledge in their thanks to her "for her many helpful suggestions" (241). The omission may be understood as related to the fact that the data the Novicks present deviate from those pre-

3. The question of the freedom that psychoanalytic trainees feel they have, and are in fact given, to actively pursue their interest in what they read is related to the question of the freedom the teacher can allow himself or herself.

sented in Anna Freud's paper regarding a matter that was central to that paper. The Novicks hold that a clear tie, through the oedipal fantasy, is maintained between beating fantasies and the later daydreams, which remain sexualized, though more remotely than the beating fantasies. Anna Freud, on the other hand, rejects (in her 1922 paper) the existence of such a tie, attributing to the daydream (or "nice stories") a "sublimatory" function, "the representation of various tender and affectionate stirrings," in contrast to the beating fantasies, which are "the disguised representation of a never-ending sensual love representation" (152 f.).

Freud's view as presented in his 1919 paper corresponds to that presented by the Novicks. He regards the daydreams, which appeared in two of his four female patients, to be "an elaborate *superstructure*" whose function it was "to make possible a feeling of satisfied excitation, even though the masturbatory act was abstained from" (190, italics mine). It seems that in this controversy between daughter and father, Anna Freud eventually realized that her father's view won the day, as substantiated by data from her Hampstead clinic.

Anna Freud did not explicitly consider her 1922 paper to be controversial vis-à-vis Freud's. Almost to the contrary, she introduces her paper as "a small contribution" to her father's 1919 paper. Moreover, the original German edition of the paper opens with an introduction (removed from the 1923 and 1974 English versions) in which she confesses that she would have preferred to continue to remain silent. And she attributes the breaking of her silence to the "strict rules" of the Vienna Psychoanalytic Society, which would not permit her to continue with her "inactive onlooking" (317): for Anna Freud was seeking membership in the Vienna Society, and this was her candidacy paper.

An Exceptional Position for Viewing Freud's Paper

The fact that Anna Freud did not remain silent makes it possible for us today to think of "A Child Is Being Beaten," to which Anna Freud's paper was a response, from an angle not usually available to us. For in the years these papers were written, Anna Freud was in analysis with her father.[4] As I shall

4. Her analysis with Freud, according to her biographer Young-Bruehl (1988), was in two phases. The first phase began in the fall of 1918: "That fall, he had a regular hour for his daughter six days a week—while, later [when his practice recovered from wartime conditions], he saw her after his full schedule, at ten o'clock in the evening" (115), and ended "around the spring of 1922." This phase of nearly four years was followed by a second phase of about two years, from 1924 to 1925.

elaborate below, central to this analysis were Anna Freud's beating fantasies, in particular her daydreams. This is demonstrated in Young-Bruehl's (1988) biography of Anna Freud and is further convincingly elucidated in Blass's (1993) recent masterful analysis of Anna Freud's paper.

The "controversy" between Freud and Anna Freud may thus be regarded as part of this extraordinary analysis, the first phase of which had just ended or was coming to an end. What has been described and analyzed by Blass (1993) as Anna Freud's "dialogue" with her father, her "struggle of creativity" in and through her paper, may be further viewed as an *enactment* of various of her experiences, conscious and unconscious, within her analysis with Freud. Her rejection, in her writing, of her father-analyst's interpretation of daydreams as being clouded by guilt over their covert sexuality—which was the view expressed in Freud's paper concerning his patients' daydreams—may be regarded, therefore, as a piece of "creative resistance" (Eifermann, 1997).

Viewed from the perspective of the exceptional analysis that Freud was conducting in the period in which he was writing his paper, an analysis in which to a large extent actual, mutual enactments would take the place of transference and countertransference, his paper may be assumed to also carry the brunt of that analysis. Matters surprisingly absent from Freud's discussion, as well as matters that received particular emphasis, may reflect the special circumstances of the paper's creation (I have elaborated on aspects of omissions and disguise in psychoanalytic writings in a recent paper, Eifermann, 1996b).

Freud derives the views that he presents in his paper primarily from his analysis of four female cases and two males, and in addition "a far larger number of cases which have been investigated less thoroughly" (191). Young-Bruehl (1988) suggests that the "fifth patient sounds very much like Anna Freud, . . . but the sixth patient is not directly described at all, and this may signal that Freud protected his daughter's privacy with silence" (104). But drawing as he was on the complete corpus of data at his disposal, Anna Freud's case was doubtless in his mind as well. He must have been aware, moreover, that she would read his paper. It would not be far-fetched to assume that these facts influenced his thought and writing. Nor would it be unreasonable to assume that he was aware of the unusual effect that the fact that his daughter was also among his cases must have had on him. More than twenty years earlier he had expressed his sensitivity, with regard to persons close to him, to what his findings and theorizing might imply about them.

Thus the senselessness of the possibility that, were he to continue to hold to his so-called seduction hypothesis, his own father would also be indicted, is mentioned among the considerations for the rejection of this "hypothesis." In his letter to Fliess of September 21, 1897 (Masson, 1985), he divulges to his friend: "I no longer believe in my *neurotica* . . . the surprise that in all cases the *father*, not excluding my own, had to be accused of being perverse made no sense" (264). It is remarkable that in that context, although already a father himself, he refers to his own father only.

Bias, De-emphasis, and Spotlighting: Illustrations

However keen Freud's awareness of the complexities involved in the writing of his paper due to its special circumstances, their effects could not be entirely avoided, nor did Freud necessarily wish to avoid these effects in every case. The following are illustrations from his paper of what appear to be a mistaken assumption, an exclusion or omission of a matter relevant to the issue discussed, a de-emphasis of another matter, and an overemphasis of yet another. I shall indicate how these biases related to the circumstances surrounding the writing of that particular paper.

Attributing a privileged position to the youngest child. Freud was aware of, and concerned about, his often-acknowledged deep attachment to his youngest daughter, nor was he blind to the complexities involved in their relationship. Young-Bruehl, Anna Freud's most recent biographer, quotes from his letter of March 13, 1922, to Lou Andreas-Salomé: "I too very much miss Daughter-Anna.[5] She set-off for Berlin and Hamburg on March the second. I have long felt sorry for her for still being at home with us old folks[. . .], but on the other hand, if she really were to go away, I should feel myself as deprived as I do now, and as I should do if I had to give up smoking! As long as we are all together, one doesn't realize it clearly, or at least we do not. And therefore in view of all these insoluble conflicts it is good that life comes to an end sometime or other" (Young-Bruehl, 1988, 117).

In "A Child Is Being Beaten" Freud presents a view that can hardly be maintained as a general rule regarding the special affection that parents "always" bestow on their youngest child: this child "attracts to itself the share of affection which the blinded parents are always ready to give the youngest child, and this is a spectacle the sight of which cannot be avoided"

5. This is the name for Anna Freud used in their correspondence.

566 / Rivka R. Eifermann

(187). This unqualified assertion, which seems like a blind spot on Freud's part, was in accord with his own experience as parent and child (his mother's favorite—having himself been the youngest child, since his younger brother Julius had died in infancy). It would seem likely that while maintaining an analytic stance in relation to his daughter's oedipal wishes, and while opposing her own interpretations of her situation, he was particularly drawn to remind himself and his readers (including Anna Freud) that his love for his daughter was plain to all. This need not have been a fully conscious move, nor was the mistake or bias that ensued necessarily confined to Freud's thought in this particular paper. Yet taking account of the circumstances surrounding the writing of this paper puts into focus the dynamics that contributed to its generation.

Below I present three additional examples, illustrating biases of various kinds. Following their presentation I shall elaborate on how the special circumstances under which Freud's paper was written—how the intertwining, specific dynamics of interaction and mutual enactment underlying the father-daughter analysis in process—contributed to the development of the "active" technique that Freud was using, and advocating, at the time. This technique was not practiced exclusively in the one analysis, of course: Freud used it in the analysis of other patients as well. In the analysis under consideration, however, the availability of the two papers here examined allows for a closer look at the dynamics that were involved. As I shall show, this study throws light on how the dynamics influenced technique. Identifying these influences is greatly facilitated by the fact that the father-daughter dynamics were, in this most extraordinary analysis, more direct, and more potent, than in analyses in which they found expression through transference and countertransference only. First, the additional three illustrations.

Absence of reference to primal scene exposure. The absence in Freud's paper of any reference to the possible effects on the child of exposure to the primal scene is remarkable,[6] especially since a number of later writers dealing with the subject of beating fantasies (for example, Kris in Joseph, 1965; Novick and Novick, 1972; Myers, 1981; Chasseguet-Smirgel, 1991) introduce this aspect as a matter of course, and in so doing they rely on Freud's paper "On the Sexual Theories of Children," published in 1908, more than ten years prior to his beating fantasies paper. Most recently Chasseguet-

6. Freud brings up the issue in a later paper (1925, 250–51). The question of later developments in Freud does not belong directly to the topic addressed in the present paper, however.

Smirgel, in "Sadomasochism in the Perversions" (1991), comments, "I think it is necessary to introduce the fantasy of a sadomasochistic primal scene into Freud's [1919] development of the subject in 'A Child Is Being Beaten' " (412). It would have been so fitting to Freud's thinking to have made the connection to the ideas presented in his 1908 paper in the context of his 1919 investigation that Myers (1981), in describing the three phases of the beating fantasy according to Freud, attributes this cross-reference to him. Describing Freud's second phase of the fantasy, he says: "Freud sees the masochistic wish to be beaten as a regressive expression of the girl's genital wishes for sexual intercourse with the father. The form of the wish is determined by her conceptualization of coitus as a sadistic attack by the father" (623).

Novick and Novick (1972), in the paper from which I quoted above, also make the connection, referring to Freud's 1908 paper in support of the findings derived from the Hampstead Index: "It is generally accepted that children form a sadistic theory of intercourse [here Freud's paper is referred to]. . . . It is via the sadistic theory of intercourse that the beating wish becomes sexualized" (238). In fact, Freud himself in his 1908 paper is more specific and cautious than is suggested by the Novicks. He discusses a number of alternative sexual theories held by children, one of which "arises in children if, through some chance domestic occurrence, they become witness of sexual intercourse between their parents"; in such cases "they adopt what may be called a *sadistic view of coitus*" (1908, 220; emphasis in original). The Wolf Man's case, which Freud published in 1919, the year in which his essay on beating fantasies was published (though he had written up the case four years earlier), also indicates such a history. Yet no mention of this source of the sadistic theory of coitus is made in "A Child Is Being Beaten."

De-emphasis of sexuality and exclusion of the mother. Related to this absence are Freud's de-emphasis of the sexual aspect of the beating fantasies in the early phase and his exclusion of the mother as having any role in their formation. Freud explores, in section 1 of the paper, the possible effects on the occurrence of beating fantasies of actually having been beaten or of having been exposed to the sight of others being beaten. Freud here focuses exclusively on exposure to the sight of the beating of *children*. This restricted perspective is doubly reinforced in section 4 of the paper. There Freud suggests that the beating fantasies are built on experiences in the children's nursery (not in the parental bedroom) and that they are connected to sibling rivalry only; it is here that the especially privileged position of the youngest child vis-à-vis its parents is presented. He insists, moreover, that "it is not with the girl's relation to her mother that the beating phantasy is connected" (187), and he concludes that being beaten by the father signifies humiliation and a deprivation of love and that hence, if the hateful sibling is being hit, the meaning of this is, "My father does not love this other child, he loves only me" (187).[7] It should be noted, once again, that Freud describes the sadistic theory of intercourse as the outcome of exposure to coitus prior to the oedipal phase (1908, 221), as was also the case in the Wolf Man's infantile history.

Freud thus de-emphasizes the sexual aspect of the early beating fantasies, attributing the rivalry for the father's love exclusively to circumstances in the nursery, to the exclusion of the mother: "The phantasy obviously gratifies the child's jealousy and is dependent upon the erotic side of its life, but is also powerfully reinforced by the child's egoistic interests. Doubt remains, therefore, whether the phantasy ought to be described as purely 'sexual,' nor can one venture to call it 'sadistic' [since the beating in the fantasy is not carried out by the child itself, as explained earlier on, p. 185]" (187). In contrast, later writers (including Anna Freud through the Novicks) in reintroducing Freud's earlier ideas and substantiating them, correct this de-emphasis.

Emphasizing the unconscious nature of the beating fantasy in the second phase. Freud regards the second, unconscious phase of the beating fantasy to be "the most important and the most momentous of all" (185). He maintains that "we may say of it in a certain sense that it has never had a real existence. It is never remembered, it has never succeeded in becoming conscious. It is a construction of analysis, but it is no less a necessity on that account" (185).[8] Notwithstanding, this unconscious phase is downplayed to the point of being ignored by later writers, even when the three phases are quoted from Freud.

Anna Freud does present the phases described by Freud, yet when describing the analysis of "the girl" she presents she does not refer to the uncovering of an unconscious phase as such. She only says that the sense of guilt that in the case of "our child, too" (in the German version) immediately attaches itself to the later, conscious fantasy "*is explained by Freud* in the following way: *He* says that this version of the beating fantasy is not the original one, but is the substitute in consciousness for an earlier unconscious phase" (1974, 139, italics mine).

7. He rather inconsistently refers, two pages on, to the fantasy of this first phase as "the fantasy of the period of incestuous love" (189).

8. Freud modifies this a few pages on to "remains unconscious as a rule" (189).

Altogether, she relates, "during the analysis the girl gave only the most cursory account of the beating fantasy—usually made with every indication of shame and resistance and in the form of brief, obscure allusions on the basis of which the analyst laboriously had to reconstruct the true picture" (1974, 143). It remains unclear whether the "obscure allusions" that the girl made were to fantasies of which she was unaware; but it sounds rather as though they had to be "reconstructed" because they were hidden from the analyst although known to the analysand. The Novicks (1972) conclude, on the basis of the Hampstead Clinic material quoted above, that "the wish to be beaten, standing for the oedipal wish, *is or can be made conscious*" (239, italics mine) after the oedipal phase and that that is the time at which the beating fantasy per se arises—in contrast to Freud's far earlier timing. In the case described in detail by Myers (1981), the fantasy of being beaten by the father was consciously evoked by the patient during masturbation, from childhood and into adulthood. Behind this conscious fantasy, a fantasy of being beaten by the mother was unraveled in the analysis. Galenson (1981), on the basis of child observations, describes "a common, and perhaps even a universal development in girls during the anal phase of psychosexual development" (651–52), namely, "the preoedipal form of the beating fantasy involving the mother" (651). That which for Freud was the "most momentous and most important," the *unconscious* phase of the beating fantasy, has as such received little attention in the work of later investigators.

THE UNDERLYING DYNAMICS AND THEIR FACILITATION OF AN "ACTIVE" TECHNIQUE

The Technique

Although in his 1919 paper there is hardly any reference to the manner in which Freud reached his clinical evidence, Freud does say, when describing aspects of the third phase of the beating fantasy, that it is "in reply to *pressing enquiries* [that] the patients only declare: 'I am probably looking on'" (186, italics mine). This active stance was his technique, as he himself describes it in the detailed paper he wrote in the summer of 1918, "Lines of Advance in Psycho-Analytic Therapy" (1919b). There he formulates his analytic task as physician: "to bring to the patient's knowledge the unconscious, repressed impulses existing in him, and, for that purpose, to uncover the resistances that oppose this extension of his knowledge about himself" (159); what the analyst does is to "teach him," to "show him" (160).

The same active stance on the part of the analyst is made explicit in the 1923 English version of Anna Freud's paper, in which the experience of "the girl" of being "induced" to relate her beating fantasies is made explicit (unlike the above quotation of the same paragraph from Anna Freud's own 1974 revision [143]). The earlier English version says, "the girl never gave any detailed account of any individual scene of beating. Owing to her shame and resistance all she could ever *be induced* to give were covert allusions which left to the analyst the task of completing and reconstructing a picture of the original situation" (93, italics mine).

Underlying Father-Daughter Dynamics

The view that Freud "induced" his patients to offer analytic material that was then "completed" or "constructed" by him more extensively than later analysts tended to do, or that (some of) his patients felt "induced" or participated in bringing about an interaction of this nature, gains further significance once we take into account that Anna Freud was describing her own analysis — that the analyst in the case described by Anna Freud was Freud himself, "the girl" in that analysis, his daughter. This has been recently substantiated in Young-Bruehl (1988). In contrast to earlier biographers of Anna Freud (Dyer, 1983; Peters, 1985), Young-Bruehl offers convincing historical data in support of this possibility, which she regards as "almost certain" (104). She points out, for example, that Anna Freud's paper was actually written six months before she saw her first patient. Blass (1993), by means of a careful study of the paper, and relying only on that text, establishes conclusively that indeed the girl whose analysis Anna Freud was describing was herself. For example, Anna Freud informs us in her paper of details that she could only have known were she herself the patient analyzed.

Here, then, we have at our disposal not only Freud's perception and understanding of the facts of the analysis of beating fantasies and daydreams but the parallel experiences and understanding of his patient, Anna Freud. Anna Freud contrasts the difficulties that were involved in bringing "the girl" to make even "obscure allusions" to her beating fantasies with the readiness with which she related her "nice" daydreams: "In contrast to this reticence, she was *only too eager,* once the initial difficulties had been overcome, to talk vividly about the various fantasy episodes of her nice stories [daydreams]. In fact, one gained the impression that she never tired of talking and that *in doing so she experienced similar or even greater pleasure than in the daydreaming"* (1974, 144, italics mine). In saying that the girl was "only too eager" to relate her "nice stories" to the analyst, Anna Freud gets across a sense of a (too?) uninhibited enthusiasm or fervor regarding the sharing of her daydreams with her analyst. This tinge of criticism (regret?) is absent from her 1923 version, in which she simply writes about the girl's "eagerness" (93) to talk about her daydreams.

In eagerly telling her daydreams, in thereby repeating the pleasure obtained in fantasizing them, the patient was enacting them in the analytic setting not only through the atmosphere she was creating in the telling but also by means of the content conveyed through relating them. For example, in most of the daydreams (or "nice stories") a knight and a youth were the two protagonists, the youth, prisoner of the knight, never making a true attempt to escape from imprisonment. The youth in these "nice stories" is under constant threat of punishment, since he refuses to betray his (family) secrets, which the knight tries to force out of him. Whereas the "nice stories" shared with the beating fantasies a period of increasing fear and tension, the major difference between the two was in their resolution, "which in the fantasy is brought about by beating, and in the daydream by forgiveness and reconciliation" (1974, 149).

All these daydreams take place "in vivid, animated, and dramatically moving scenes. In each the daydreamer experiences the full excitement of the threatened youth's anxiety and fortitude. At the moment when the wrath and rage of the torturer are transformed into pity and benevolence—that is to say, at the climax of each scene—the excitement resolves itself into a feeling of happiness" (147).

Blum (1995) reminds us that "in treatment, the daydream always has a transference dimension, and the patient's attitude toward the daydream, the telling of the daydream, and the style of daydreaming, are replete with significance" (43). Freud, the analyst, must have been aware of the complex relationship of father-analyst to daughter-analysand expressed in and through the telling of these daydreams in the analysis. In attempting to actively— perhaps at times eagerly or forcefully—"show," "teach," and interpret, in stripping the daydreams of their "niceness," Freud could not help, however, but enact the knight of his patient's tale. This is, indeed, how Anna Freud, in a letter to Lou Andreas-Salomé of January 25, 1924, describes her experience and its disappointing curative results: "I am impressed by how unchangeable

172 / Rivka R. Eifermann

and forceful and alluring such a daydream is, even when it has been—
like my poor one—pulled apart, analyzed, published, and in every way
mishandled and mistreated. I know that it is really shameful . . . but it
was very beautiful and gave me great pleasure" (quoted in Young-Bruehl,
121).

No wonder "the girl" sought a solution to her predicament—of being
overly preoccupied with her daydreams—in an act of writing down one of
her "nice stories," that is, in an attempt to communicate to people other than
her analyst-father. This attempted solution—elucidated by Blass (1993),
who also points to significant deviations of her one written story from her
daydreams—could not but fail.

Freud must have been aware of many of the complications and difficulties
that the analytic relationship would introduce into their lives. This is evident
from his 1919 paper on technique, in which he chose to spell out specifically
one of the evolving "quite definite rules of procedure" (162) that the new
field of analytic technique must work over. This "fundamental principle
which will probably dominate our work in this field . . . runs as follows: *Analytic treatment should be carried through, as far as possible, under privation—in a state of abstinence*" (162; emphasis in original). Thus, in addition
to dealing, rather forcefully, with his patient Anna's resistances, Freud was
also aware of and must have practiced, at least in the context of the analytic
setting, greater abstinence than was habitual in their relationship prior to
having taken upon himself the additional role of being her analyst. This was
surely a privation for him, not only for his patient. In a sense, once analysis
had begun, the father was less of a father because he had also become the
analyst, just as he remained less than fully analyst since he could not shed
his role as father. When Freud proclaims in "A Child Is Being Beaten" that
with regard to analytic work "at the present time theoretical knowledge is
still far more important to all of us than therapeutic success, and anyone who
neglects childhood analysis [removing childhood amnesia] is bound to fall
into the most disastrous [theoretical] errors" (183), he is not only distancing
himself from his concern for his daughter but also expressing conflicting
aims that may arise between treatment and research.

Anna Freud's and Other Patients' Analyses

Thus, not only the analysis but the research, too, suffered from inevitable
biases. The attribution of a privileged position to the youngest child, the

absence of reference to the primal scene exposure, the de-emphasis of sexuality and the exclusion of the mother, and, finally, the highlighting of the unconscious nature of the second phase of the beating fantasies are all connected to the mutual enactments played out in this father-daughter analysis, influencing the technique and facilitating its practice. Identifying these biases and how they came about was possible through an examination of the two papers and the themes and circumstances presented in and through them. Because father and daughter were involved, the underlying dynamics were expressed more directly and more intensely than in the transferences and countertransferences of other analyses of the time. Yet similar biases must have intervened: although Freud and his daughter both maintained her privileged position in relation to her father in having been the only one of Freud's children in analysis with him, a similar though less conspicuous "privileged" position was held (or upheld) by many of his other patients, drawn from his circle of friends and acquaintances. Furthermore, Freud's active technique achieved its aim—the affirmation on Anna Freud's part that fantasies of being beaten (by the father?) were part of her experience. The technique may have acted both to increase repression (for example, regarding the role of the mother in the pre-oedipal phase) and resistance and to promote a desire to actively, though ambivalently, protect secrets, to have them "beaten out." The same technique, when applied to other patients, will have had similar, if milder, effects. The exclusion or underplaying of certain themes (the primal scene, the role of the mother) by both patient and analyst is here seen to have occurred in an analysis guided by active "showing" and "teaching," in which, moreover, the direct mutual enactment of themes that were explicit concerns of the analysis left little room for whatever appeared irrelevant, not "connected" (Freud, 1919, 186). By its nature such disconnectedness, as well as collusive avoidance, splitting, and other mechanisms, were more of a necessity in the analysis under consideration than in other analyses.[9] Yet, as is evident from what is said (and left unsaid) in Freud's paper, the same trends appear to have been present to some extent in these other analyses as well.

Asch (1981) comments that Freud's paper was "conceived too early in the development of analytic theory" (653). Some light may be thrown on *why* Freud had to conceive it when he did once we regard the paper as having

9. Simon (1992) addresses the issue of "symbolic incest" in the analysis of family or acquaintances.

been in part an enactment of Freud's role as an active, teaching analyst of his analysand-daughter.

RELATED COMMENTS ON
LEARNING AND TEACHING

My discussion of aspects of the relation between the papers by Anna Freud and Sigmund Freud, as well as the prior description of my preparation for the seminar and of the way I eventually came to follow my own "hidden track," pave the way for some related comments regarding learning and teaching at our institutes.

Transgressions. Problems that arise in analyzing family or friends—the difficulties in maintaining boundaries and the resulting transgressions—may be closer to our doorstep than we would like to think with respect to psychoanalytical trainees in analysis. In allowing ourselves the "transgression" of investigating analyses of the more extreme cases of our "forefathers," we may come closer to facing truths concerning our own errors with our students in analysis. Young-Bruehl (1988) relates that Anna Freud thought that the mistaken idea that Lou Andreas-Salomé was her analyst "persisted because people were scandalized by the thought that her father was her analyst" (112). I am aware that some of my readers, if not scandalized, may nonetheless consider it inappropriate or unnecessary to put under scrutiny, as I have done, aspects of that analysis and to suggest, as I have, that the issues discussed here may be focused on in a seminar.

Yet Gabbard (1995), in his recent examination of the history of boundary violations in psychoanalysis, shows how much of value can be learnt from these early transgressions. He argues that "institutional resistance to addressing these difficulties in contemporary psychoanalytic practice may relate in part to the ambiguities surrounding boundaries in the training analysis itself" (1115). Some of the difficulties in maintaining boundaries at our institutes today are inherent in our teaching framework, which often requires that the training analyst be teacher to his or her analysand. Whether addressed directly or by implication in the course of a seminar, the confrontation with such thorny issues through study of the more extreme cases—opening up to related, disturbing, ever-present but "hidden questions" (Gardner, 1994)—facilitates awareness and reexamination of the inherent limitations of training analyses.

Hidden questions. Such questions are matters that are with us constantly, and as I have illustrated here, may have their roots, as well as their effects, in the process of preparation for a seminar, long before entering the class to teach. In the course of my repeated reading of "A Child Is Being Beaten," various reactions to the text, such as a lack of interest or enthusiasm, an unwillingness to get involved, and a severely critical stand toward the text, emerged. Once I reached my turning point, I recognized that personal sources accentuated these reactions (Eifermann, 1996b). I was reluctant to confront, or even to identify, "hidden questions" that the text had evoked in me and to open these to public scrutiny even indirectly, through my examination of the relation between the two texts discussed here. Such unrecognized sources, inhibiting as well as inspiring, are always present: no learning is conflict-free. Gardner (1994), in his recent book, speaks of the centrality of "hidden questions" to any process of learning and teaching. He says, "I have found repeatedly that my students' and my hidden questions, like our responses to them, are elaborate expressions of our inclinations both to advance and to obstruct learning" (145). Awareness of this complexity, within ourselves and our students, may contribute to a greater readiness to be in touch with these questions and, in particular, to allow room for them in the process of learning and teaching.

It is more difficult, of course, to be attuned to individually motivated hidden questions when teaching a large group in a seminar. No wonder the two distinguished teachers who were asked to write on how they teach for *International Psychoanalysis* (Gray, 1995; Joseph, 1995) opted to focus primarily on the individual supervisory situation.

"Showing," "inducing," "seducing," and "beating out." My description of the course of my preparation for this seminar, which only eventually led me to the perspective development here, was based on the assumption that other teachers at our institutes (and outside) share similar experiences. To have gone though the intensive and extensive process of learning and relearning served as an effective reminder that true learning requires, on the part of teacher and student alike, considerable investment. Spoon-fed summaries or reviews, because they may be useful organizers, because they also save a great deal of effort, are often the preferred mode of learning and of teaching. Our attempts to circumvent inherent difficulties in a process that cannot be smooth and easy may, however, render our teaching less than satisfactory. We may fall into too active a method of teaching, convincingly showing, perhaps inducing students to accept our view—or even seducing our students

into believing our view to be their own; indeed, we may beat it out of (or into) them. We may thus deprive our students of the privilege to search, to be in a state of not-knowing, and to have the freedom to pave their own way and ourselves of the privilege to be surprised, to learn what their way might be. Parallels in the psychoanalytic process—"active" or otherwise—are not hard to seek.

Overzealousness, or a "furor" to teach. Just as, in the practice of psycho-analysis, overzealousness to cure—or to research (and was not Freud's "A Child Is Being Beaten" caught by such zealousness?)—is counterproductive, so is a furor to teach unlikely to attain the results sought. Matters of the utmost importance to the teacher, offered with great zeal, may be regarded as unimportant by his or her students. The fact that most if not all participants in seminars at our institutes are in analysis must be taken into account. What personal issues, perhaps burning issues for each of them at the time, introduce a very strong slant to what they attend to concerning psycho-analysis and how they attend to it? Another central, easily traceable influence is that of parallel seminars, particularly if one has just been attended; the carryover is often apparent, and a rude switch may be unwelcome. Gardner (1994) comments in this connection: "I find myself repeatedly pushing subjects and progressions considerably more fascinating to me than to my students" (53). Our own deep interest may blind us to that of our students and, realizing this, students may avoid raising certain questions or issues, and thus our zealousness may constrict our own view as well as theirs. We may inadvertently create an atmosphere of tension and resistance, arousing feelings of being "mishandled and mistreated."

Keeping these precautions in mind, I would be ill-advised to rush into a seminar, eager to teach on "the exceptional position of 'A Child Is Being Beaten,'" before the dust of my enthusiasm settles.

REFERENCES

Asch, S. 1981. Beating fantasies: Symbiosis and child battering. *Int. J. Psychoanal. Psychotherapy* 8:653–58.

Blass, R. B. 1993. Insights into the struggle of creativity—A rereading of Anna Freud's "Beating Fantasies and Daydreams." *Psychoanal. Study Child* 48:161–87.

Blum, H. P. 1995. The clinical value of daydreams and a note on their role in character analysis. In *On Freud's "Creative Writers and Daydreams,"* ed. E. Spector Person et al., 39–52. New Haven, Conn.: Yale University Press.

Chasseguet-Smirgel, J. 1991. Sadomasochism in the perversions: Some thoughts on the destruction of reality. *J. Amer. Psychoanal. Assn.* 39:399–416.

Dyer, R. 1983. *The work of Anna Freud.* New York: Jason Aronson.

Eifermann, R. R. 1993. Teaching and learning in an analytic mode: A model for studying psychoanalysis at university. *Int. J. Psycho-Anal.* 74:1005–15.

———. 1996a. Ambivalent sibling rivalry: Latent concerns in Anna Freud's candidacy paper. In *Psychoanalysis at the political border: Essays in honor of Rafael Moses,* ed. L. Rangell and R. Moses-Hrushovski, 133–45. Madison, Conn.: International Universities Press.

———. 1996b. Uncovering, covering, discovering analytic truth: Personal and professional sources of omission and disguise in psychoanalytic writings and their effects on psychoanalytic thinking and practice. *Psychoanal. Inq.* 16:401–25.

———. 1997. Countertransference in the relationship between reader and text. *Common Knowledge* 6:155–78.

Eifermann, R. R., and Blass, R. B. 1992. Manifeste und latente Inhalte in Anna Freud's "Schlagephantasie und Tagtraum." Presented at the international symposium *Über Masochismus,* Munich, 1992.

Freud, A. 1922. Schlagephantasie und Tagtraum. *Imago* 8:317–32.

———. 1923. The relation of beating-phantasies to a day-dream. *Int. J. Psycho-Anal.* 4:89–102.

———. [1922]. Beating fantasies and daydreams. *The Writings of Anna Freud.* New York: International Universities Press, 1:137–57 (1974).

Freud, S. 1907. The sexual enlightenment of children. *S.E.* 9.

———. 1908. On the sexual theories of children. *S.E.* 9.

———. 1919a. A child is being beaten. *S.E.* 17.

———. 1919b. Lines of advance in psychoanalytic psychotherapy. *S.E.* 17.

———. 1925. Some psychical consequences of the anatomical distinction between the sexes. *S.E.* 19.

Gabbard, G. O. 1995. The early history of boundary violations in psychoanalysis. *J. Amer. Psychoanal. Assn.* 43:1115–36.

Galeson, E. 1981. Preoedipal determinants of a beating fantasy. *Int. J. Psychoanal. Psychotherapy* 8:649–52.

Gardner, M. R. 1994. *On trying to teach.* Hillsdale, N.J.: Analytic.

Gray, P. 1995. My teaching self. *Int. Psychoanalysis* 4:21–23.

Joseph, B. 1995. How do I teach? *Int. Psychoanalysis* 4:23–25.

Joseph, E. D. 1965. Beating fantasies. In *Monograph I of the Kris Study Group,* ed. E. D. Joseph, 30–67. New York: International Universities Press.

Masson, J., trans. and ed. 1985. *The Complete Letters of Sigmund Freud to Wilhelm Fliess: 1877–1904.* Cambridge, Mass.: Harvard University Press.

Myers, W. A. 1981. The psychodynamics of a beating fantasy. *Int. J. Psychoanal. Psychotherapy* 8: 623–47.

Novick, J., and Novick, K. 1972. Beating fantasies in children. *Int. J. Psycho-Anal.* 53:237–42.

Peters, U. H. 1985. *Anna Freud.* London: Weidenfeld & Nicolson.

Simon, B. 1992. "Incest—see under Oedipus Complex": The history of an error in psychoanalysis. *J. Amer. Psychoanal. Assn.* 40:955–88.

Young-Bruehl, E. 1988. *Anna Freud: A biography.* London: MacMillan.

Construction of
a Fantasy
Reading "A Child Is
Being Beaten"

MARCELO N. VIÑAR

Commenting in 1996 on a text written by Freud in 1919 is not so straightforward a task as it may appear. It is essential to specify our perspective if we are not merely to add to the mushrooming literature on the original work, a literature spawned by the diversity of regional cultures and the rivalry between schools and personal styles that are currently creating a confusion of tongues within the psychoanalytic movement. At the same time, it is important not to stifle, in the name of whatever orthodoxy, a reader's or author's freshness and possible creativity of approach to the oral or written transmission of Freud's oeuvre. I will try to distinguish between exegesis of the original text and the expression of the ideas aroused in me by Freud's paper. Yet there is no clear line of demarcation. In reading Freud today, one is never merely reciting his words but is engaging in a dialogue with his concerns and bringing his thought into the present. Whether our reading of a canonic text is wise or foolish, we may agree that we as author use its referential function to express what worries us, what we think, and what we wish to investigate; this inevitably gives rise to a diversity of

Translated by Philip Slotkin, MA MITI.

approaches, as is surely reflected in the conception and structure of this monograph.

Another difficulty occasioned by a dialogue with Freud's work stems from the same source. Freud announces and concentrates upon one or two central ideas (in this case, the genesis of perversion and masochism), and, in the course of his search for synthesis and systematization, the restlessness of his explorer spirit overflows on all sides, so that the reader, in following the development of Freud's ideas, may well encounter themes that engage his attention more than the author's manifestly central focus.

Such was my experience with this particular paper: in the midst of the ostensible theme of perversion and masochism, I discovered a key of unparalleled clarity to the genesis and architecture of fantasy—that is, to the constitution of the subject—that emerges from the vicissitudes of the Freudian experience.

Discussion of what actually constitutes the central topic of one of Freud's texts, whether "A Child Is Being Beaten" or any other, is by no means idle. The theoretical elaboration of Freud's writings may be likened in some respects to those fruitful moments in the work of analysis when, in attempting to say one thing, the patient or the analyst in fact says or finds something else.

We have also learned, not without difficulty, to see Freud's concepts in the context of their gradual development over time: rather than coming into being by an instantaneous act of parthenogenesis, they evolved by a slow, step-by-step and sometimes contradictory process in which Freud combined in his unique way his capacity for coherent systematization with the nomadism of an indefatigable explorer of the mind. To me, "A Child Is Being Beaten" is a paradigm of a synthesis of wandering and coherence.

The greatest difficulty confronting the would-be interpreter of and commentator on such a text seventy years on, however, is the giddy pace of the ongoing cultural transformation since its composition. Anthropologists and historians increasingly stress the importance of allowing for the effect of the cultural gap between author and reader in one's approach to and understanding of a text. Every text derives its meaning from a specific cultural code, whereas the significance and resonance of every term depend on the particular vision and explanatory stance of the relevant interpretative, cultural, and scientific community.

Inevitably, therefore, the two central concepts of Freud's paper, perversion and masochism, have a very different ring in the polyphonic confusion of our own time from their connotations in 1920s Vienna. As the historian Nicole Loraux eloquently put it: "We must investigate the past out of the fire of the present" (1994). Can the relation between sexuality and culture be understood today in terms of the codes that prevailed seventy years ago? The distinction between normal and pathological sexuality was hard and fast in those days, but now it would be necessary at least to specify the defining criteria. Again, I doubt that there is consensus within the analytic community as to whether psychoanalysis could or should be performing normative, classifying functions.

In "A Child Is Being Beaten," the clinical treatment of perversion and masochism is considered from the point of view of biological constitution and of the erogenous body negotiating the vicissitudes of the Oedipus complex. A decade later, in *The Future of an Illusion* (Freud, 1927) and "Civilization and Its Discontents" (Freud, 1930 [1929]), the emphasis was to shift to the interface between sexuality and civilization.

In our own time and culture, Daniel Gil's large-scale study of the genesis of the moral sense in the Western world stresses the links among pleasure, guilt, and sin (Gil, 1996). Guilt appears not only as the cause of pleasure but as its very condition, so that sexuality becomes more a matter of culture than of any psychopathology of biological constitution.

The conceptualization of masochism and sexual deviation has been a task for psychoanalysts from the beginning, but we should be remiss if we were to adhere rigidly to the original norms and adopt an attitude of exaggerated orthodoxy. It is essential to take account of the temporal, linguistic, and cultural gap between the background against which "A Child Is Being Beaten" was written and our own situation and to spell out not only these differences but also the criteria for diagnosis we use today. Measuring the gap between 1920s Vienna and our present global village, however necessary, is a task so difficult that it could take a lifetime. Let us at least remember Freud's dictum that, if we cannot see clearly, we should at least be more aware of the obscurities.

Today's views on the relations between sexuality and culture are more variegated than those prevailing in Freud's day, when the standard medical view of a polarity between normality and pathology afforded a certain guide. When the psychopathology of neosexualities (McDougall, 1980) raises its head in the psychoanalyst's consulting room, the clear—albeit stupid and hypocritical—precepts of Victorian morality that psychoanalysis itself helped to demolish prove not to have been replaced by a new but equally coherent framework.

In our present-day world of apocalyptic concerns, it is not easy to arrive at a consensus on sexuality, an area now in ferment as nonconforming minorities seek the legitimation of deviation and challenge the received medical and legal wisdom. Normalization as the purpose and objective of psychoanalytic treatment no longer seems to be the most reliable and fruitful criterion of success. And if, as Freud noted, therapeutic effects are also demanded, it is now incumbent upon us to deepen our understanding of the place of sexuality, its pathology, and its possible creativity in mental life.

BETWEEN AUTHOR AND READER

Although the principal subject of "A Child Is Being Beaten," according to the paper's subtitle and Strachey's commentary, is the genesis of perversion and the conversion of the drive into its passive form (masochism), I was struck most in my rereading by Freud's discussion of the architecture of fantasy in the relation between the conscious and unconscious systems—that is, by what he calls the "transformations" of the *Schlagephantasie* (beating fantasy) (Freud, 1919, 179). Freud describes and "places in order" a succession of three phases that form the links in a dialectic movement of subjective positions and in which repression and the burial of the Oedipus complex act as the fundamental explanatory factor resulting in the "interrelations and sequence" (Freud, 1919, 186) whereby the observed clinical stages are integrated with an intelligible chain of contents and transformations.

In this key text, which is perhaps unfinished or unfinishable, Freud discusses the work of fantasization and establishes a polarity between the reality of consciousness and that of the unconscious wish, not as a formal abstraction but out of the immediacy of his patients' material. A notable feature of this text is the powerful scenic element in the narrative: the suggested visual aspect is a telling component of the construction of meanings.

Another reason "A Child Is Being Beaten" is so important is that it shows how Freud combined clinical work, which is observable, with metapsychology—a conjectural activity and mental construction of the investigator—so as to make the observed facts intelligible and preserve them from anarchy. His demonstration, however, is not of the kind used in the empirical sciences. Freud's aim is the production of meaning, which is here taken as self-evident, with no aspiration to the validation and verification demanded by the positivistic natural sciences, from whose norms he here departs.

Consider, for example, the second phase, "I am being beaten by my father," which Freud asserts is *the most important and the most momentous of all.* But we may say of it in a certain sense *that it has never had a real existence.* It is never remembered, it has never succeeded in becoming conscious. It is a construction of analysis, but is no less a necessity on that account" (Freud, 1919, 185, italics mine). This passage constitutes one of those clear instances in which Freud breaks with the naturalistic realism of clinical medicine and exhibits the specificity of analytic observation and understanding. Although elsewhere in the same paper he adopts the ordinary clinical style, emphasizing the statistical element of the number of cases observed, at this crucial and decisive juncture in his explanation his argument is not statistical but logical; the formulation is based on the need for internal coherence in his reasoning and not on considerations of evidence concerning the observed data.

Jacques Lacan (1994, bk. 4), commenting on this text, sees the sequence of phases as logical rather than genetic in nature. He describes the first phase as "nominate" and triangular, bound up with the history of the subject. It features the hated rival, usually a sibling; the subject acts as a symbolic mediator between the punishing father and the victim. The *telos* (aim) of the fantasy is explicit: to oust the rival from the place of love so that the subject can occupy the privileged position, the throne on which he is loved and desired. The subject himself stands in a relation to the other two protagonists. By virtue of its triangular character, the work of symbolization expresses the present plenitude of the subjective and ternary intersubjective structure. The plenitude of this ternary relationship is the characteristic feature of the neurotic fantasy.

From the second phase on, the number of protagonists is reduced to two—the subject and the punishing father. The situation is confined within a sadomasochistic circularity.

The salient feature of the third phase is the dilution and blurring of the characters on the stage, or indeed their removal from it, and the work of symbolization that constitutes them. The father is transformed into a substitute, the victim lapses into anonymity or multiplication, and the subject himself is reduced to an eye, a mere unconcerned spectator, no longer a symbolic mediator between the punishing figure and the victim.

Lacan regards this breakdown of symbolization (dilution and blurring of the subject and of the characters on stage) as essential and specific to the fantasy and the perverse structure. Although the representative figures and the dramatic action are the same, a process of desubjectification has taken place because they are no longer sustained by the subject function of the neurotic organization.

Lacan concludes that Freud's famous aphorism "neuroses are the negative of perversions" should be understood as meaning not that perversions clearly exhibit what is concealed by repression in neuroses but that the polarity has to do with the internal texture of the fantasy organization, which is ternary and involves subjects that are complete in neurosis but desubjectified and diluted into anonymity in the perverse fantasy.

THE ARCHITECTURE OF FANTASY

What is fruitful and telling is not only the content of each of the three phases, which Freud describes with his characteristic zeal and tenacity, but also what he calls their "interrelations and sequence," whose dialectic makes for unity of understanding (1919, 186).

The second phase, being unobservable, would have remained but an arbitrary, dilettantish, and capricious solipsism had Freud not imposed a necessary structure on it—not now from the point of view of clinical observation but in terms of his metapsychological hypothesis—and thereby achieved a unified understanding of the narrative. This is the very essence (the *eureka*) of Freudian *Deutung* (interpretation). In a masterly explanation, Freud combines the oedipal mechanism with the process of psychosexual development to account for the enigma of the transformation of suffering into pleasure or enjoyment; he thereby seeks to resolve the paradox.

The basis of Freud's demonstration is the combination of guilt at the incestuous wish with regression to a pregenital stage, in which pleasure is constitutionally sadistic: "This being beaten is now a convergence of the sense of guilt and sexual love. *It is not only the punishment for the forbidden genital relation, but also the regressive substitute for that relation....* Here . . . we have the essence of masochism" (1919, 189).

Two positions are possible: the explanation may be deemed correct and exact; or seeking specifications, additions, or refutations may be regarded as irrelevant. I feel no need to espouse either of these stands. In reading this work, I can only allow myself, once again, to be surprised and captivated by the enormous importance Freud assigns to an unsuspected facet of sexuality in human mental life—and, in particular, by the manner in which its opacities and enigmas harass and challenge the subject as he suffers from and enjoys them in his actions and thoughts.

In other words, the merit of this work lies not only in the precision of its result but also in the way it focuses on what might appear to be an insignificant detail of psychic life. The specific treatment of the theme itself and the way it is developed are more important than the correctness of the answer. Freud places pregenital sexuality in the context of one of its most opaque and enigmatic manifestations; and, as he negotiates these uncharted waters, he succeeds in his aim of bringing about understanding.

An element lacking in Freud's text that would probably be a central aspect from today's point of view is a consideration of the patient's place and role in the production of knowledge rather than as merely the bearer of a complaint. After all, even if the investigator's constructions are by no means to be deprecated in explaining the genesis of masochism, the point is surely to determine the position of the suffering subject, assailed as he is by his inability to resolve the recurring diabolical temptation of an excitation that he cannot satisfy but does not wish to forgo. The subject is exposed to the contradictory slings and arrows of his fantasy but is unable to achieve the same coherence of intention as he does on other levels of his psychic life. What prevails is this contradictory aspect of mental life, with its particular capacity to harass the subject.

My experience of ordinary life and my clinical practice do not bear out Freud's claim that the beating fantasy is literally universal. Was it merely a passing phenomenon? Perhaps the official "black" teaching of those days has now been superseded by more indulgent patterns, in which genuine progress in relations with small children blends with a sham attitude in which educational authority has not changed in character but is diluted and ineffective. A dialectic between adults and children that, although laborious and contradictory, is vigorous and does not preclude clear values and convictions on the part of the adult (however erroneous) is not the same thing as a posture of withdrawal, abstention, or vagueness espoused in the name of spontaneity. At any rate, although *Les Malheurs de Sophie* and *Uncle Tom's Cabin* (referred to in Freud, 1919) are read less often nowadays, the practice of sadism is abundant and strident, not only in fiction but also in reality. Through television, information on terror is accessible and available at all times, and unfortunately the reality is always more horrible than fiction.

If the stimulus changes, so too will its figurative expression. Freud's concerns are therefore still valid, and although the trappings may be different, our present-day culture retains at its core the universal psychic experience of algolagnia—sexual excitation through pain—even if no longer in the form of beating fantasies.

The idea that the search for pleasure is an important component of mental life does not fly in the face of common sense. What intrigued Freud is the enigmatic combination of pleasure and suffering. Adopting a simple and perspicacious approach, he focused on an ordinary, frequent experience that constitutes a typical daydream. Its suggested universality is not readily demonstrable because the phenomenon is manifested only in the intimacy of Freud's psychoanalytic setting and clinical style. Despite the differences in the trappings and configurations of this fantasy today, there is nothing obsolete about the interest in the way every individual handles his masochism according to his own psychopathology and the means of expression favored or inhibited by his specific culture. Although the expressive form changes, the structural elements of the enigma remain.

Concerning the relationship between the cultural background and the nature of fantasy production, it is important to note that Freud certainly possessed the conceptual tools needed to distinguish clearly between life experience (biography) and fantasy activity. Beating fantasies, he said, are independent of "real corporal punishment": the individuals concerned "were very seldom beaten in their childhood, or were at all events not brought up by the help of the rod" (1919, 180).

IS THERE A PATIENT'S POINT OF VIEW?

The patient wonders—and asks us—how and why it is that certain representations that give rise to rejection, loathing, or terror in him also attract him and repeatedly impose themselves on his mind—sometimes as glaringly and insistently as in the *Zwang* of obsessional neurosis, impelling him to recreate fantasies in which pain and excitation assume blurred, ambiguous, and perhaps bivalent outlines. Lacan draws attention to the subtle difference between the mental use of images (accompanied by pleasure and not by guilt) and their spoken formulation (which gives rise to aversion, repulsion, and guilt). The boundary is a matter of behavior: *playing* mentally with the fantasy is not the same thing as *speaking* about it (Lacan, 1994, 113).

It is important to watch for the emergence of such material not for the purposes of scatological contemplation (to which our work also exposes us) but because sometimes—perhaps even frequently—the psychic series of masochistic fantasies and sublimatory activity are close together, interact with each other, and because their working through often opens up pathways to beneficial psychic achievements and change.

As with the triangular space of the direct and inverted Oedipus complex, when Freud here postulates a triptych (whose decisive central figure is conjectural and not observable) rather than a single figure for masochism, he is describing a movement whose convertibility is just as important as, or even more important than, its intrinsic characters. The situation is analogous to music in which the melody matters more than its constituent notes.

There are two simultaneous actions: (1) that of the active-passive couple of violence inflicted and violence suffered, and (2) that of the subject's place in the violent scene as a central protagonist in the repressed phase and a passively uninvolved, less responsible spectator in the conscious phases. If the aim of analytic treatment is to make the unconscious conscious (and I do not agree with this risky formulation), this is to be understood as meaning that the subject must be taken or accompanied to the central position of responsibility and not remain a mere spectator.

In the scene presented by the third phase, the subjects of the action are anonymous, variable, or erratic, and Freud, who considers the second phase to be "the most important and the most momentous of all" (1919, 185), postulates that the truth lies in that which is most avoided. In the conscious phase the person having the fantasy is *never* the beater or the one who is beaten (185), and the object of the analytic operation is to undo the dilution and bring the subject to the central position from which he is deemed to have excluded himself—that is, to a position of participation in and responsibility for the violence suffered and inflicted.

The "never" of the conscious phases seems to foreshadow the "no" on which Freud was to write six years later in his paper on negation (1925). The concept of projection, which Freud had had at his disposal since Schreber, is not mentioned in the paper here under discussion.

As a restless investigator eager to explain the facts, Freud did not make explicit the position of his patients, who, in addition to suffering from a symptom, must theorize about it in order to overcome it. This one-person psychoanalytic approach has been criticized by many authors and is transcended in Willy and Madeleine Baranger's notion of the bipersonal field (1961–62).

188 / Marcelo N. Viñar

In conclusion, I contend that Freud's investigation of beating actually reveals a universal human element of cruelty, not confined to an endopsychic causality of drives and to the internal world of the individual but involving a transpersonal dynamic that includes the father and the culture. After all, a plurality of characters actually take the stage in the most intimate and unconfessable confidences of the beating fantasy.

The paper on beating contains one question concerning *action,* violence suffered and inflicted, and a second question, on the *identity of the victim* and of the *perpetrator,* which fluctuates between extraneous characters—anonymous characters or family members—and the fantasizer himself, who manufactures the fantasy in order to disclaim responsibility for his place in the scene even to the point of denying its authorship. When Freud refers to "the most important and the most momentous [phase] of all" (185), he is in turn indicating the direction of the analytic work: from the fantasizer's "never" to the status of author—that is, responsibility. Can this be relevant solely to the genesis of perversion, or is it a universal human attitude toward intolerable violence? It is surely appropriate not only to apply the model of oscillation between concern and abstention to sexual sadomasochism but also to see it as a universal foundation of violence in the social field.

Baranger, W., and Baranger, M. 1961–62. Problemas del campo psicoanalítico. Kargieman/*Revista Uruguaya de Psicoanálisis* 4(1).

Freud, S. 1919. A child is being beaten. *S.E.* 17.

———. 1925. Negation. *S.E.* 19.

———. 1927. The future of an illusion. *S.E.* 21.

———. 1930 [1929]. Civilization and its discontents. *S.E.* 21

Gil, D. 1996. São Pablo: *La carne y el espíritu.* Unpublished.

Lacan, J. 1994. *Le séminaire.* Paris: Editions du Seuil.

Loraux, N. 1994. Entrevista de la prensa. *Le Monde Diplomatique.*

McDougall, J. 1980. *A plea for a measure of abnormality.* New York: International Universities Press.

Contributors

ISIDORO BERENSTEIN is a training and supervising analyst and professor at the Institute of Psychoanalysis at the Buenos Aires Psychoanalytic Association and has served as chair of its Institute. He was awarded the Sigourney Prize by the Mary S. Sigourney Trust in 1993.

RIVKA R. EIFERMANN is an academic associate professor in the Department of Psychology of the Hebrew University of Jerusalem, a training and supervising analyst at the Israel Psychoanalytic Institute, and past president of the Israel Psychoanalytic Society.

MARCIO DE F. GIOVANNETTI is a training and supervising analyst of the São Paulo Brazilian Society.

PATRICK JOSEPH MAHONY is a fellow of the Royal Society of Canada, a full professor of English literature at the Université de Montréal, and a training and supervising analyst of the Canadian Psychoanalytic Society. He was awarded the Sigourney Prize by the Mary S. Sigourney Trust in 1993.

ARNOLD H. MODELL is clinical professor of psychiatry at the Harvard Medical School and a training and supervising analyst of the Boston Psychoanalytic Institute.

189

JACK NOVICK is a clinical associate professor in the Department of Psychiatry at the University of Michigan and at Wayne State University, a training and supervising analyst of the New York Freudian Society, and a supervising analyst of the Michigan Psychoanalytic Institute.

KERRY KELLY NOVICK is on the faculty of the Michigan Psychoanalytic Institute and is clinical director of the Allen Creek Preschool.

ETHEL SPECTOR PERSON is a training and supervising analyst of the Columbia University Center for Psychoanalytic Training and Research, a former director of that institute, and a professor of clinical psychiatry at Columbia University. She is a vice-president of the IPA and chairperson of the Publications Committee of the IPA.

JEAN-MICHEL QUINODOZ is a training and supervising psychoanalyst of the Swiss Psycho-Analytical Society and consultant at the Department of Psychiatry of the University of Geneva.

LEONARD SHENGOLD is clinical professor of psychiatry at New York University, a training and supervising analyst, a former director of the New York University Psychoanalytic Institute, and a former vice president of the International Psychoanalytical Association.

MARCELO N. VIÑAR is a full member of the Uruguayan Psychoanalytic Association and a training and supervising analyst.

Index

Melancholia, 124
Meltzer, D., xix, 97
Memory, xi, 32; and deferred action,
 35–36; malleability of, 35, 81; recovered memories, xv, xviii, 35, 81
Merkin, Daphne, 72–73
Meyers, H., 43
Mirror fantasy, 128
Modell, Arnold, xiii, xvii–xviii
Mortality, childhood discovery of, xx,
 100–1, 104–8
Mother: experienced as "dead" object,
 73; masochism linked to, 62;
 neglected in Freud's analyis of beat-
 ing fantasies, xvi, 40, 119, 167–68,
 173; pre-oedipal mother in beating
 fantasies, 62, 73, 119; as sexual
 object, 105–6, 107, 119; in superego
 formation, 125–26
"Mourning and Melancholia," 124, 135
Murder, 78, 91
Myers, W., 62, 167, 169

Nachträglichkeit. See Deferred action
Narcissism, 56, 79; curiosity in,
 99–100; hermaphrodite, 123; infantile, 103–4; in sadomasochism,
 xiv–xv, xvii, 37, 41; in the second
 phase of beating fantasies, 51, 139
Necrophilia, 108
Neurosis: Oedipus complex in the
 formation of, xiv, 32, 102, 117;
 perversion distinguished from, 68,
 70, 123–24, 125, 184; sexual difference in the formation of, 55; superego in, 125–27
"New Introductory Lectures on Psycho-
 Analysis," 120
Nietzsche, Friedrich, 64
Novick, Jack and Kerry Kelly, xiv–xvi,

62, 79n2, 84, 161, 167, 169; Anna
 Freud's help in research by, 162–63

Object relations, 141; fear of object
 loss, 84, 124; and sadamasochism,
 37–38. See also Sexual object
Oedipus complex, 16–17, 98–99;
 aggression in, 91–92; and the castration complex, 105–7; in female sexuality, 135; inverted, 120–21, 123,
 129; in neurosis formation, xiv, 32,
 102, 117; in perversion formation,
 55–56, 89, 102, 116, 117, 142; positive experience of and the maternal
 superego, 125–26; and sexual difference, 103–4; in the sexualization of
 beating fantasies, 32, 38–39; superego formation after, 101, 141
"On Narcissism," 98
"On the Sexual Theories of Children,"
 98, 166
"On Transformations of Instinct as
 Exemplified in Anal Eroticism," 98
Oral phase, 40
Orgasm, vaginal vs. clitoral, 67–68
Ornston, D., 60
Orwell, George, 80, 82

Paranoia, 32, 38
Passivity, 18; in boys' beating fantasies,
 116; equated with femininity, xvi,
 40–41
Penis envy, xx, 114
Perversion, 15–17, 100, 137; as denial
 of difference between sexes, xx, 89;
 as deviation from genital union, 67;
 as eroticized hatred, 72; infantile,
 5–6, 67, 79, 80, 118; and mortality,
 xix; neurosis distinguished from, 68,
 70, 123–24, 125, 184; oedipal origins